# The Bible According to Jim

The Bible You Never Hear Preached in Church!

December 8, 2014

Revised September 2015

Rev. Dr. James K. Stewart

authorHOUSE®

AuthorHouse™
1663 Liberty Drive
Bloomington, IN 47403
www.authorhouse.com
Phone: 1-800-839-8640

Published by AuthorHouse  08/22/2016

ISBN: 978-1-4969-4927-1 (sc)
ISBN: 978-1-5246-2598-6 (hc)
ISBN: 978-1-4969-4926-4 (e)

Library of Congress Control Number: 2014919473

Print information available on the last page.

Any people depicted in stock imagery provided by Thinkstock are models,
and such images are being used for illustrative purposes only.
Certain stock imagery © Thinkstock.

This book is printed on acid-free paper.

Unless otherwise noted all Biblical quotations are from the King James Version.

# Contents

# Acknowledgements

I would like to acknowledge all my friends who encouraged me to write The Bible According to Jim. In particular, I owe a debt of gratitude to the following for their encouragement and editorial assistance.

Patricia Mandy          RN BA MPA CHE
Andy Downes             CLU, CH.F.C. CFP. (Retired)
Ruth Ann Woods          RN

*To all who helped make my first printing a success I extend my sincere gratitude.*

# Prologue

One of the most important Biblical considerations is how you believe God's Word has been transmitted to you and who transmitted those words. Most congregations sit week after week listening to what is supposedly "God's word." They never ask why Luke records Mary as a single woman at the birth of her illegitimate son, while Matthew is emphatic that Mary and Joseph were in fact married and that Jesus was born "according to the law." In the Old Testament, 2 Samuel 24:1 has David number the people on instruction from God. In 1 Chronicles 21:1 Satan's encourages David to number the people. If you consider the fact that Israel underwent punishment for the numbering it makes you wonder if both are "God's Holy Word." Genesis 1:1 – 2:3 comes from the Elohists tradition of God creating man and woman as equals. Genesis 2:4 – 2:24 is the Yahwist tradition of creation stating that the woman was subservient to man. The Roman Church and fundamentalist religions have chosen to believe this version.

I firmly believe that God's Word is contained within both the Old and New Testaments. Many of the stories have you believe that God functions under a cause and effect mandate. That is, if you are bad, God inflicts punishment. If you are good, God blesses you. That is how the ancients and the church have presented God over the ages.

However, if you examine the stories you will notice that free will is at the heart of the human struggle for peace and happiness. You will notice that when Israel was disobedient, God's protective hand was removed and they suffered from whatever power was in the land at the time. When Israel was obedient to God, they were impervious to subjugation. Within the Biblical stories God's word becomes clear. Simply, obey God and live in peace. Disobey God and you will suffer the worldly consequences of your actions. I believe Mark's Gospel imitates that philosophy by saying, believe my witness and live, or, believe it not and die.

Most Sunday morning sermons would have you believe we are all sinners. That is true, we are all sinners. We are imperfect people continually eroding away a perfect world. However, contrary to what the church has taught over the centuries, the battle within scripture is not with Satan and sin. The ongoing battle is between Baal and God, now known as YHVH. The sin of the Old Testament is not simply that the people sinned but that they continually returned to Baal worship. All warring madness, all heinous crimes, all human subjugation is a return to Baal worship, or any other god for that matter. This book will walk you through the passages that are never preached or preached incorrectly, enabling you to understand the power dynamic contained within the human story of Israel's relationship with God. There are only two commands in the Bible. The first is to love God. The second is to love your neighbour. Simple! The way you demonstrate that you love God is to love your neighbour. If you do not believe this statement then find for yourself where Jesus told you to do anything else.

The Bible, as we know it, is a canonization of many different oral traditions comprising a single body of work. These Holy Scriptures are a witness to God at work in the world. Christians and Jews believe the Bible contains God's inspired word to the people of the world. The first way of understanding God's Word is verbatim or word-for-word dictation. Fundamentalists believe Moses received the Pentateuch directly from God. Moses then had these words written on a scroll. The second way of understanding the Bible is inspired (2 Timothy 3:16). Notice that Timothy does not say dictated. Most clergy believe the Bible to be the inspired word of God. However, they do not believe inspired is to become overwhelmed as a poet or an artist with an idea or experience that comes to be penned from the author's heart and mind. These clergy understand inspired as the spirit breathed word, which is one in the same as verbatim. If scripture is the spirit breathed word of God how then could it be anything but flawless? Even though I firmly believe the Bible to be God inspired I do not believe it is God dictated. This work will try to shed some light, in the Hebrew context, upon the common understanding of many scriptural passages.

The Rev. Dr. Peter Gomes of Harvard Seminary has stated that the Bible sheds light upon God's word, as does a streetlight in the night. Christians must learn to see in the light, not use the pole to lean upon like a drunk. As such, I have not set out with a theological agenda to prove, but rather to enlighten the interested reader beyond the Sunday school gospel preached in our Christian churches. It has always bothered me that clergy take a literal scriptural statement and then say, "we take this to mean" as if God's dictation was not definitive. The church has always used this statement in place of their lack of evidence to support what they want us to believe. Martin Luther knocked the Roman Catholic Church on its backside when he questioned the Popes extra-scriptural interpretation of scripture. His defense was simply, sola scripturea "by scripture alone." In other words, "what does the Bible actually say?"

After many years of listening to clergy tip-toe around the truth within the scriptural stories I have decided to write an exposé, from a forensic perspective, using only Hebrew and Greek texts. This kind of investigation not only uncovers male bias but also causes one to reflect upon the scriptural statements made about a person or an event in juxtaposition to their actions. In other words, the Biblical motive for an event may not correspond with the resulting actions. Nor will the acclaim accorded a person correspond with their conduct.

This book will:

- discuss topics rarely preached upon by clergy;
- reveal the ongoing war of the gods between Yahweh and Baal;
- elaborate on the chauvinistic tribal culture of the Old Testament;
- bring to light the feminine voice in scripture;
- expose the fight for dominance of Yahweh as God's name and not Eloheem;
- make clear that God's Word is found in the Bible, not "is the Bible"; and
- explain how humans demonstrate their love for God by loving one another.

**According to Jim**
**"Laws have turned faith into religion."**

**"The church of Christ has survived in spite of the Christians."**
**The Late Rev. Dr. Les Renault**

Unless otherwise noted all Biblical quotations are from the King James Version.

# CHAPTER ONE

## Genesis

### In the beginning God

The opening words of scripture are most often translated as "in the beginning God." In Hebrew, these simple words set forth the greatest love story ever told. Ancient people could not have possibly understood the complexities nor could they comprehend the intricacy of a DNA building block. Nevertheless, they did know there was a creator and they called this creator El which is the ancient name of God. Scripture also testifies to the fact that other people knew the God of creation before God's self-revelation to Abram. Two others were Job in Mesopotamia, and Melchizedek in Salem.

El was so woven into the Hebrew culture that parents used the ancient name of El and the post Moses name of Yah as a prefix or suffix to proper nouns. Example names are; Eliymelek, (el-ee-meh'-lek) meaning "my God is king." Naomi means "my delight." Melek is the ancient word for king. The name Samuel, Shemuw`el, (sehm-oo-ale`) means, "his name is El." Cities, such as Bethel, (Beyth-`El) means "house of God." The name Israel (Yis-raw-ale) formerly Jacob (yah-ak-obe) means "God prevails." You will notice how the suffix for Samuel and Bethel is El, whereas the suffix for Jeremiah and Elijah (ay-lee-yaw) is Yah. The use of El or Yah indicated the men were named by either Elohists or Yahwist followers. It is also important to note that each name has a literal definition which plays a part and helps tell the story.

In the Book of Ruth, the two sons of Eliymelek and Naomi died. This would not have surprised Hebrew children as Mahlon (Makhlone) means sick, and Chilion (Kil-yone) means pining or to ache. The Hebrew language and form of literature is not only fascinating, it is beautiful. Hebrew poetry is full of alliteration and rhyme, creating a unique way of storytelling.

Biblical students need to recognize that, like the books of the New Testament, there is a plurality of voices in the Old Testament. These voices convey the most compelling love relationship story in all of history. The first voice in scripture is that of the Elohists. One can recognize the Elohists' voice by how the storyteller communicates the ancient name of God (El). Genesis 1:1 - 2:3 is the Elohists story of creation. Some translations put a noticeable space between verses 3 and 4, while other translations use the ¶ to identify the beginning a new chapter. Look at your own Bible to see if you can spot the chapter or paragraph changes and why. It is worth noting that scholarly commentators used the King James Version for so long that changing chapter and verse numbers would create confusion beyond description.

The second voice in scripture makes its appearance in Genesis 2:4, the Yahwist creation story. Take a moment if you wish to see why. Notice how the voice now refers to the creator as "LORD God." LORD meaning YHVH and God meaning El; Yehovah is God. As an aside, Professor Patricia Dutcher-Walls was emphatic in her teaching that the name "Lord" (Adonay) in the Old Testament was not a reference to Jesus. She would often say, "Jesus is not in the Old

Testament." Furthermore, Chapter 2 is not a repeat or a continuation of Chapter 1. Many clergy believe that Chapter 2 simply adds more detail to Chapter 1. This is incorrect. Chapter 2 clearly belongs to a group referred to as Yahwist. YHVH was unknown to the people prior to Moses' encounter with God at the burning bush. In addition, the proper noun "Jahwist" is actually "Yahwist" as the letter J does not exist in Hebrew, Greek or Latin. The letter J is a western (German) invention. All proper Hebrew nouns beginning with the letter J are incorrect. Ironically, the Jehovah Witnesses use this corruption to designate their faith group. Too bad, so sad.

The Hebrew name of Jesus is actually Yehowshua (Yeh-ho-shoo-ah) meaning "Yehovah is salvation." St. Jerome, in 382, corrupted Yehowshua (Joshua) to Jesus of Nazareth. The name "Jesus" is a corruption of the Greek name for Yehowshua which is Iesous (ee-ay-sooce). The name change came during the reign of Pope Damasus who had been charged with murder and adultery. After all, it was ok to have a murderous Pope but they could not have a Jew as the saviour of humankind - IHS. Some denominations translate the IHS monogram as "In His Service". In Greek the monogram means Iesous Hominum Salvator (Jesus Saviour of Humanity). At the time of St. Jerome there was only one Christian Church. In 380 Emperor Theodosius named Nicene Christianity as the official religion of the Roman Empire. The Emperor Constantine had only established a tolerance for Christianity in his Edict of Milan of 313.

God's Word

Now that I have retired, the opportunity to visit many different denominations for Sunday Worship presents an interesting revelation of clergy understanding of the Bible. Most congregations hear their minister preface the reading of scripture with "this is God's Word."

The statement means God has transmitted scripture directly to the writer. Therefore, scripture is infallible. Unfortunately, scripture is the inspired testimony of a chosen people and their relationship with God. Those who try to say otherwise have not read all of the passages or they have failed to understand what they have read. Had God's Word been communicated verbatim there would not be so many errors in the Biblical text. Later in this work, I will discuss the tension between the Elohists voice and the Yahwist. Suffice to say there are four main sources/traditions in the Scripture. The other two are the Deuteronomists (lawgivers) and the Priestly class (Levites.)

Have you ever wondered why some of the books in the Bible seem to repeat themselves with conflicting details? It is because there are different voices telling the same story. They are like the stories at your family reunion. One uncle will tell a slightly different fishing story than another, or an aunt will remember your mother's first date differently than your mother. This is human. It is natural. Each detail is not as important as is an understanding of the overall story. Information is simply a recollection of details surrounding an event. Not everyone remembers every detail or in the same way. As in a family reunion, scripture calls us to dialogue with our brothers and sisters of long ago because the stories are coming to us through their many experiences with God. This personal dialogue helps us to feel their pain, rejoice in their celebrations, share in their faith and most of all understand why it is important to remember God.

Even though they lived worlds apart, Abram and Melchizedek both knew the same God. I will discuss their meeting later, but for now will look at the origins of our Christian communion which Moses called Passover. Try to understand what the Passover must have meant to Jesus and his disciples. Christians fail to realize that the sharing of bread and wine is the most ancient human celebration that publically acknowledges that the sharing parties believe in the same God (El) the one true living God, creator of heaven and earth. When Melchizedek realized Abram believed in his God, he immediately invited Abram to share the bread and wine with him as an affirmation of their fellowship under God (El). Moses renewed this symbolic acknowledgment at the first Passover in Egypt. As the blood on the lintel divided believers from non-believers so communion unites Christ believers with God's promise of salvation.

## Understanding God's Word in Scripture
## Daw baw Eloheem

A true Presbyterian/Church of Scotland preface to a scripture reading from days gone by was "let us listen for God's word contained within Holy Scripture." This statement acknowledges the fact that scripture was inspired by God, not dictated. Many clergy say "inspired," then go on to tell the congregation that God telepathically beamed the story into the writer's head from on high (verbatim). Is it any wonder people do not know what to think? This book is not an attempt to question the existence of God. Nor does it attempt to change the fact that God's word is contained in scripture. Rather, it will demonstrate how human self interest turned God's love relationship with creation into 632 rules and laws. I will demonstrate how the church has preferred one story over another; how male bias has turned the equality of our human male/female relationship into one of dominance ordained by God. More importantly, by manipulating Biblical knowledge in order to maintain power over humanity the church has used this bias understanding of scripture to usurp humanities freedom to be the children of God.

It has been said, "any religion that pits brother against brother is not of the father." Jonathan Lockwood Huie writes, "true love is a process of co-creation in which neither feels ownership or superiority." The one true living God is a God whose never-ending love for humanity is essentially unexplainable. God's love transcends a mother's love. In times of extreme duress, God has displayed human characteristics. In times of unexplained acts of kindness, humanity has displayed Godly characteristics. God created humanity in God's own image and likeness. In addition, God said, "let us make man in our image, after our likeness. So God created man in his image, in the image of God created he him; male and female created he them" (Genesis 1:26-27 KJV.) Notice the plurality of the statement. Notice too the lack of superiority and dominance in the Elohists version of creation which states "in the image of God created them male and female" (Genesis 1: 27.) Notice as well that God was not talking to himself or speaking into empty space. The Elohists make us aware of a heavenly host.

Note!

The only time the phrase "Son of God" is used in the Old Testament is when Nebuchadnezzar notices there is a fourth man in the furnace with Shadrach, Meshach and Abednego (Daniel 3:26). All other references are plural, "sons of God." Considering there is only one son of God in the furnace, it does not refer to Jesus. Son of God is used 47 times in the New Testament. The phrase Sons of God is used 243 times, in 3 forms, throughout the Bible.

Humankind

Genesis 1 is an interesting passage to study in Hebrew because of the plurality and in consideration of how it has been translated. The English words "man" and "Adam" are translated from the Hebrew

Aw-dawm which can mean human or humankind. In Genesis 1:26 God said, "let us make man in our image, after our likeness." In my opinion and in consideration of the fact that this is a conversation with others, the words "us" and "our" dictate that Aw-dawm means mankind (male and female). The Elohists tradition reads, let **us** make "mankind" or "human kind" after **our** divine or "heavenly kind" image. The Yahwist translation is singular with God saying, "I will make him a helper" (Genesis 2:18). This version creates a separation by superiority between male and female. Unfortunately, in the Yahwist version, the woman was the last choice as God made every other living creature before taking Adam's rib and making woman. Can you see how the traditions collide? It can be compared to the Baptists (Elohists) arguing that there is no scriptural directive to baptize infants and the Roman Catholics (Yahwist) countering with the weakest of all defenses "we take scripture to mean".

In Proverbs 8, the voice of wisdom (khok-maw) speaks out to tell us how wisdom was with God in the beginning. The writer of the Gospel of John seems to have plagiarized this verse from Proverbs 8 replacing Wisdom with Jesus. Wisdom is the feminine aspect of God and she was the one with God before creation began, not Jesus.

This work is not a Sunday school ratification of a bias interpretation of scripture. It is about how I have been inspired, through the reading of scripture, to understand God's love and God's wrath upon those who have chosen to walk in their own way, outside the love of God. It will also demonstrate why religions follow human design. Lutherans follow some of the teachings of Martin Luther; Presbyterians follow some of the teachings of John Knox; Roman Catholics follow the decrees of the Pope. Over the course of time, I have come to believe that "rules and laws have turned faith into religion."

It is not the intent of this book to deal with every chapter and verse. Discussion will centre on an understanding of what specific texts actually say in the Hebrew and Greek context. While studying at Knox College, our Old Testament professor, the Rev. Dr. Patricia Dutcher-Walls, impressed upon her students to "listen to what the words say." Rev. Dr. Dorcas Gordon, our New Testament professor, called it a "close reading of the text." This I intend to do. Further references to Dr. Dutcher-Walls and to Dr. Gordon will be shortened to "Patricia and Dorcas."

Elohists or Yahwist

In the introduction, I spoke of two voices, the Elohists and Yahwist. As difficult as it may be for some to comprehend, the creation story is actually two different stories. Genesis 1 ends at Genesis 2:3. To demonstrate I will have to explain Hebrew literary practice. Biblical Hebrew has no periods or lower case. Vowel pointing was a relatively modern invention of the Masoretes (the copyists of the Hebrew Scriptures). Genesis 2:1 ends with a final tsadi noting the end of the events of the sixth day. Genesis 2:2-3 is the seventh day story ending with "God rested." This ends the Elohists story of creation. Some copyists put a Peh between Chapter One and Chapter Two. KJV translators mistook Genesis 1:31 as the end of the first creation story.

The last word at the end of a paragraph or story is also identifiable by a slight change to the shape of five particular letters. They are termed final letters and are as follows:

Khaf כ changes to a final khaf ך    Mem מ changes to a final mem ם
Nun נ changes to a final nun ן    Tsadi צ changes to a final tsadi ץ
Peh פ changes to a final ף peh.

It is also noteworthy to say that the literary practice in the Hebrew culture is to address only the male, even in a mixed audience. If a speaker is addressing a thousand women and there is one man in the audience the speech is masculine. When the audience is comprised solely of women then the speaker will use feminine terminology.

The Yahwist story of creation begins at Genesis 2:4. As I have said, the information, the amount of information and dare I say, the male bias of information varies depending on the tradition. The writers of the Hebrew canon, the Masoretes, did not attempt to judge which tradition was correct so they included both stories in their sacred writings. Throughout the Old Testament you will see that the Yahwist tradition dominates. This is also a convenient tradition for those who agree that women were created as helpers, incubators for her husband's seed, and the person to take the blame for man's sin. Ask yourself, was it God's intent to make Genesis 3:16, "and he shall rule over you" the most obeyed command in the Bible? Sorry ladies, the Bible says it and you know that your husband would never disobey the Bible. But take not of the Yahwist version which says that a husband and wife will be one (Genesis 2:24).

Considering our oneness, "did God's inspired word say women were to be subservient," or did God say that men and women were equal? After all, Adam received the punishment as well as Eve. O yes, and notice Adam's answer when asked why he did not obey God. Adam, in Genesis 3:12 put the blame back on God and onto Eve by saying "the **woman** whom **you** gave to be with me" gave me the fruit. Do you ever wonder if the male of the species has changed from the time of creation until now?

The Elohists make no such claim. Genesis 1:26-28 states that God said, "let us make humankind in our image, after our likeness… so God created humankind in his image, in the image of God created he him; male and female created he them." Notice the plurality in the text where God is speaking to others. Notice how the creation of humankind was both male and female in the divine image. Notice the words "his" and "he" in reference to God. A wooden translations however, states, "God created Aw-dawm in image, image God created male female created (Genesis 1:27). Hebrew does not definitively refer to God as "he" and "his." Also note how Chapter 5:1 reverts to the Elohists tradition. The Yahwist's, having placed the cause of sin on the female, go on to record for eternity the growth of humanity prior to Noah and the flood story.

Proverbs 8:22-30 states that wisdom was in the beginning with God. Before creation, wisdom was with God. Some commentaries state that wisdom is Christ. Unfortunately, Wisdom (khok-maw) is feminine. Hebrew is gender specific. Wisdom is the feminine aspect of God. Sorry all you fundamentalists who want to put Jesus at creation. Jesus was God's Son. Even though the story was coming out of the Yahwist chauvinistic tradition, they could not hide the fact that Wisdom is feminine.

As knowledge of plants and animals evolved it is easy to see why the Yahwist tradition treated women as incubators. People could see and understand the results of planting a seed of corn in mother earth. The sun and water caused the seed to be transformed into a stalk of corn. In a like manner, they understood that the man planted the seed in the woman where it grew into a boy or a girl after nine months. Today, we would refer to the woman as the host. To the ancient people, the woman was like mother earth. The woman had no part in the genetic formation of this tiny human within her. She was simply the host. Consequently, and contrary to God's word concerning adultery, men created two sets of moral standards. Leviticus 20:10 states that, "the adulterer and the adulteress shall surely be put to death." Adultery, on the woman's part, meant the child inside the woman was not the real heir to her husband's fortune and land. This is the real dilemma in the story of Ruth, Boaz and the kinsman. I will discuss her determination later.

Prior to the flood story, Chapter 6:1 relates an ancient tale with overtones of Greek mythology. As humanity began to flourish the heavenly Sons of God (plural) saw that mortal women were beautiful. These heavenly beings took wives (plural) "of all they chose." The overriding theme is, "a man can take whatever woman he chooses." The Bible also claims the children of these amorous relationships "were the heroes of old, warriors of renown" (Genesis 6:4). Could it be there is a link to the Greek pantheon, to Achilles and Hector? We are reminded of these heavenly beings in the Jacob's ladder story (Genesis 28:12). Also, all Biblical angels are masculine. Maybe it is not such a wise idea to tell your girlfriend that she "looks like an angel."

The Flood

Noah built the ark to withstand the flood God was sending to destroy a sinful humanity. The flood was not a worldwide catastrophe. The reader should understand that the whole world was not flooded. Only the world of the people who lived at the eastern end of the Mediterranean was destroyed. One only need question the rationality of that much water over the whole earth. If the whole earth were covered where would that much water subside? Joshua, when speaking of Terah and Abram in Mesopotamia reminded the people that "your fathers dwelt on the other side of the flood in old time" Joshua 24:2-3, 14-15. Joshua was telling the people to choose the god they would serve and then said his now famous quote, "as for me and my house, we will serve the LORD." That is to say, "we will serve Yehovah," not El. Moses is the one who introduced YHVH to Israel. Many of the people however continued to remain Elohists.

What is interesting about the flood is that it appears to have taken place in what is now Palestine. The land beyond the flood was Mesopotamia. Mesopotamia means the land between the two rivers. The two rivers are the Tigris and the Euphrates each of which flow into the Persian Gulf. Patricia explained that, over centuries people moved down from the mountains where they had lived in caves and began to build communities on the fertile plains. The caves near the modern Turkish city of Hasankeyf will be flooded when the Ilisu Dam is completed. This site dates back 12,000 years but the need for electricity is apparently more important than the archeological significance of this region. It is quite possible that this is the area Terah chose to settle when he left Mesopotamia. By this time, people had learned many of the aspects of agricultural husbandry. Through irrigation they were able to plant and harvest large quantities of wheat and corn. They began to build cities with walls to protect the community. Possibly, the founding of Sodom and Gomorrah took place after the flood and before Abram.

Genesis 11 tells us that people journeyed from the east; (antiquity) learned how to make bricks and burn them thoroughly. Next, they set their eyes on God by building a tower to reach heaven. The term "Canopy of Heaven" comes from this time when people thought a large canvas was above them and the stars were but pinholes in the canvas. Heaven was a literal place on the other side of the canvas. The Bible also tells us that after speaking to other divine beings God made the decision to confound the language and scatter the people. Some families however did not move into the cities, they remained in tents living like gypsies. These non-conformists became the scapegoats for urban crimes and subsequently moved away out of fear. This historical evidence coincides with the Biblical Tower of Babel. Terah was one of those people who, in this time, moved his tribe from Ur of the Chaldees to an uncertain location in Turkey, possibly Hasankeyf. Abram and sister/wife Sarai, as well as Lot, were part of the family tribe. Travel in those days was a slow process. The straight-line route from Bagdad to Damascus would have been 500 miles across the barren wilderness. The ancient trade route followed the Euphrates River north to Aleppo, then south to Damascus and on down the coast of the Mediterranean coast to Egypt. Caravans and armies alike would have taken this route. You can see how and why Terah ended up in Haran, now part of Turkey.

At this point in Genesis 11, it is necessary to touch on an age-old Biblical debate. Some scholars believe the story of Job to have taken place around 600 BC, in the time of Solon of Athens. I side with scholars who believe the story of Job predates Abram and took place in Mesopotamia or just south of Turkey prior to the year 2000 BC and before Joseph was sold into Egyptian slavery. In any case, Job did not live in a city but on the plain. As such, the placement of the Book of Job in scripture should be prior to Terah's story in Genesis 11. The first 11 chapters of Genesis are termed prehistory. Chapter 12 begins history or relatively sustainable written evidence.

When Terah left Mesopotamia, he settled in Haran, in what was to become the nation of Turkey. Terah named this settlement Haran after his dead son. Lot was the son of Haran. It is from Haran that God called Abram to leave his father Terah, his brother Nahor and family. Scripture records Abram as moving south bypassing Damascus as it was a thriving metropolis at this time. Abram, being from a tribal nomadic clan did not go into Damascus but stayed well to the east of the walled city, which dates back to 6300 BC. Water from the Ural Mountains flowed under the Steppes of Russia and percolated up from the porous rock causing Damascus to stand out as a green pearl on a golden desert.

## Detective Work

Two happenings caused me to understand scripture in a different manner than the dictated "party politic" (denominational dogma). Firstly, there was my theological education at Knox College, Toronto. This is where Dorcas would tell her students to "pay attention to the women's stories because they were important." The stories of women in scripture were not only interesting but also fascinating. In a world dominated by men, a good understanding of woman's stories is imperative. Women have an important place in scripture. Often scripture does not name the woman in a story but God spoke with many of these women and these women spoke with God. It took courage to step out of the fragile female subservient mold and do as God directed.

Secondly, a book called *The Red Tent*, by Anita Diamant influenced my thinking. Her understanding of the male bias and her conclusions based on the actions of Jacob's sons were the incentive for me to look closely as to the why Jacob's sons deceived and brutally murdered the men in Shechem. On a close reading, I discovered my findings paralleled many of Diamant's. Other scholars believe Shechem denotes Jacob's aversion to inter-tribal marriage as Abram, Isaac and Jacob all married their sisters/cousins. Remnants of this tribal mentality still plague inter-racial marriages. There are cults in existence today where marriage outside of their patriarchal community is forbidden? Humanity has come a long way from creations' story. Unfortunately, it has a long way to go before true equality is achieved. I invite you to open your eyes in the story of Dinah.

Dinah – Genesis 34

Simply reading the story of Dinah for information deprives the reader of the cultural interaction and family dynamics at play in this brutal reprisal for an offense that may not have been what the male bias would have the reader believe. Rebekah, Rachel and Dinah, to name a few, make interesting studies in terms of a woman's place in scripture. Rebekah and Rachel were not stereotypical women. Their stories are not examples of total submission, they have a voice. Read the story of Dinah, and then ask yourself, "where was her voice?"

Jacob's first wife Leah bore him six sons, and then she bore Dinah. Now, appreciate the family system dynamics at work in the story of a beautiful young woman with six older [protective] brothers. Jacob moved his family/tribe to the region controlled by Hamor, then settled on Hivite land in order to pasture his sheep. People from each tribe began mingling and the inquisitive Dinah wandered into the marketplace where she met Shechem. It was love at first sight. Verse 2 becomes the justification for the heinous acts which followed. Scripture says, Shechem seized Dinah and "lay with her by force." Professor Anna Carter Florence always tells her students to "pay attention to the verbs." In a text where the justification for the action rests so heavily upon a proper translation of the verbs, it is important to research the meaning of each verb used. In the story, Shechem "seized" her, "lay" with her, and "defiled" her. Neither seized or lay, has a direct sexual connotation. The word defiled in Hebrew means to be unclean but in this story it means "to be occupied." Had she been raped, an appropriate word would have been used specifying forced sex. Rape would have been the verb, not defiled. The story is clear that there has been an offence committed. Yet the word raped does not appear in this story and interestingly enough it is not used in the whole of the Bible. The Bible does not record men raping women; it only records women leading men astray.

In Hebrew, the story goes, "raw-ah law-kakh shaw-kab aw-naw. (Say the words out loud and listen to the rhyme). In English, Shechem, "saw, took, lay, defiled." The NRSV translates this passage as "he seized her and lay with her by force." However, seized is the fourth most common translation of law-kakh. Also, law-kakh (took) is the same word used when the sons of God took wives. According to word use does it mean the sons of God raped the daughters of men? The most common uses are; to take, to take away by hand, and to carry off. I tend to shy away from the incorrect use of the word force, as the next verse (34:3) tells us that he spoke his heart to her, that he was head over heals in love with her. So much so, Shechem went to his father Hamor to encourage him to ask Jacob for Dinah's hand in marriage because "he loved her." Diamant appears to be on to something tangible in terms of the male bias. The conflict within the story is that a prince of the people thought so little of this foreign damsel that he raped her. Then, all of sudden, he wants to marry her. Rape demonstrates a complete disregard for the woman and a spoiled prince would feel that women were there for his pleasure without the consequence of reprisal. After all, tribal cultures condone the sexual miss-use of women without male accountability.

To support the theory of love, verse 3 verbs tell us that Shechem's soul was "drawn" to her. He "loved" the damsel and he "spoke" with her. There is a certain incongruity in the story and the relationship which had developed between Shechem and Dinah. The murderous acts of reprisal (34:27) do not match the love expressed by Shechem (34:3). Even Shechem's directive to his father, "get me this damsel to wife" suggests that he asked his father to pay the bride price, no matter how high. Remember, the reader has very little peripheral information other than the fact that Dinah went off by herself to visit the women of the village. (This may sound all too familiar to parents of young girls who dream of excitement?) We really do not know whether the defilement of Dinah was with consent or not. I believe it speaks of love and consensual sex with someone outside the family.

Consider the fact that Dinah did not tell her father (Genesis 34:5). In Hebrew culture, if a raped woman did not scream or otherwise resist, she would be stoned as an active participant. In order to save her life, Dinah was required to scream for help (Deuteronomy 22:24) and report the matter to her father. However, the Bible tells us that Jacob received the information via another source. In Dinah's time, the loss of virginity changed the ability of the father to marry off a desirable daughter and receive a large dowry. Therefore, the question that seeks an answer is, "were there another reasons involved?" The answer is, "yes." The offence was the proposal of inter-tribal marriage and but the real reason was the plundering of Hamor's wealth.

This is supported by Hamor's inter-tribal marriage proposal to Jacob. Hamor said it would unify the two tribes and maintain a peaceful relationship (Genesis 34:9). In a world that now embraces inter-racial marriage, this seems insignificant. Nonetheless, think about warring families in the United States who would sooner murder a child rather than let them marry a neighbour. In Israel's tribal culture, incest was preferable to inter-tribal marriage. Thus far in the lineage, Abram and Sarai, Isaac and Rebekah, Jacob and Rachel, were all of the same family. Remember Abram's words to his servant "and I will make thee swear by the Lord, the God of heaven, and the God of the earth, that thou shall not take a wife unto my son of the daughters of the Canaanites, among whom I dwell. But thou shall go unto my country, and to my kindred, and take a wife unto my son Isaac" (Genesis 24:3-4.)

Sadly, Dinah's story could have had groundbreaking ramifications. Unfortunately, tribal purity was more important to Simeon and Levi than was the happiness of their sister. I say that because the supposedly raped damsel does marry Shechem although scripture does not record the explicit details. Only the plea of Hamor to unify the tribes and Jacob's condition of circumcision occupy the reader's attention in an attempt to justify the deceit. This is also supported by the fact Jacob condemned his sons for making him "as stink" among the surrounding nations (Genesis 34:30). As the men of the village were still in pain from their circumcisions, Jacob's sons, Simeon and Levi, organize the attack that murdered all the men. Then, Jacob's other sons plunder the city, all because their sister was "defiled." Bear in mind defiled here means "unclean," and not violated. Scripture does not deny the sexual act between Shechem and Dinah. However, I propose that the evidence of their love for one another is in Shechem's soft words of love and their marriage. Again, in a story where Dinah is the main character, where is her voice? She does not report the indiscretion. She does not have a say in a marriage to a man who supposedly raped her. Finally, ripped away from her wedding bed, the voiceless Dinah fades into history.

In a police investigation, the resulting actions often determine the motive for the crime. Read what scripture records as the results of Simeon and Levi's heinous action. Genesis 34: 26-30 states, "they killed Hamor and his son Shechem with the sword, and took Dinah out of Shechem's bed, and went away. The other sons of Jacob plundered the city, because their sister had been defiled. The sons took their flocks and their herds, their donkeys, and whatever was in the city and in the field. All their wealth, all their little ones and their wives, all that was in the houses, they captured and made their prey." Then Jacob said to Simeon and Levi, "You have brought trouble on me by making me odious to the inhabitants of the land." As he lay dying, Jacob chastised his sons Simeon and Levi for their anger and cruelty (Genesis 49:5). Could it be that Jacob was not totally opposed to inter-tribal marriage? It is clear that Jacob's sons are saying, "you cannot take our women in marriage, but we can take yours." Remember, the woman was only the host and men liked to have many fields in which to plant seeds.

Lot

When God destroyed Sodom and Gomorrah, Lot took refuge in a mountain cave with his two daughters. The Bible tells how his daughters, realizing that Lot was old and there were no men to be found, said, "let us make our father drink wine, and we will lie with him, that we may preserve the seed of our father" (Genesis 19:31-32). Two children were the result of those incestuous relationships. The first was Moab (of his father). Moab became the progenitor of the Moabites. The second was Benammi (son of my people) who became the progenitor of the Ammonites (tribal). This is why, the Hebrews considered these people detestable.

This story became suspect to me as I thought about the abhorrent incidents of incest from Abram to present day. Look at this story through the eyes of a sexually abused woman. How do you think an abused daughter would interpret Lot's father/daughter sexual relationship? It makes more sense to me that Lot got into the wine and then he lay with his older daughter one night and the other daughter the next night. Possibly, there were several encounters over the course of time. I realize this proposal is heresy. But consider the male bias in the story. Blaming the girls for the pregnancies would justify Lot. Women did not have any rights or voice. All instances of infertility are attributed to the woman. To me, it is just a convenient way to shift the blame from the man to the woman. Throughout scripture women have always received the blame for man's sin (Genesis 3:12 and Nehemiah 13:26).

Consider also the time element in the story. Lot finds for himself and his two daughters a cave in which to dwell on the mountain of Zoar. Living in isolation, his daughters somehow find wine. Considering the length of time needed to plant a vineyard, harvest grapes and age wine you can see the story is not told in real time. Also, Lots daughters were married but the sons-in-law thought him crazy and did not leave Sodom (Genesis 19:14). Maybe I am a heretic in suggesting this but read the whole story, understand the cultural dynamics in place and then ask "do all the statements sound plausible?

The mistreatment of women is common in scripture. Consider the Genesis 38 story of Judah and Tamar. Judah's son Er married Tamar but God killed him because of his wickedness. Judah told his other son Onan to "go in unto her" that she might bring forth a child. He did, but spilled his seed on the ground. When Tamar complained, Judah told her to wait until his very young son Shelah was old enough to make her pregnant. When this did not happen, Tamar learned that Judah had gone to oversee the shearing of his sheep. So, she dressed up as a harlot and lay with Judah who promised to send her a kid from his flock as payment for her service. Tamar asked for a pledge and received Judah's signet ring and bracelet (Genesis 38:18). Then she went away and hid in her father's home.

Many months later she was found to be pregnant and accused of being a harlot. She was brought to Judah to be sentenced to death by fire. Tamar then produced the signet and bracelet of the one who fathered the child. When Judah discovered that he was the father and shamed because he did not fulfill his responsibility of making sure his sons gave her the seed in place of Er, Judah confessed and repented. Many Old Testament stories reveal women struggling from suppression and taking the blame for man's sin. As you pay attention, two standards emerge in scripture. One for women and one for men and you begin to see why men did not feel their infidelity was adultery. Men were allowed many wives but women were only allowed one husband.

Rebekah - Genesis 24:15

Immediately upon her entrance into the scriptural story, the writer identifies Rebekah as a virgin. Dinah never did receive the same designation as she was not the real objective of the story. Family honour was more important and the thought of inter-tribal marriage was repulsive. Also, the storyteller had to account for Jacob's new found wealth and women. Rebekah enters the story as a woman of action. Unlike other Biblical women, she makes non-traditional decisions. Not only does she respond to the stranger's requests but converses with him. The social culture of the time was primarily tribal. A woman would not dare speak to a stranger out of fear for her life, nor would she allow him to put jewelry on her. Rebekah broke the traditional mold. She was a woman who should have known her place. Pay attention to her as she is an important person in the story, and, she has a voice.

Notice also the importance of this story as it is told in real time. First, the servant of Abraham relates the story to Rebekah and then the servant recites it again to Laban. After the servant praises God for directing him to Rebekah he eats and drinks with the family then requests his leave. The family wants to keep Rebekah for ten more days but the servant is determined not to wait. In terms of voice and decision-making, the story differs drastically from that of Dinah. Laban calls Rebekah back into the conversation. Rebekah is required to make a decision, which turns out to be contrary to her father's. She has made the decision to leave her family and marry her cousin Isaac.

Isaac

Isaac was the child of Abraham and Sarah and is the second of the three patriarchs. A close reading of the text with regard to Isaac reveals that although he spoke to God in prayer, God only spoke to him twice. Once, in a time of famine, God directed Isaac to move the tribe to Gerar, and then later directed him to move to Beersheba. In both instances scripture records Isaac's obedience to God. The part of the story that remains untold is "why did God not tell Isaac to bless Jacob and not Esau?" If Isaac was obedient then why did a woman have to resort to conspiracy and deceit to accomplish God's plan? The only thing that makes sense is that Isaac refused to listen to God.

Rebekah, on the other hand, not only spoke with God, but God spoke with her more than once. Scripture tells us that Isaac prayed for his wife because she was barren and God answered his prayer, Rebekah conceived. Writing the passage in this manner suggests that Isaac was a prayerful man. However, actions always tell a more truthful story than statements. The reality is Rebekah was his first (prime) wife, the one from whom his descendants were to come. Rebekah appears to have had a difficult time carrying the twins so she prayed to the Lord, and the Lord answered her saying, "two nations are in your womb, and two peoples born of you shall be divided; the one shall be stronger than the other, the elder shall serve the younger" (Genesis 25:23.)

Next, the story moves to Esau and Jacob as adults. Esau was a skillful hunter who sold his birthright to Jacob for some bread, lentil stew and drink. Birthright is the right of the first-born male child. The first-born male child inherits everything. If born to a farmer, he inherits the farm. If born to a king, he becomes king. Patriarchs did not divide farms, estates or kingdoms. We know, through God's conversation with Rebekah, that Jacob was to receive the blessing. The question is, "why is Isaac about to pass the blessing on to Esau?" Possibly, he did not want to listen to God; Rebekah did. Now her strength of character begins to shine. Overhearing Isaac speaking with Esau, she prepares a stew for Isaac while Esau is out hunting. Then she has to coax a fearful Jacob into tricking his father. Jacob whined so much that Rebekah made him arm coverings so that he would feel hairy to his father, and then sent the trembling Jacob into Isaac's tent to receive the blessing. Once all was accomplished, Jacob's fear caused him to run away. The point is just how are we to understand a scripture passage when the words collide with the actions? This has always been termed "Jacob's deceit," but was it? I believe the strength of Rebekah shines through the male bias. It should be Rebekah's deceit.

I must admit that the mysterious way in which God works in the lives of people never ceases to amaze me. The people God has chosen are far from perfect, yet Christians want to make everything in scripture perfect. God does not need us to make scripture perfect; make it accurate in every detail, or justify differences by making up outlandish scenarios to satisfy our desire to make perfect what God has chosen to leave a mystery. God has always been at work in the world among sinful people, not perfect people.

The story of Jacob gives an account of the life of the third patriarch whom God later named Israel (God prevails). This is why Jacob is revered by the Hebrew people. After steeling the blessing, Jacob ran away and we find ourselves asking, "what is next?" The answer is more intrigue and mystery. Jacob saw angels (sons of God) coming and going from heaven to earth on a ladder; he finds his uncle Laban, and falls in love with his cousin Rachel. All in the Family should have been the heading for this portion of scripture. The highlights of Jacob's sojourn with Laban are:

- Jacob desires to marry Rachel, but does not have a dowry;
- he works for seven years as the bride price;
- on the wedding night, Laban substitutes his elder daughter Leah for Rachel;
- in the morning, a hoodwinked Jacob realizes Leah is not Rachel;
- Laban chastises Jacob for bypassing the family custom of birth ordered marriage;
- Jacob still desires Rachel so Laban tells him to complete the required matrimonial time with Leah and he can then marry Rachel;
- he has to work another seven years as the bride price for her;
- Jacob worked a total of twenty years for Laban;
- Jacob's wives give him their handmaids Bilhah and Zilpah in order to have more children.

## More Deception

As time moves on, Jacob struck a deal with Laban for wages because Laban's flocks had increased so much under Jacob's care. Jacob agreed to take as wages only the sheep and goats that were speckled or spotted. Jacob then took rods of poplar, hazel and chestnut to mark and spot the livestock. When Laban's sons realize Jacob was pulling a fast one, Jacob packed up and headed for home not realizing that Rachel had stolen the family gods. When Laban heard that Jacob had run away with his flocks, he also learned that his household gods were missing. Catching up with Jacob, Laban accused Jacob of theft, then searched everywhere for the missing gods. When he came to search Rachel's camel, she said she could not dismount her camel because "she was in the way of a woman." The one thing you have to love about the Bible is the way it tells the family stories. Once again a named woman is part of the action and decision making process of the story. Some stories are biased, some so brutally honest we can only smile. There is also a brutal honesty in their relationship with God and God's relationship with them. There is a brutal honesty in their relationship with each other and with other people. When you read the stories, you simply say to yourself, "well, that's family for you." Clergy who attempt to censor these stories conceal the truth.

As you read the story of Jacob, the thought must come into your mind, "why did God choose this guy to name Israel?" The reality is, no one knows. After twenty years of serving Laban Jacob decided to return home and meet Esau, whom he still believed wanted to kill him. To appease the wrath of Esau, Jacob sent messengers ahead bearing gifts for his brother. Jacob also sent his wives and children across the Jabbok River; divided his tribe, flocks and wives into several small groups, but he stayed behind out of fear. This is where Jacob wrestled with an angel until daybreak. As the sun was dawning, Jacob would not let go or give in so the man struck Jacob and dislocated his hip joint. Peniel (facing God) is the name given to that place because Jacob said, "I have seen God face to face, and my life is preserved" (Genesis 32:30). When Jacob finally met Esau his fears dissipated. Esau did not harbour any ill feelings. With Jacob gone, he had carried on as the family patriarch, and did not want anything from Jacob. The two brothers' part and the story of the patriarch Israel is about to begin.

I have already spoken about Dinah and Israel's aversion to inter-tribal marriage. Maybe now you can understand why. Had you read all of the stories you would have noticed the close relation of Abram & Sarai, Isaac & Rebekah, and Jacob & Rachel. So close that we now call it incest. In 2001, I started ministry in Bathurst, New Brunswick, on the south shore of Bay Chaleur. Up until very recently the road between Bathurst and Caraquet was cut off from civilization during the winter because of severe snowstorms. The incidences of incestuous births in this region are among the highest in Canada. Just ask any minister who has served in that area. What you need to realize is, incest in a tribal culture is and always has been common. Revisit stories like Dinah and read what the words say. Let the actions speak for themselves. If the words say, "he was a nice guy," but the actions demonstrate that "he was a psychopathic killer," there is something wrong with the story.

Genesis has taken us from prehistory to Abram (exalted father) who was renamed Abraham (father of the multitude) to the death of Jacob (supplanter), now called Israel (God prevails,) to the story of Joseph (Yehovah has added) and how they ended up in Goshen. Please understand that the world was bigger than Abram could imagine, bigger than the story tellers could imagine. Genesis gives the reader the background to the growth that will take place in Egypt. God is going to transform the smallest, the weakest, and the most detestable people and make a great nation of them. I would caution you to read the story carefully as there were dozens of family/tribes just like Jacob's in Goshen.

Egypt is where the sons of Jacob begin the great transformation from tribe to nation with the story of Joseph and his coat of many colours. In his old age, Jacob gave his youngest son a colourful coat inciting the jealousy of the other children. The jealous sons sold Joseph to a slave caravan headed for Egypt. Joseph went from good fortune to bad and to good again, ending up as an advisor to Pharaoh. The Biblical story of Joseph and the historical evidence of the Hyksos invasion of Egypt correspond. The Hyksos were warriors, not administrators. They used anyone who had administrative ability. So it was that through the injustice perpetrated upon Joseph God turned evil into good. Jacob moved his tribe to Egypt because of the great famine in the land (Chapter 41).

Unfortunately, the Bible does not make clear the fact that dozens of families and tribes, like that of Jacob, moved to Egypt in the great famine. During Israel's sojourn in Goshen the Hyksos were eventually driven out of Lower Egypt into Palestine. The Egyptians put all the foreigners into one city called Goshen and made slaves of them. Most everyone is familiar with the story of Moses and the Exodus. Considering the fact that the Bible is the story of the Hebrew people, the Exodus reads as if it were about Hebrews alone. This is not true, but it does reveal the idol worshipping tension which from that point forth, plagued Israel. What followed during and after the Exodus was an ongoing battle for godly supremacy. There were a multitude of religious beliefs among the people in Goshen and God's struggle for supremacy is brought to light in the Chosen People. When the people finally crossed into the Promised Land, they encountered Canaanites who worshiped the god Baal (Lord). The battle against Satan (the tempter) pales in comparison to God's war against Baal.

Baal with Egyptian crown.

There were many gods in Baal's court, including Yah, but the main deities were Baal and Ashtoreth whose poles (phallic symbols) were a source of God's anger in the era of Kings. Realize that in the Canaanite pantheon of gods Baal was El's son. Realize as well that common practice was to have images of bronze or clay, much like those of Laban. When this melting pot of people crossed into the Promised Land they were returning to their Canaanite roots and Baal worship. Baal is mentioned 63 times in the Old Testament, whereas Satan is only mentioned 15 times. The first two chapters of Job mention Satan 11 times, once in 1 Chronicles, once in Psalm 109 and twice in Zechariah 3:1-2. In fact, an argument could be made that Baal is actually the Satan in Job!

In Genesis, El and Yahweh have two differing creation stories. Moses on the mountain came face to face with Yahweh. When Moses commanded the people that "you shall have no other gods before me" in Exodus 20:23 he was not only directing the people away from Baal's court but instituting the true name of God, which was YHVH and not El. With this understanding the Schema takes on a whole new meaning, "Hear, O Israel: The LORD our God, the LORD is one LORD. You shall love the LORD your God with all your heart and with all your soul and with all your strength" (Deuteronomy 6:4-5). [Hear O Israel, Yahweh is El. Yahweh is one]. Please read the scriptural words! Moses is saying "the LORD our God" and "you shall love the LORD your God." Notice the use of the words "our" and "your." He is directing the people away from Baal.

God's greatest adversary was not Satan, (Saw-tawn) it was Ba`al (Lord). Satan means adversary or the one who withstands as we learn in the opening of Job. The person of Satan, the devil as we know him today, has evolved over the course of time. During the second millennium, the devil grew more grotesque at the design of humans to the benefit of a Roman Church who desired to fill the people with fear rather than love. The easiest way to get people to adhere to your religion is to frighten them into faith by using scare tactics. Scripturally, Satan only has the power to tempt, not cause. This relationship is explicit in the Book of Job. If the Book of Job were to be placed after Genesis 11, then the next time Satan would be mentioned is 1 Chronicles 21 where he enticed David to number the people.

Genesis ends with the establishment of the 12 tribes of Israel. The names of the 12 sons of Jacob are: Rueben, Simeon, Levi, Judah,

Issachar, Zebulon, Dan, Gad, Asher, Naphtali, Joseph and Benjamin. Joseph however does not have a tribe named after him. Joseph's two sons, Manasseh and Ephraim comprise two half tribes. The following is a list of Jacob's sons by his four wives:

Jacob (heel holder) and Leah (weary) gave birth to:

| | |
|---|---|
| Reuben | (behold a son); |
| Simeon | (heard); |
| Levi | (joined to); |
| Judah | (praised); |
| Issachar | (there is recompense); |
| Zebulun | (exalted). |

Jacob and Rachel (ewe) gave birth to:

| | |
|---|---|
| Joseph | (Yehovah has added); |
| Benjamin | (son of the right hand). |

Jacob and Bilah (troubled) gave birth to;

| | |
|---|---|
| Dan | (judge); |
| Naphtali | (wrestled). |

Jacob and Zilpah (a trickling) gave birth to:

| | |
|---|---|
| Gad | (troop); |
| Asher | (happy). |

# Exodus

Let my people go into wilderness to worship

Genesis ends with the tribal patriarch Jacob dying in Egypt surrounded by his children. His son Joseph is still in Pharaoh's favour. At this time the Hebrew people were primarily herdsmen. Pharaoh separated these lowly people from the Egyptians confining all foreign people to the fertile land east of the lower Nile, in the region of Goshen. Through a divine turn of events, the children of Israel escaped a deadly famine and ended up inhabiting fertile farmland in Egypt. At this point Biblical history and world history merge. The famine that drove Jacob, his seventy children, their spouses, children and slaves, into Egypt also drove many other groups of people to the land of plenty. The Bible simply says, "there was a famine in the land" (Genesis 12:10) and that "the entire world came to Joseph in Egypt to buy grain, because the famine became severe throughout the world" (Genesis 41:56).

One must remember that the Bible is the story of a direct relationship between God and the chosen people. As such, Biblical storytellers were only concerned with events that involved them, their relationship with God and not with others. The great famine caused dozens of tribes and families to immigrate to Egypt but the Bible makes it sound like it was only the children of Abraham. History also records the splitting of Egypt into two kingdoms, Upper Egypt and Lower Egypt. This gave rise to the two different crowns seen on images of Pharaoh. In the movie, "Exodus" Rameses II (Yule Brynner) wore the crown of Lower Egypt – north.

Exodus is more than likely one of the most misrepresented stories in the Bible. The movie *The Exodus*, although a great movie, did not completely reveal the truth of scripture. Charlton Heston played the role with much dignity but he did not leave the audience with a true picture of Moses, nor the reason why Pharaoh acquiesced to the request to "let my people go."

Prior to the time when Joseph's brothers sold him into slavery, the Hyksos (sea people) had taken control of Lower Egypt. The Hyksos were a warring people, not skilled in agriculture or administration. In the mysterious way in which God works in the lives of people, one can see, in the natural events of life, a situation which brought thousands of people together. After the Hyksos were driven out of Egypt, north into Palestine, the people in Goshen became slaves. Exodus 8 reveals that "a new king arose in Egypt that did not know Joseph." The famine was over. Political leadership had changed and the Egyptian army was once again strong. Tens of thousands of non-Egyptians had become part of the fabric of the land. Fear of reprisal and the need for slaves to renew the pyramid building were required. Centuries of slavery served to forcefully integrate the immigrants. As everyone cried out to their god it was time for Yahweh's revelation to Moses and the people.

The Egyptians were elitists and the religious practices of this mosaic of immigrant people were detestable to them, especially the monotheism of the Hebrew people who professed a belief in (El) God most high. Mountains were the high places. Moses met God on the mountain. Elijah met God in a mountain cave. Sages in every age have gone to the mountains to meditate, to be with God. Mountains were as close to the presence of God as mortals could come. Take note that our God, the God whose presence was revealed to Abraham, to Moses and to David desires to live in human hearts. This is not a casual incidental statement. It defines the one true living God. All other cultures worshipped gods who desired human sacrifice.

Melting Pot

Goshen had become a melting pot of cultures and religious beliefs. Remember that Rachel had stolen her father's idols when she left with Jacob. Every family had at least one idol. Families also kept the name of their idols secret lest a neighbour made better prayers and sacrifices to entice the spirit of your god into their home. It is fair to say that the lessons learned in our childhood become the foundation of our adult beliefs. This has always been the problem with religions. Rather than admit their faith belief might not be correct people would rather murder their neighbour than change.

Christians will understand this dilemma in the context of trying to make change within their own church. People will fight to the death rather than change what they have done or believed in the past. The thought of being wrong is the underlying implication to change. The Exodus was not just about freedom from slavery, it was about change. It was about unifying all of God's people under one faith belief, one God. This will be discussed further when Pharaoh finally relents and allows the people to leave Goshen to worship in the desert. Remember, the Hebrew people were not the only people in the Exodus.

Unfortunately, as with many historical movies, Hollywood takes many liberties. The movie Exodus, starring Charlton Heston as Moses, is no exception. The Biblical record is all too short with regard to the information from the time of Moses' birth, his youth, murder of an Egyptian, marriage to Zipporah and birth of his son Gershom. Hollywood has cemented the image of a benevolent Pharaoh named Seti who loved Moses more than his own flesh and blood son Rameses. The movie version has Moses expelled from Egypt. Rameses presented Moses with a staff to rule over the scorpions, and then sent him into the desert to die. The Bible however records Moses running away to Midian after Pharaoh learned of his crime. It is worth noting once again that God used the most unlikely people, at the most unlikely times, to fulfill the divine covenant made with Abram.

Moses and God

Most people know this part of the story. While in Midian, Moses ascended Mount Horeb and experienced God speaking to him from a flame within a burning bush. Presbyterians have adopted this image as a symbol of the church with the Latin inscription *Nec tamen consumebatur* (and the bush was not consumed). Upon meeting God at the burning bush, Moses covered his face. While reading the passage, notice the real time dialogue is first person omniscient. This dialogue goes on for one and a half chapters. Here is where we learn for the first time, the Tetragrammaton, the YHVH (Yehovah). This four-letter name of God would not have had any vowels in the ancient writings and would have therefore been ineffable unless someone knew the proper pronunciation. Only a few priests would have known the pronunciation of the ineffable name. Remember, the proper pronunciation of the name of their God was a closely guarded secret. Most scholars believe the ineffable name was lost during the two generations of priestly captivity in Babylon.

Hebrew is a guttural language. As the storyteller was reciting Moses' encounter with God, his voice would have become firm and resolute as he said (hayah hayah), "I am that I am." Moses knew the people would ask who had sent him, so God told him to say "Yehovah, the Eloheem of your ancestors." That is, the El of Abraham, the El of Isaac and the El of Jacob has sent me to you. In the past, El was God's name, but now, the proper name of God, Yehovah was to be his name forever. Note that the name Yehovah was unknown until revealed to Moses. The name LORD was later injected the into Yahwist stories. The Elohists continued to use El.

Now we come to the part that clergy either do not know or purposely leave out of the story. That part is, God sent Moses to request permission from Pharaoh's to go into the desert three day's journey to sacrifice to Yehovah (Exodus 3:18-22). God knew that Pharaoh would never acquiesce to a demand to free the slaves. God had to perform many miracles just to force Pharaoh to let the people go into the wilderness to worship. God also told Moses to have the Hebrews plunder the Egyptian gold and jewelry. This was the source of the gold used to cast the golden idol. Unfortunately, the truth of the story puts a whole new spin on "let my people go."

From the very beginning, Pharaoh was under the impression that the Goshen slaves would return; they were only going into the wilderness to sacrifice to their God, an act detestable to the Egyptians. Just as God had predicted, Pharaoh would not allow this to happen until the consequences became unbearable. It took many plagues and the death of the Egyptian firstborn during the Passover before Pharaoh yielded to the request.

Christians need to understand Communion in the context of the Passover. The bread and wine are not a newly instituted act of faith, but an ancient symbolic act of faith in the one true God, creator of heaven and earth. As I mentioned, there were a multitude of idols, images and gods in Goshen. The lamb's blood on the lintels was the outer sign of faith in Yehovah the El of the Hebrew people. The bread and wine of communion has become the Christian symbol of salvation paid for by the blood of Christ, the sacrificial lamb.

The sacrificial lamb was a remembrance of a tribal people pinning their sins to a lamb, and then sending it out into the night so the wolves might consume it. It is a foretelling of the Messiah, the Lamb of God. Most importantly, the bread and wine would continue through the millennia as a remembrance of this horrible night and what God had done for all people. It would also serve as a remembrance of the Messiah's death, that the empty cross might save all who believe that death was conquered by the Son of God. Again, I say might be saved. As you can see, the design of this work is not to refute one's faith in Jesus or God. It seeks to bond all who believe that Yehovah is your El. It may also be of interest to note that God commanded Moses to consecrate all firstborn children. Notice, it does not say baptize. Baptism does not exist in the Old Testament. Jesus' consecration to God took place on the eighth day. Jesus chose to set the example of an adult baptism in the River Jordan. Sorry main line religions, the Baptists are right, children are to be dedicated, not baptized.

It is fair to say that more of this generation have seen the movie The Ten Commandments, starring Charlton Heston, than have read the Bible. Referring back to the movie, we watched as Pharaoh (Yule Brenner) changed his mind, deciding to go after the Hebrews and kill them. Remember, the Biblical request was to go three days journey into the desert to sacrifice for three days and take three days to journey back to Goshen. Hollywood has clearly distorted the Biblical story. Ten days later the report came back to Pharaoh that there was no sign of the Hebrews. When the Egyptians realized the slaves were not coming back there was not enough time to gather the army and take on enough provisions to pursue the slaves. The only alternative was to give chase with the 600 chariots. The Egyptians caught up to Israel at Baalzephon, (lord of the north) beside the Red Sea. Trapped between the sea and Pharaoh's chariots the people could not see any means of escape. It was then that Moses prayed, held out his hand over the sea and witnessed God's wind (Ruwach) part the waters so they could cross. The Egyptians gave chase for the last time. The collapsing wall of water destroyed Pharaoh's chariots, his desire for revenge, as well as any hope of recovering the stolen treasure.

Before you look at "Moses' song of victory," look back to Moses' encounter with God on Mount Horeb. Do you remember Moses' fearful reply to God when the enormous task of deliverer was bestowed upon him? Moses replied, "O my Lord, I have never been eloquent, neither in the past or even now that you have spoken to your servant; but I am slow of speech and slow of tongue" (Exodus 4:10). Now read Exodus 15:1-19. Above the pericope, you will read the caption "The Song of Moses." If you read the caption above Exodus 15:20 it will read "The Song of Miriam." That verse also says Miriam (rebellion) led the women "and Miriam sang to them." It seems strange that a man who was slow of speech should have the capacity to write and lead in the singing of such a beautiful hymn. In all probability, Miriam wrote the song and male bias attributed the hymn to Moses.

## The Human Likeness of God

Next comes a very interesting part of scripture. The storyteller cannot hide God's exasperation as humanity's sin boils over the limits of divine tolerance. Finally, the Israelites are free. They make camp below Mount Sinai to rest and celebrate their freedom. Moses goes up the mountain to speak with God. Then, some of the foreigners try to revert to idol worship. It is important to remember that God has never asked for, or desired, anything but the love of the believer's heart. Any monuments made to God were to have been of uncut stones. There is nothing in God's creation from which humanity can make an image of the creator. Unfortunately, foreigners forced Aaron to help them make an idol, a golden calf. Do you remember how and where they got the gold? On one hand, this was an act of deception and theft. One could argue however that it was payment for the years of slavery. All the people had to do was get to the Promised Land with their new-found riches without reverting to Baal worship and they would be set for life.

In every age, people cry out for evidence of God. People want to see something tangible. The Exodus does not get any more tangible. The evidence is clear and distinct. The miracles come to us through scripture and in some cases historical evidence. Nevertheless, people today still cry out "where is God," they want to see evidence of God at work among the nations. How much more evidence did the people of the Exodus need in order to believe God was at work among them. There is always someone wanting to take the power and control away from those who have it. The Golden Calf is a perfect example. The Baal cults are a perfect example of erroneous faith overriding physical evidence.

While Moses was on the mountain talking with God, these people had Aaron make a golden calf for them. The golden calf was not an image of their deity. I was the seat upon which Baal was expected to sit when he came to them. There are however, no records of Baal ever coming to the people. I rather suspect that Aaron acted out of fear and not desire. As I have pointed out, the gold to make the idols came from the Egyptian households. This should also remind people that governments and religion have always been bedfellows. Whoever controls the religion controls the people. Pharaoh believed he was a god; Xerxes believed he was a god; French kings believed they were divine descendents of Jesus. Like the Jerusalem of David, the palace of many a king and Caesar was attached to the temple treasury. This created an additional fear as the theft of gold from the kings treasury was not only a crime against the king but also an offence against the god they worshiped.

The Humanity of God

When Moses came down from the mountain has saw what the people had done. Not only did Moses break the two tablets upon which were written the Ten Commandments, he proceeded to burn the golden calf in the fire, ground it to powder, strew it over the water and made the people drink of it. (Exodus 32:20) In Numbers 16:28 Moses tells us "the earth opened her mouth and swallowed them up."

Prior to this however, God's displayed a fierce humanistic wrath against the sinful people. Exodus 32:10 states "now therefore let me alone, that my wrath may wax hot against them, and that I may consume them: and I will make of thee a great nation." To paraphrase Moses, it may have sounded like this, [who on earth do you think will ever want to follow you if you consume these people? The Egyptians will say you brought the people out to slaughter them in the desert]. Moses repeated this story in Deuteronomy 9:24-28 and in Numbers 14:16. Moses came to be one of the greatest prophets in history but God did not allow him to cross the Jordan River to die in the Promised Land. Moses had sinned. God said, both you and Aaron "broke faith with me among the Israelites at the waters of Meribath-kadesh in the wilderness of Zin, by failing to maintain my holiness among the Israelites. Although you may view the land from a distance, you shall not enter the land I am giving to the Israelites" (Genesis 32:51-52). When the Exodus began, Joshua and Caleb were adults. They were the only two adult males allowed to cross into the Promised Land. The forty year desert sojourn had consumed every other adult male.

Let us take a moment to look at human longevity at the time of Moses. As punishment for their sin (the Golden Calf) God said, "your children shall wander in the wilderness forty years, and bear your whoredom until your carcasses be wasted in the wilderness" (Numbers 14:33). This was the punishment accord every adult male "and he made them wander in the wilderness forty years, until all the generation, that had done evil in the sight of the Lord, was consumed" (Numbers 32:13). Those not of age were spared punishment. God said "but your little ones… them will I bring in" (Numbers 14:31). Anyone older than 13 years of age died in the wilderness. (At thirteen, a Jewish boy comes of age – bar mitzvah). Forty years in the wilderness means that male longevity in the time of Moses was fifty-three years. Life span for an adult male was fifty to fifty five years. The year of crossing was 1406 BC. As there is discrepancy among scholars as to the date of crossing I would point out that the fourth year of Solomon's reign was 480 years after Israel crossed the Jordan River (1 Kings 6:1). Biblical dates are conflicting but it is fair to say that approximately 450 had past between entering the Promised Land until King David's death.

When Abram left his father Terah, he had a small family and servants. When Jacob left his father in law Laban, he left as a small tribe with wives and servants. After the massacre of the men of Shechem, the women and children of the village added to the numbers of Jacob's tribe. In Egypt, people from many nations lived among the Hebrews in Goshen. However, the storyteller is only concerned with God's chosen people. That is why there was so much trouble with idols in Israel. It is also why modern-day Biblical students think Jacob's sons multiplied themselves into hundreds of thousands of people while in Egypt. Over the course of 430 years, Goshen had become a multi-cultural melting pot. The sojourn in

Egypt turned Israel into a multi-cultural nation. It is important to remember the Old Testament is about God's relationship with the Hebrew people. As such, the story-tellers have Moses organize all the people into twelve tribes.

Love or Destroy

Genesis 1 tells us that creation was (Tov) good. At the end of the sixth day, Genesis 1:31, after the creation of man and woman in God's image, God declared everything to be "very good." Please bear in mind there is a difference between good and perfect. When I speak of God's humanity, it is the context of the range of divine emotions. Humans are capable of the same fierce wrath as well as the same unexplainable grace to love and forgive. In Exodus 32:12, God's promise to Abraham was about to be broken as it was in 2 Samuel 24:16, 2 Kings 13:23 and 1 Chronicles 21:15. If you do a word search of "destroy," you will find it occurs 261 times in 246 verses. Destroy is a major theme in scripture. Love however, is a more dominant theme occurring 310 times in 280 verses. From the anger that flares a Rabbi's nostrils, to the love that bent down to comfort a woman caught in adultery, God's emotions are very human. On the other hand, should I say, human emotions are very God-like. The salvation and punishment that took place in the dessert were both miraculous and devastating. Nevertheless, people continue to look for evidence of God. But "God is not in the world as evidence. God is in the world a promise" (Tom Long).

Before we leave Exodus, let us look at another fallacy about God. Pastors and people alike believe that you cannot look upon the face of God and live. While this sounds awesome, it is a human fallacy as it denies God the omnipotent power to allow that person to live upon seeing God's face. Scripturally, God invited Moses into the divine presence several times. The closing chapter of Deuteronomy states, "never since has there arisen a prophet in Israel like Moses, whom the Lord knew face to face." Having said this, most pastors know Exodus 33:20, "you cannot see my face; for no [sinner] one shall see me and live." What they overlook is the part of the story just prior to the glory of the Lord passing over Israel. That part is about the tent in the wilderness, the holy of holies. Exodus 33:11 states, "thus the Lord used to speak to Moses face to face, as one speaks to a friend." Also, Genesis 32:30 states, "and Jacob called the name of the place Peniel: for I have seen God face to face, and my life is preserved." Had this been God's verbatim word to Moses there would not be so many contradictions dictated in the stories within the Pentateuch.

Exodus is a book of wonders and miracles. The story flows from love and compassion to hate and destruction, then back again to a renewed covenant, a major theme in the Old Testament. As you read, feel God's humanity; understand the tension the people placed on God. Never forget that you and I still do the same thing. Please listen to the scriptural voices telling the stories. Do not listen to a male biased church that twists the truth to suit their dogma. Remember, the dominant voice is that of the Yahwist, whether they are Deuteronomists or of the Priestly class. Also, remember that scripture is the story of a relationship between God and a specific group of people, a chosen people. God had chosen the smallest, most vulnerable group of people (Abram) and promised to make a great nation of them.

It is sometimes difficult to comprehend why God created men and women "very good" and not perfect. When you realize that making creation perfect would be like making puppets you can understand why intellect and free will were more important to God. Creation must of itself understand that loving God and loving one another is the only way to become one with God. Humanity is not perfect but we are getting better. As humanity consciously eliminate bias, chauvinism, racism, prejudice and greed from our nature, we will come closer to meeting God face to face. Never forget, that God has exhibited many characteristics that humanity also struggle with. In this context we need to see Jesus as more than just the Messiah, the one sent to redeem us from our sins but the one who will one day lead us back into the presence of God's love. Let me ask, "if everyone and everything were perfect, would life not be boring?" Cattle in the field have the capacity to be bored. Humans do not. Humans are inquisitive and creative. Although our relationship with God is truly a mystery, one day we will understand. For now, all we can do is wonder and keep the faith.

# Leviticus

### "God spoke to Moses face to face"

Levites are the descendants of the tribe of Levi. Moses set them aside to serve in the Tabernacle. Leviticus (of the Levites) is a book of law, rules and duties. There are 613 laws or commandments therein contained. When a Jewish boy reaches the age of 13, a girl 12, they take the "Bar/Bat Mitzvah. (Son/Daughter of the commandments) It is a coming of age ceremony. It means a son/daughter who is subject to the law. Bar is son and Bat is daughter. It is worth noting that the term Jew first appears in the Book of Esther and is the English derivative of the Hebrew word "Yehudi," meaning Judean. I will discuss the split between Judah and Israel later.

The parents of Moses, Aaron and Miriam were both of the tribe of Levi. Amram (exalted people) and Jochebed (Yehovah is glory) were their names. Aaron was the first priest and Miriam (rebellion) was the woman in charge of the song and dance during the Exodus. Leviticus is an example of what happens when humans need clarification with regard to God's two basic laws. First law, love God. Second law, love your neighbour. Part of the irony of the Luke 10 story is that a lawyer, wouldn't you know it was a lawyer, had to ask the eternal question "who is my neighbour?" Think about this for a moment, "if every human on the planet obeyed this one command would religions have been the cause of such catastrophic devastation and death over the ages? The other consideration is; how better could human beings show their love for God than by obeying the one commandment to love their neighbour?

Everyone knows the Leviticus 24 command, "an eye for an eye, and a tooth for a tooth." Look at the verse again; see that you are also responsible for your actions. Understand the time and conditions in which the people lived. The lawyer in the Lucan story understood the meaning and relationship of neighbour as far as the children of the covenant were concerned. Maybe he was asking the question "does it extend further?" Leviticus deals the law, with petty crimes and with heinous crimes such as murder. God instructed Israel to put to death those who murder. To prevent false accusation or circumstantial evidence from wrongly convicting anyone, God later directed in Numbers 35:30, not to apply capital punishment on the witness of only one. Today, society will not apply capital punishment on the witness of a thousand. Pity! Later in this work, I will discuss the two types of Biblical sin. They are sin unto death and redemptive sin. Jesus came to redeem sinners, not those who committed heinous crimes against their neighbour.

Leviticus speaks of rules, sin, and acceptable offerings for sin. In order to understand the mind set of the priests and Levites at the time of Jesus you need to understand Israel's history and traditions. What began as something divinely beautiful turned into rules and regulations. Behind all human indifference and greed, God was constantly struggling to be at one with this chosen people and with the land. Land is a major theme in the Old Testament. The earth belongs to God the Creator. It is from this perspective that God instituted the Year of Jubilee.

Leviticus 25:23 states, "the land shall not be sold into perpetuity, for the land is mine." God gave the Promised Land to the children of Israel. What this means is that a father cannot sell the family farm and land. It means the unborn children from generations to come will always have land on which to farm and raise a family. Verse 25 states that a family in difficulty must lease the land to the next of kin. The way Jubilee worked is, the land was sold for the value of what could be farmed and harvested in the years from the sale until the year of Jubilee. At the time of Jubilee, all land was returned to the family who sold the property. This is what is happening in the story of Ruth and Boaz. The problem was, there was not a male to inherit the land. This caused Ruth to sleep with Boaz, the kinsmen redeemer, on the threshing floor after the harvest.

Unfortunately, the people forget how they came into possession of the land. God had warned Israel that others would eat of the seeds they planted if they were not obedient (Leviticus 26:16.) This is the reverse of the promise made to Israel that they would eat what others had planted and dwell in homes others had built. Joshua had to remind the people that God had given Israel "a land for which you did not labour and cities which you built not, and you dwell in them; of the vineyards and olive yards which you planted not do you eat. Now therefore fear the Lord, and serve him in sincerity and in truth: and put away the gods, which your fathers served on the other side of the flood, and in Egypt; and serve you the Lord" (Joshua 24:13-14). The battle of the gods rages on.

God has always demanded obedience but rarely received it. God had always warned against false gods but the people continued to worship Baal. Had Israel remained obedient by worshiping only God they would never have to fear any other tribe. Chapter 26 tells how five Israelis would chase 100 of the enemy and how 100 Israelis would chase 10,000 enemies. If Israel did not remain faithful then God's protection would cease and their enemies would overtake them. From a purely practical perspective, it makes sense to have one God; one form of worship; one set of rules; one form of government that is fair for everyone. In Canada, liberal politicians led the Canadian people into a bilingual society, which is nothing more than dividing one country in two. The Canadian Government now insists that Canadians forget Christianity as the basis of the countries laws and culture. After all, Canadians would not want to offend people of other religions who seek to make Canadians accept fundamental principals which are totally contrary to equality and liberty. Canadians have made radical steps in areas such as women's equality (Elohists) and social reform. The Bible dictates that more than one witness is required in a capital trial to assure integrity (Numbers 35:30). God's laws have provided for fairness in Canadian life. Now others are fighting to have women's rights thrown back to the Stone Age where a husband can treat a wife like a chattel, able to murder her at his sole pleasure. This is what God's laws were trying to prevent – men playing God.

Leviticus ends with instruction regarding tithes. First, the 10% tithe was agricultural in nature. Moses is speaking prior to 1406 BC. King Croesus minted the first standard quality gold coin, circa 550BC, in what is now Turkey. Tithing signified obedience, gratitude and faith. Tithes went to the Levites, as they did not have arable land. Considering the fact that the Levites were the smallest tribe, it is easy to see that 10% from the other 11 tribes was more food than could be consumed. So why so much tithe? The tithe was also the source of food supply at the festivals. A student of the Bible should realize that part of the reason for a festival was God's way of making sure that the poor received meat from time to time. They poor did not have livestock.

The sacrificial fire did not consume the whole animal. The fire consumed only the entrails. The pleasing aroma wafting heavenward was from the roasting carcass. This is not to say there were never any whole sacrifices because there were. Leviticus 2:3 states that "the remnant of the meat offering shall be Aaron's and his sons: it is a thing most holy of the offerings of the Lord made by fire." Leviticus 7:31 states that "the priest shall burn the fat upon the altar: but the breast shall be Aaron's and his sons." It would be most unlikely that the prime of the herds, the 10% of all flocks, to have been simply burned up in the altar fire. Festivals were a time when God looked after the poor, the widow and the orphan. Tithes supported the Levites whose duty it was to look after the tabernacle in the wilderness.

# Numbers

"Because you believed me not"

The Book of Numbers is an important part of the Pentateuch. Overlooked because of the repetitious genealogies and the numbering of the tribes it seems unimportant. Patricia explained that a people without a history do not have a sense of foundation, of being. The ability to trace your heritage, your family history, gives one a sense of belonging. In order to be a nation three things are necessary. First, the people must have a history to know they are part of and belong on the land. Second, they must have a king to conscript men into an army and make concubines of their daughters. Third, they must have a god whose decrees set in place the law of the land. It is also necessary for the king to have a direct relationship with their god.

Knowledge of past generations gives assurance for a family future. Marcus Garvey wrote, "a people without knowledge of its past is like a tree without roots." The closest analogy would be the life long dilemma of an adopted child attempting to find their birth mother. Knowing where you come from sets the human heart at rest. Genealogies, such as those in the Book of Numbers signify a giant shift from family (Abraham) to tribe (Jacob) to nation (Israel.) Hence, Moses conducted the first census, setting in place the organizational structure of a nation without land. Next, God gave instruction for something very important, the redemption of the firstborn. Biblical students must never forget that ancient cultures believed in the sacrifice of the first-born male. God abolished this abhorrent practice with Abram. Human sacrifice is far more prominent in scripture than is clearly evident.

Human sacrifice is part of the history of humanity. It is in this context that Abram was willing to sacrifice Isaac to God. In this context Abram would have had to have sacrificed Isaac in order to establish himself as the tribal king; the one to whom god had spoken. The purpose of God's command was not just to test Abram, as any father of the time would have obeyed the voice of God. The purpose was to make a once for all statement; "NO MORE HUMAN SACRIFICE." Sacrificing back to God the children of God's creation is a hideous act to God. The abolishment of this repugnant act separated and distinguished God (El) from every other god. It is also important to remember that it also separated Abram from every other people.

As God began to build the nation of Israel, the first act was to wean the people off human sacrifice and replace it with animal sacrifice. Later in scripture, the revealing of God's heart becomes evident in the Hosea 6:6 passage, "for I desired mercy, and not sacrifice; and the knowledge of God more than burnt offerings." This is the evolution of love. The sacrifice of Christ on the cross was not just an obscure arbitrary whimsical act, but one with a significant reminder to the Hebrew people of the evolution of love. To the Romans, this punishment was to act as a deterrent. To God, this was the final, "once for all" vicarious sacrifice for the redemption of the people as instituted in the Book of Numbers.

God Speaks

The forty year sojourn in the wilderness would be difficult to comprehend in a twenty first century society. Tens of thousands of people walking, always searching for water and food and remember, portable toilets had not yet been invented. Certainty in Egypt had been replaced with uncertainty in the wilderness and the thought of wandering for decades was incomprehensible. Overwhelmed with problems the people resumed their complaining. Family jealousies flared up. Miriam and Aaron began bickering and started to speak against Moses. Like a father, God called Miriam, Aaron and Moses to the entrance of the tabernacle. Speaking directly to Miriam and Aaron God told them that revelations come to prophets by visions and dreams, but with Moses God speaks mouth to mouth (peh to peh) so that Moses can behold the form of the Lord (Numbers12:5-8.) Prior to this, the burden of caring for the people had become too much, so God established an eldership to assist Moses. In Numbers 11:16 we learn that 70 Elders were appointed. Moses was the high priest and Aaron was the assistant high priest. This information becomes very important in Ezekiel 8 as 72 elders comprise the total priesthood.

Israel's wilderness experience was also very trying for God to say the least. Once again, Moses had to intercede for the people. One of the most revealing passages in the Bible occurs in Numbers 14:14-16 with regards to the relationship between God and Moses. It is where Moses has to use reasoned logic to talk God out of destroying all of the people in the Exodus. Moses spoke to God face to face. The Hebrew word *paniym* means face. When speaking with Aaron and Miriam God told them he spoke to Moses mouth to mouth. The Hebrew word peh means mouth and is the root word for face. The Hebrew peh is shaped like the human face. The Hebrew letter peh is used in words to signify "in front of" or "face to face."

It may seem strange to suggest, but I believe God's frustration with humanity initiated plans for a Messiah. I say that because there is a huge disconnect between the divine and the mortal. Jesus was not only humanities redeemer in terms of his once for all vicarious sacrifice, he was also God's means to reconnect with creation. Jesus has the ability to stand before the Father and say on behalf of each individual, "[Father, I have walked in their shoes, experienced their pain, shared in their earthly struggles, therefore my suffering on the cross was for the redeemable. Please forgive her/him]. After forty years in the wilderness the people still found it difficult to trust their lives to God. Our lesson is that we must have the faith to trust our eternal salvation to God through Christ.

Following God's command to Moses in Chapter 13, to send men from each tribe into the land as spies, God's anger turned to rage. After forty days, the spies returned with their report that the land was truly flowing with milk and honey. They also reported that the people were strong and the cities well fortified. To describe the giants (Nephilim) the spies said they themselves felt like grasshoppers. Again, the people cry out against Moses causing God to come to the entrance of the tabernacle.

To paraphrase Numbers 14:11-31, in the presence of all the people the glory of the Lord appeared in the tabernacle and asked Moses, "how long will these people despise me and refuse to believe in me in spite of the signs and miracles?" God threatened to strike a pestilence among the people and disinherit them. Moses replied saying, "but then the Egyptians will hear of it and of how you brought them into the wilderness to kill them yourself." Moses continued, "now if you kill this people all at one time, then the nations who hear of it will say that you could not make good on your promise to bring them to the land you swore to their forefathers."

In this passage, we find Moses giving God advice saying: "the Lord is slow to anger, and abounding in steadfast love, forgiving iniquity and transgression, but by no means clearing the guilty, visiting the iniquity of the parent upon the children to the third and fourth generation. Forgive the iniquity of this people according the greatness of your steadfast love, just as you have pardoned this people, from Egypt even until now." Then God said, "I do pardon just as you have asked but none of the people who have seen my signs and wonders shall inherit the land promised except for Caleb, Joshua and your little ones, they shall know the land you have despised. (Little ones were 13 years or younger, plus 40 years in the wilderness equal a male longevity of 53 years.) In Numbers 20:12 we learn the reason Moses was not allowed to enter the Promised Land. Moses did not believe nor did he sanctify God before the children of Israel.

The sad part of reading the Book of Numbers is that you realize the backsliding of the people never did come to an end.

All of the ceremonies, the remembrances, the sacrificial offerings were meaningless to the people. Women continued to be second-class citizens and idols continued to be worshipped. In an effort to insure that one tribe did not swallow up another tribes' inheritance, especially the Josephite clans, God forbid the transfer of land from one clan to another. The tribes were to remain separate entities, yet have the ability to unite when dangers such as war and famine were imminent. God was to be their king. God's kingship was an important aspect of their relationship.

The Book of Numbers ends with a faithless Israel in the wilderness and Moses at his wit's end trying to keep God from destroying the people. Try to understand why people do not read the Pentateuch. It is difficult to comprehend. Chapter 35 reinforces the consequence for premeditated murder as well as the directive that more than one witness is required to impose the death penalty. Difficult as it is to read, the rewards will become evident as you come to understand the magnitude of the grace of God in the sacrificial death of his son as atonement for your sin. Never forget, we may not think that we do the same things as Israel in the wilderness, but we are sinners just the same.

The oldest and one of the best known blessings is given in Numbers 6:22-27, "The LORD spoke unto Moses, saying, speak unto Aaron and unto his sons, saying, on this wise ye shall bless the children of Israel, saying unto them, "The LORD bless thee, and keep thee: The LORD make his face shine upon thee, and be gracious unto thee: The LORD lift up his countenance upon thee, and give thee peace." Continuing, the LORD said, "and they shall put my name upon the children of Israel; and I will bless them." Notice two things. First, the exclusive use of the name LORD (Yehovah) and the absence of God (El). Second, the command to "put my name upon the children" is the ordinance to dedicate children to the LORD and not to baptize them.

Modern archeology has unearthed much historical evidence that coincides with our Biblical witness. Discoveries include:

The Narmer Palette – two tablets;
Jericho which was destroyed just prior to 1400 BC;
Hyksos expelled 1550 BC;
Merneptah Stele mentions Israel; and the
Basalt Stele.

# Deuteronomy

The words Moses spoke to Israel

The extent of the Promised Land was not to have been the patch of ground Israel came to inherit. The Promised Land was only the next step in the process of taking the smallest, most detestable of all people and making them into the largest most respected nation on earth. God does not think small. The extent of the Promised Land was to be from the Transjordan in the east to the Great Sea in the west; from Arabia in the south to Lebanon in the north (Deuteronomy 1:7.) The sin of worshipping Baal and the disobedience of the people prevented Israel from taking possession of all the Promised Land.

Deuteronomy is a continuance of instruction from Moses. The nature of this book although similar to Numbers is noticeably different. Repeated in their entirety are the Ten Commandments. Having read the first four books of the Bible, take notice how Israel's relationship with God takes on more detail and how no explanation for murder, adultery, theft, false witness and coveting are necessary.

In preparation for the people to cross the Jordan River into the Promised Land Moses must once again explains the nature of Israel's relationship with God. Moses emphatically attempted to settle the Elohists/Yahwist argument by instituting the Schema (Teaching).

The Schema is not a simple statement of faith. Moses desperately tried to eradicate the Elohists voice before Israel crossed the Jordan River but he never did totally eliminate it. Throughout the Old Testament the Elohists tradition keeps appearing.

To understand the Schema correctly it is first necessary to start with a wooden translation. A wooden translation is a technical term and the first step in translating Hebrew to English. Hebrew is a tri-literal language. Most words consist of three consonants. The proper Hebrew name (DVD) translates to "David" in English. By adding a prefix or suffix to the three consonants, such as in the word "heart" (LBB) it then becomes "heart of you" (LBBN). Hebrew also reads from right to left.

A wooden translation sounds odd but does have a tendency to make clear what the Hebrew writer was trying to say, not what some modern translators try to make it say. I would also note that many clergy use the term "word study" then rattle off the names of three or four translations. This is not a word study. It is a translation's study. Clergy are looking at what translators have determined the text to say. Word study means the clergy are competent enough to look at the original Biblical languages, Hebrew or Greek, and determine the meaning and choose the most appropriate word based on context.

From the following you will see how translators take the Hebrew words in their "wooden or literal form" and convert the sentence structure (syntax) into English. Notice the New Testament addition to the three main nouns in the Schema, "heart, soul and might." New Testament scribes added the word "strength" to the above three.

Jesus would not have made that mistake or that kind of change. Remember LORD means Yehovah and El means God. The Schema is a command directing people away from the worship of Eloheem in favour of Yehovah.

The Schema in Deuteronomy 6:4-7 is as follows:

4 Hear, O Israel: The LORD our God is one LORD:
5 And thou shalt love the LORD thy God with all thine heart, and with all thy soul, and with all thy might.
6 And these words, which I command thee this day, shall be in thine heart:
7 And thou shalt teach them diligently unto thy children, and shalt talk of them when thou sittest in thine house, and when thou walkest by the way, and when thou liest down, and when thou risest up.

For the following example of the Schema, I have used the NIV Interlinear wooden translation of John R. Kohlenberger III.
Deuteronomy 6:4-7

4 hear – Israel – Yahweh – God of us – Yahweh – one
5 and you must love – the – Yahweh – God of you – with all of – heart of you – and with all of – soul of you – and with all of – might of you
6 and they must be – the commands – the these – that – I – giving you – this day – on heart of you
7 and you must impress them – on children of you – and you talk – about them – when to sit you – in house of you – and when to walk you – on the road – and when to lie down you – and when to get up you.

In the above passage, each time the word "God" appears the Hebrew word is Eloheem. Eloheem means ruler, judge, or divine. The word LORD means Yahweh, the existing one and is the proper name of God, YHVH. As the name consists of consonants only, humans do not know how to pronounce God's proper name. Only Moses knew how to pronounce the divine name and legend has it that Moses passed the pronunciation down through the Levite priests who attended within the Holy of Holies, the inner sanctuary of the tabernacle and later the Jerusalem temple. As there was no temple in the two generations Israel spent in Babylonian captivity, the priests would not pronounce the word and it was lost. Again, this is legend and not fact.

Once again, Moses repeats God's words of utter frustration with the people saying, "let me alone that I may destroy them and blot out their name from under heaven; and I will make of you a nation mightier and more numerous than they" (Deuteronomy 9:14). Think of the temptation that Moses had to endure. Imagine yourself in his sandals. First, living in the lap of luxury in Pharaoh's household. Next, fleeing to Midian for his life where he married Zipporah (Bird). Content to live in the tribe of Reuel (friend of God) and tend his flocks, God calls him to go back to Egypt to help free the people. Who could have imagined that listening to God would bring over four decades of headaches and Tylenol was still 4,000 years away? Imagine the resolve it must have taken not to give in to temptation and say to God, "ok, get rid of them, I've had it as well. Yes, build a nation of my children." The Hebrew people do not only revere Moses because he spoke with God face to face, but because of his inner strength and courage. As the Schema says, "with all your heart, with all your soul and with all your might, shall you love the Lord your God. In Moses' life, God was first.

Nearing the end of his life Moses told the people that God will raise up a prophet like him (Moses) from among the people (Deuteronomy 18:15). The people became concerned about the means to identify a true prophet so God said, "if what the prophet speaks comes true, the prophet speaks in my name." If it does not come true, "kill him." I wonder how many television evangelists and ministers would be alive today if that were still in effect. The television ministers that make me shake my head are the ones who tell their listeners to plant the seed of faith by sending them $1,000.00. Wow, if you are that stupid please send the money to me. If you want to plant a seed of faith, send the money to any of the main line denominations who have an administration structure in place so that over 95% of your money will go to the work of helping the widow and the orphan, as well as the homeless and victims of disaster or famine. If you want to love your neighbour, do not send television evangelists money to build air-conditioned dog houses. Do not send to those who spend $43,000.00 a night in foreign hotels for their own personal pleasure and the comfort. When you send to registered charities, first find out how much the CEO makes in salary and benefits. You will be surprised to know that some very well known charities pay their CEO's such an enormous salary that just a little more than half the money you send to them gets to the designated famine relief.

The closing chapters of Deuteronomy speak of curses and blessing. You will also notice that the woman is still the property of the male, and female virginity is still a valuable commodity. The last half of Chapter 27 details a series of curses. Of note is verse 22, which curses sister and brother sexual relations (incest) but says nothing of a father's responsibility not to have sex with his daughter. As Deuteronomy ends, God through Moses is telling the people to love the Lord thy God with all your heart and with all your soul "is not too hard for you" (Deuteronomy 30:11.) God holds out life and prosperity to those who obey and love God. If the people choose to be like every other nation, then death and adversity will forever plague them. Chapter 32 is a beautiful example of Hebrew poetry attributed to Moses. Chapter 33 is the poetic blessing Moses recited over the tribes and then in Chapter 34 "Moses went up from the plains of Moab to Mount Nebo, to the top of Pisgah, which is opposite Jericho, and the Lord showed him the land." There Moses died at 120 years of age died and Joshua, son of Nun assumed the leadership of the nation of Israel. Verse 34 states, "never since has there arisen a prophet in Israel like Moses whom the Lord knew face to face.

Christians, if you really want to know what is going on in the Bible, read the Pentateuch. Feel the love. Feel the pain. Feel the human anguish. Feel God's pain. It will help you understand the reason for the Lamb of God, who takes away the sins of the world.

# Joshua

An era had passed. Moses had died. A nation without land waits on the Transjordan. Joshua, the man who was faithful to Moses and God from the beginning now takes on the responsibility of leading this stiff-necked mix of people. Joshua was not only brave but also curious. In Exodus 33:11, we find Joshua hiding in the tabernacle while Moses and God were speaking. Possibly, this experience accounts for his enormous faith in God. Moses and Joshua become the paradigm of faith. Only Joshua and Caleb had the courage to advance into the land of the Nephilim knowing that God was the head of their army and could slay any number of giants. Their faith allowed them to be the only two adults over the age of 53 to enter the Promised Land.

Students of the Bible should also be aware that women as well as men have played a prominent role in the growth of Israel as a nation. Bearing this in mind, take special notice in passages where the feminine voice and the divine voice are absent. Women have listened to God and been obedient. Oddly enough, there are no stories where the woman was not obedient to God's voice. Now, as the new era begins, a non-Israeli woman risks all she has in order to help strangers. Having heard of the mighty deeds of God, she believes God is at work in the lives of this new people who are camped on the other side of the Jordan. Rahab (wide) is her name. She is a prostitute or more correctly speaking, the Madame. When the king's soldiers come to her house of prostitution looking for the Israeli spies, Rahab hid them in the stalks of flax. Then, she sent the soldiers on a wild goose chase into the wilderness. When Joshua and the army finally take the city of Jericho, Rahab's life, as well as the lives of her family, is spared.

The Book of Joshua mentions Rahab (raw khawb) five times. Her name means wide, which suggests that Rahab the prostitute was a big woman. Three other Old Testament books mention Rahab but write her name as Rah hab, meaning breadth. In the context of the Promised Land passages, Rahab (Rah hab) actually symbolizes the emblematic name of Egypt or a mythical sea monster. Used twice in the New Testament (Hebrews and James) Rahab refers to the prostitute in both instances. Rahab and the spy story takes place in the year 1406 BC and we must remember that human longevity has dropped to the middle fifties. This is important as David's genealogy traces back to Rahab who became the wife of Solmon. David died in 970 BC. There is a span of 436 years between Rahab and David. With male longevity being 53 years and arbitrarily setting the fathering of a child at 23 years of age it would require 12 generation from Solmon to David. I will discuss this subject later. Again, exact details are not a requirement of story; beginning and ending are.

So it was, a non-Hebrew woman was instrumental in the taking of Jericho. Take note of the non-Hebrew genealogy. God is the Father of all people. Jesus came to save all who obey God. Confessing Christ is not the way to salvation. Obedience to God is the way and it is something you choose. We will never know what prompted Solmon to marry Rahab. However, from the offspring of these two people came the line of David, which in turn becomes the line of Jesus. One of the qualities I like about scripture is that it is so blatantly honest. Real people, kings, prostitutes, soldiers, widows, and prophets (male and female) were all part of the lineage of Jesus. If this were of human origin it would have been fabricated blemish free; a prince and princess tale. Everything would fall neatly in place. Our Bible is not picture perfect. Male bias infests scripture and the Masoretes wrote the stories as the various traditions presented their versions. They wrote the stories as were transmitted to them from the scrolls of the past. Each time one engages scripture, the ugly truth of God's relationship with Israel unfolds before the reader's eyes. I believe that the story of God's relationship with this backsliding people keeps shining through even though obvious errors and bias are evident. In the past, an enlightened Presbyterian minister would say, "let us listen for God's word contained within the scripture reading this morning." This preface to the reading of scripture acknowledges God's presence but does not attribute the authorship of scripture to God.

## Crossing the Jordan

Stones, twelve uncut stones were placed in the River Jordan prior to Israel's crossing and then later taken to Gilgal. God does not tolerate graven images. God does not tolerate any visual images as they are of human desire and creation. The implements used in the tabernacle and later the temple were not images. Images are a representation of deity. One might wonder why the Christian church has so many images to venerate. From the very beginning, God has desired to live in our hearts but the church has chosen to venerate images as did the children of Israel. The image of Christ on a cross is a detestable image meant to shame people into remembering what Jesus did for them. Those who believe in faith do not need an image as a reminder. The empty cross however, is not an image of deity; it is a reminder that death (the cross) has lost its hold on the redeemed through Christ.

Scripture should be reminder enough of the miracles performed by an omnipotent God. Bear in mind that a miracle is something beyond the power of a human to accomplish. Humans can be part of a miracle or benefit from the miraculous outcome, but they do not work the miracle. Miracles are of God. Such was the miracle that Joshua prayed for at Gibeon. He prayed, "sun, stand still at Gibeon, and moon, in the valley of Aijalon." God answered, "and the sun stood still, and the moon stopped, until Israel had taken vengeance on their enemies" (Joshua 10:12-13). Humans pray, but God works the miracle.

Obedience is the key. Joshua obediently followed all of God's instructions. Chapter 11 talks about the many kings Israel defeated. God told Joshua to burn the chariots and hamstring the horses. Joshua obeyed and more victories followed. If you can recall King Saul's disobedience, you will see the difference. As you read the Bible, you will notice that Israel did not have any horses or chariots. Horses and chariots do not appear until the time of King David and Solomon. Even then, they were negligible. Kings put their trust in horses and chariots; Israel was to have put their trust in God. What becomes evident is that when Israel remained faithful to God they were able to defeat the Egyptians, the Philistines and the Canaanites, all of whom had many chariots.

Chapter 31 records the defeat of 31 kings. Bear in mind that the name king in this context should actually be termed tribal leader, or clan leader. Each of these clans occupied a small area of land. Egypt and Babylon were nations. The emerging nation of Israel entered Palestine as a nation with no land. Israel was to have swallowed up these tribes, taken their land, lived in their houses and harvested their crops. They were a people with a God, with a past, and now were to become a people with land, houses and crops. Notice the absence of the words "government" and "king," synonymous terms.

An idea worthy of consideration and one that Patricia proposed to the class was that the fact that Israel was already a conglomeration of tribes and people. In this context, this newly formed nation was to have been a positive influence on the conquered people in terms of the worship of Yahweh. Although it was not overtly evident, Patricia taught that evangelism was to have been part of Israel's mandate. They were to have led the other nations to the worship of Yahweh, the creator of heaven and earth. Problem was, Israel wanted to be like those nations who worshiped idols housed in temples and had a human king. Reading the Old Testament reveals that God prohibited the creation of any tangible representation of God's self. God is to live within the human heart and soul. The Roman church has the human representation of the crucified Christ on a cross to shame parishioners. The problem is, with the body of Christ still on the cross it is essentially saying, "look what I have done for you." Christ on the cross nullifies the glory of the empty cross. If Christ is still on your cross then he has not risen. Protestants removed Christ from the cross for that very reason. The glory of the cross is an empty cross and a risen Lord. Death did not defeat the son of God, nor can it hold the faithful. Consider, if you will, the idea that the cross becomes an idol when a human image is affixed to it.

Faithfulness is a major theme in scripture. Had Israel been faithful they would have inherited all of the land but they were not. Israel, under Joshua's leadership, defeated thirty-one kings, but there was still much land to conquer. The Book of Joshua does not say why they did not continue and finish the conquest. The remainder of Joshua details the division of the conquered land between the tribes. As Joshua's life ebbed to a close, he called the people together at Shechem. He said, [you have to make a choice between worshipping the gods of your ancestors or Yahweh.] Then Joshua made his own personal declaration, "as for me and my house, we will serve Yahweh" (Joshua 24:14). The people then answered, "far be it from us that we should forsake the Lord to serve other gods." At that point, the people became witnesses against themselves.

Joshua, being 110 years old, died. His burial took place in the hill country of Ephraim. After transporting the mummified body of Joseph for over 400 years, burial took place in the plot of land Jacob had "purchased" from Hamor while in Shechem. Like Joshua, Joseph also lived for 110 years.

# Judges

The Book of Judges is more than likely one of the most fascinating books in the Bible. The people who judged Israel were the most unlikely group of people one could imagine. Their stories have supplied the material for the making of movies which extend from the miraculous to the bizarre, to the incomprehensible. Judges are exactly what the word implies, someone who sits in a seat of authority whose function it is to settle disputes fairly and impartially. These people were more than judges; they were people of action, military leaders. Judges did not determine punishment, they determined guilt. God determines the punishment. This is something modern courts have forgotten.

After Joshua died, the fighting continued. The tribe of Judah attacked Jerusalem, slaughtered the people and took the city (Judges 1:8). The back and forth tension continued. The people fell away from God and returned to worshiping Baal and Ashtoreth. Ashtoreth is comparable to Dionysus in Greece where the use of intoxicants freed the spirit to engage in uninhibited sexual activity. The Apostle Paul fought this free spirited sexual activity strenuously in order to promote Judo/Christian monotony.

## Ehud

As you read Judges, you see how Israel blamed God for all their ills. This is where people get the notion that God does things to test us. Judges 3:1 reads, "the Lord left [these nations] to test Israel." There is a big difference between testing and letting humanity suffer the consequences of its unfaithfulness. I know that the Bible uses the language of blame but you will also observe that when God is with Israel they have good fortune. When God is not with them, they suffer from the oppression of surrounding tribes. Personally, I do not believe God needs to do anything to test us. As the prayer goes, "lead us not into temptation, we can find our own way."

King Eglon of Moab defeated Israel suppressing the people for eighteen years. The Lord raised up Ehud, a left-handed man. Bear in mind, left handed was a curse in many cultures. In Latin left and right are termed sinister and dexter. Parents would often strap the arm of a left-handed child to their side so they could only use the right hand. However, left-handed to God is not a curse.

Called by God to take the tribute of his tribe to King Eglon, Ehud fashioned an eighteen-inch sword and strapped it to the inside of his right thigh. After delivering the tribute, Ehud said to King Eglon, "I have a message from God for you, O king." This appealed to the king's ego so he sent everyone out from his chamber. In those days a secret message from god proved to the people that god was with their king. King Eglon was a very fat man. When Eglon stood up so that Ehud could whisper the message in his ear, Ehud reached into his robe, pulled out the short sword strapped to the inside of his right thigh and drove it into Eglon's belly. Even the hilt was swallowed up in the fat, "and the dirt came out" (Judges 3:22). To cover his escape Ehud put the king into the toilet chamber and closed the doors. When Eglon's servants came into his room they saw the door to the chamber was closed so they thought he was "relieving himself" (Ibid. 3:24) so they waited until the wait was embarrassing. When they opened the chamber door, Eglon was lying dead of the floor.

## Deborah

Israel continued to do evil in the sight of the Lord. The phrase "Israel did evil" is used six times in the Book of Judges. The evil was Baal worship. After Ehud delivered Israel from King Eglon, they continued their evil ways and King Jabin of Canaan invaded the land and suppressed Israel. The commander of King Jabin's army was a man called Sisera. This is an interesting woman's passage about Deborah (bee) and Jael (mountain goat). Judges 4:2 informs the reader that the men were taken captive by King Jabin. All able-bodied men were pressed into forced labour, leaving only the women and children to work the farms. It is in this situation that Deborah rose up as prophet. Please appreciate the courage of Deborah to take on the role of prophet. Appreciate as well a woman to whom God had spoken and given instructions and yet Deborah's acknowledgment does not exist. Appreciate how she summoned Barak with two tribal leaders delivering to them a specific battle plan. This story demonstrates how, under the kingship of God, the tribes were to unit and help each other. The tribes of Naphtali and Zebulun responded to the call with 10,000 men.

Scripture is not clear on the battle plan of Deborah. It simply says, Sisera and all his chariots and all his army were thrown into a panic (Judges 4:15). If you look at a map of the Jezreel Valley, you will see the Wadi Kishon runs east to west through the valley. (Wadi is a river that dries up in the summer.) About ten miles from the coast, the Wadi comes very close to the mountain range. The best battle plan against charging chariots would have been to line the men up so the enemy could not see the riverbed. As the chariots charge, step aside as best possible, letting the chariots fall into the dry riverbed. I believe this is what happened. Charging chariots could decimate thousands of foot soldiers, but once on uneven ground they would fall prey to the foot soldiers.

Deborah's prophesy was about to come true. Sisera was obviously not leading the attack. He escaped the battle on foot finding refuge with a woman whose husband was a captive of Jabin. Her name was Jael (mountain goat). Giving Sisera a skin of milk to drink she covered him. Sisera asked her to stand guard at the entrance of her tent. She agreed and said, [trust me.] Exhausted, Sisera fell asleep. Jael quickly picked up a mallet and a tent peg, walked softly into the tent, put the peg on his temple and drove it through his head and into the ground saying, "got ya." When Barak finally showed up to inquire if she had seen Sisera Jael replied, "come and I will show you the man whom you are seeking" (Judges 4:22). Once again, God delivered the people. As Will Willomon would say, "you have to love a woman who knows how to get the job done." Following this story is the Song of Deborah. Songs and poetry were the means by which successive generations received their ancestral history. As in the Song of Miriam, much information is contained in the victory song of Deborah. Notice in verse 5:30 how each man took one or two women for himself. Women were for a man's pleasure and to bear his children.

Gideon

By this time, the student of scripture should be wondering if the Hebrew people had been plagued with an early form of Alzheimer's disease. There is a pattern developing, not unlike the backsliding that had taken place in Exodus. In this pattern, God performs a miracle (evidence), Israel rejoices in God's blessing (acceptance), then turns away (backsliding) in a desire to be like everyone else by worshipping Baal. In the time of Gideon, the Midianites and Amalekites were suppressing Israel. These easterly tribes would come at harvest taking the crops and livestock leaving Israel impoverished (Judges 6:6). Each time God left Israel to their own devices they became victims of ruthless tribal kings, as was the case of King Jabin and King Eglon. The story of Gideon is not just a story of what God can do, but a reminder of what God had done with Abram. Never forget that Abram was the patriarch of a small nomadic family when he left his father Terah. God said to him, "I will make a great nation of you" (Genesis 12:2).

In the same way God is about to use Gideon as Israel cries out once again. God heard and came to Gideon saying; "go in this might of yours and deliver Israel from the hand of Midian" (Judges 6:14). In Judges 6: 22-23 we are told that Gideon stood face to face with the angel of the Lord and is told that he will not die. The conversation is also reminiscent of "the lowliest of all people" passage (Deuteronomy 7:7) as Gideon replied, "how can I deliver Israel. My clan is the weakest in Manasseh, and I am the least in my family." Thus assured, Gideon took his father's bull and pulled down the altar built unto Baal and the Ashtoreth pole (phallic symbol). Second, he called upon the tribes of Asher, Zebulun and Naphtali for help. To ensure that God was really with him Gideon placed a fleece on the threshing floor and said, [if the fleece is wet in the morning and the floor is dry, then I will know you will deliver Israel.] In the morning, Gideon wrung out enough water to fill a bowl. Gideon then said, to be doubly sure, [do the same things again, only let the water be on the threshing floor and the fleece be dry.] Oddly enough, like a patient father, God was acquiescent to the request.

Next was a demonstration of proof/evidence that God's hand was in the victory. Gideon sent twenty two thousand Israeli soldiers home, keeping ten thousand to fight. The remaining troops went down to the water to drink. Three hundred soldiers drank by lapping the water with their tongues like a dog. The remainder cupped their hands to lift the water and drink. God said, "keep the 300 and send the rest home" (Judges 7:7). Gideon then took his servant Phurah (bough) with him to spy on the enemy camp. There, they overheard one of the enemy soldiers interpret a dream in favour of "the sword of Gideon." Thus assured, Gideon placed his 300-man army strategically around the enemy camp and on his signal they started to blow trumpets and smash jars. Thrown into disarray by the noisy deception the enemy panicked and fled. Again, the Bible demonstrates how Israel was a nation unto itself. As Israel chased the enemy, Gideon and his men came into two villages to ask for bread. The villages of Succoth and Penuel refused Gideon's men sustenance. On his victorious return, Gideon trampled the elders of Succoth with thorns and briers. He then went to Penuel, pulled down their tower and killed all the men. Sadly, the backsliding in Judges 8 became a recurring pattern with the children God had claimed as family. As soon as Gideon died the Israelites relapsed and "went whoring after Baalim (lord) and made Baalberith (lord of the covenant) their god" (Judges 8:33). Mossad is the modern day equivalent of the Sword of Gideon.

Abimelech

Abimelech (my father is king) became king and convinced the men of Shechem to follow him. He then went to his father's house at Ophrah (fawn) with his band of worthless hired men and murdered all seventy of his brothers. Only Jotham (Yehovah is perfect) the youngest brother escaped. Abimelech spent his days fighting. During the siege of Thebez, a woman threw a millstone off the tower crushing his head. While he was still able, he told his young armour bearer to kill him with his sword so people would not say a woman killed him.

Tola, (worm) of the tribe of Ephraim then judged Israel twenty-three years. Following Tola, Jair (he enlightens) judged Israel for twenty-two years. Israel continued to do evil in the sight of the God, and continued to fall victim to their own devices. If you are a student of the Bible this is a good time to reflect upon your theological perspective. Was God the cause of Israel's afflictions? It is evident that Israel benefitted from the countless victories under the leadership of the Judges who obeyed God but what about the times they were disobedient? Where I differ from the Biblical storytellers is, God sending foreign kings to punish backsliding Israel. The view I have always taken is that the protective hand of God was withdrawn, leaving the people victim to their own desires. As you read these recurring themes, ask yourself whether or not it is fair to blame God for Israel's disasters. Ask yourself, "is God is that vengeful?" God has demonstrated many human qualities but God's desire is not to have a fearful despotic relationship. God desires a loving relationship with children who willingly obey commandments made for their own well-being. We fear God, not because God punishes us but because the rejection of God leaves us without protection from the ungodly.

Jephthah

By now, you may be wondering why they did not call this book "Generals" rather than "Judges" as all of the judges have been military leaders. Jephthah is no different and every bit as interesting. Judges 11 begins the story of the outcast son of Gilead born of a prostitute. As I have said, you have to love the Biblical storytellers for their blatant honesty. When Gilead's sons, by his real wife, became adults, they drove Jephthah away, saying to him "you shall not inherit anything of our father's house for you are the son of (a whore) another woman." When he left his father's village Jephthah gathered around him a large number of followers whom the Bible calls "outlaws." (By definition an outlaw is an individual who is outside the protection of the law). As time passed, the Ammonites made war against Gilead forcing the Gileadites to find Jephthah and ask him to lead their army. Jephthah's gang must have been sizeable and well skilled in battle. Possibly the conversation went something like this, [we know we kicked you out of town because you are the son of a whore but we need you now so will you come back and fight for us]?

The reply would have been hard to accept but the people did not have a choice so when Jephthah said, [I will come back and fight against the Ammonites and if I am victorious I will become your leader]. Mizpeh was the site of the promise to Jephthah. Mizpeh was the place, at the foot of Mount Hermon, where Jacob and Laban built a rock heap and made the following promise, "the Lord watch between me and thee, when we are absent one from another" (Genesis 31:52). Taking command of the army, Jephthah sent messengers to the king of the Ammonites wanting to know why they had come to fight Israel and take their land. The king claimed Israel had taken the land from his ancestors when they came into the land. A hard reality pill to swallow is that by not killing off your entire enemy succeeding generations take retribution against you. If I were to ask you when peace will come to the people of Palestine, what would your answer be?

Jephthah realized that war was imminent so he prayed to God for victory. He vowed that, "should God grant him victory, he would offer a burnt offering of the first person to come out of his house on his return". After inflicting a massive defeat upon his enemy Jephthah returned home. Overcome with excitement and before the selected servant girl could come out, his daughter rushed out to greet her father dancing and shaking her timbrel. However distraught Jephthah was, he kept his vow. Even though this is written as a Yahwist story, the observant reader can see that the Canaanite custom of human sacrifice to Baal was still being practiced. Note also, the absence of God's voice and the presence of total male domination. Male bias has a habit of leaving God's voice and the feminine voice out of stories with questionable actions. Please learn to recognize who is speaking in a story and more importantly, who is not. When a story is about a female, ask yourself, "where is her voice"?

Jephthah's only daughter requested two months to wander on the mountains near Mizpeh with her friends to bewail her virginity (Judges 11:37). When she returned Jephthah carried out his vow to God. Scripture is clear that "she had never slept with a man. So there arose a custom that, for four days every year the daughters of Israel would go out to lament the daughter of Jephthah the Gileadite" (11:39-40).

Samson

The story of Samson (like the sun) has motivated Hollywood to make many movies about this wonder child. Samson's mother remains nameless even though an angel of the Lord appeared to her foretelling the birth. Again, scripture tells a story of a barren nameless woman chosen to be the mother of a special child, a child of destiny. This is more than a divine intervention pattern. It is a familiar story of God at work in the lives of a chosen people. When the angel of the Lord appeared to the woman she was informed that she will bear a son. She is not to drink wine or consume strong drink, and no razor is to come upon the child's head. He is to be a Nazarite. (One consecrated to the Lord).

Note!

By now, the Biblical student should have noticed a pattern developing; a pattern of barren women becoming the progenitors of the chosen people. The overriding theme is that of God at work in situations where human efforts are fruitless. Like creation itself, ex nihilo.

When the woman informed her husband Manoah (rest) of this revelation, he prayed that the angel of the Lord return. The angel reappeared and Manoah offered to cook a kid but the angel would not eat thereof. Manoah asked the angel's name only to be met with the reply, "it is too wonderful" for you to comprehend. The prophesy came to pass, the woman bore a son and they named him Samson, meaning "like the sun." In a culture where dark hair was the norm, a blonde haired boy would be an anomaly. The blonde haired Samson was special gift from God. The same was true of a red haired boy, like David, the hair designated a gift from God. Notice how the mothers remain nameless while Manoah is mentioned 14 times.

As a young man, Samson saw a young Philistine woman and wanted to marry her. His parents wanted him to marry one of his kin but he was insistent. Notice again, the desire to marry a cousin (intra-tribal) or as a last resort, within the tribal family. Samson more than likely realized his marriage to a Philistine woman would cause animosity with the Philistine men. During this time, Samson killed a lion with his bare hands and later found that honeybees had made a hive in the carcass. Prior to the wedding Samson made a feast and proposed a riddle to the guests. He said if they could guess the riddle within seven days, he would give them 30 linen garments and 30 festal garments. If however they could not, they were to give him 30 linen garments and 30 festal garments. The men agreed. The riddle was, "out of the eater came something to eat. Out of the strong came something sweet" (Judges 14:14).

After three days, they could not explain the riddle so they said to Samson's wife, "coax your husband to explain the riddle to us, or we will burn you and your father's house with fire." So it was that she nagged at him for three days until he finally gave in and explained the riddle. She told the men and they repeated the answer to Samson, "what is sweeter than honey, what is stronger than a lion." Samson said, "if you had not ploughed (devised) with my heifer you would not have answered the riddle. In order to pay the debt Samson went to Ashkelon, killed thirty men, took their garments and paid the dept.

A short time later Samson went to visit his wife but her father would not let him see her as she had been given to Samson's best man. He did however offer him his younger, prettier daughter. At this insult, Samson caught 300 foxes, tied two foxes together by their tails, attached a torch to their tails and set them loose in the fields of grain. When the villagers learned what had happened they burned father and daughter, which is what they were going to do if she did not cooperate. The war Samson wanted had started. The Philistines came to Judah demanding the capture of Samson. After allowing the men of Judah to bind his hands, the Philistines carried him off to Lehi (jaw). As the men of the town were coming out Samson broke the ropes that bound his arms, picked up the jawbone of an ass and killed a thousand men. Needing some R & R he went in unto a prostitute in Gaza. The men of the town decided to gather at daybreak and take Samson as he left the prostitute but he left at midnight, pulled down the gate of the city and carried it off.

As you read a story like Samson, you have to wonder how enjoying prostitutes was consistent with being chosen by God. Raised as a Nazarite, possessor of the gift of strength, what went wrong? Surely, his parents must have been puzzled as have the thousands of parents who raise children in a Godly home, then watch as the child turn to the ways of the world. Samson would have been the modern day equivalent of a sports celebrity, literally, the golden boy, but now the golden boy falls in love (lust) again. This time we learn the name of the woman immediately. She is Delilah. We are told that Delilah led Samson astray, deceived him. Now go back and read the story. Do the actions match those of a hero who listened to God? The only things that led Samson were his lust for wine, women and fighting. No leading astray was necessary but the woman gets the blame anyway.

It is difficult to say if Delilah was a prostitute but when the Philistines came to her with an offer of 1,100 piece of silver, she did not hesitate. Wine and women became Samson's downfall. Notice how God's direction and presence is absent. First, Samson says, [bind me with seven new bow stings and I will become weak.] Delilah bound him then shouted "the Philistines are upon you" but Samson broke the strings with ease. After whining about the mockery, Samson told Delilah to bind him with new ropes and he will become weak. The same thing happened. Next, he told Delilah to brad his hair into seven locks and weave them together, securing them with a pin. Again she shouted, "the Philistines are upon you," with the same results. Samson must have really loved this woman or he was intellectually challenged. As the saying goes, "strong as an ox and just about as smart."

Delilah nagged him for days until he finally revealed the secret of his strength. No razor had ever touched his head from his birth until now. Cutting his hair would cause him to become as weak as any man. After falling asleep on her lap, Delilah called her servant to cut Samson's hair. This time, when he awoke, the Philistine fell upon him, took him captive and gouged out his eyes. Taking their prize to Gaza, the Philistines shackled him to a millstone where he ground grain day after day. Once the golden boy of the Nazarites, now the object of mockery, Samson finally decided to pray to God for revenge.

Having kept Samson alive until the festival and prior to sacrificing him to their god Dagon, the Philistine positioned him between the two pillars that supported the temple. The temple was full, the time for the vengeful sacrifice of Samson had come, but they had not anticipated Samson's plea to God. His hair had grown, his strength was renewed. Samson pushed over the two pillars and the temple came crashing down killing its occupants.

Chauvinism

Following Samson are two Levite stories. One is the story of Micah (who is like God) the Levite for hire who sold his Levitical service for gain. The other is about a Levites concubine. They are stories of murder, deception and idol making. As you read each story you cannot help but ask yourself, "what on earth are these stories doing in the Bible?" One consideration is the thought that the writer was trying to establish the need for a human king. In preparation for Israel's desire for a king, Chapters 18 and 19 open with "in those days, when there was no king in Israel." Just when you think these stories could not possibly get anymore bazaar, Chapter 19 proves you wrong. For centuries, scholars have been puzzled by the inclusion of this story in the Bible. They have marveled at the violence reminiscent in the Sodom and Gomorrah story.

From a societal perspective, the story dramatically illustrates what happens when a culture dictates that men are to have complete control and authority over women. As previously stated, the actions and outcome of an incident demonstrate the truth of the matter. Please take the time to read this story and determine whether you agree this story is an appalling demonstration of the male bias infused into the Yahwist interpretation of Genesis 2:20. Remember, the Yahwist version of creation demonstrates that woman (ish-shaw) was created as a helper (azar)e. In the Adam's rib story, the Hebrew language clearly demonstrates the relationship of man and woman. Man is eesh and woman is ish-shaw, meaning "taken from man." The word helper (azar) does not mean servant. The word for servant is (eh-bed). A proper Biblical understanding of biased male superiority is critical to understanding the repugnant revelation of the following story.

The Levite's Concubine

Unlike the story of Dinah, the female victim in the Levite's Concubine is nameless. Surprisingly, the male characters in the story remain nameless as well. As previously mentioned the Masoretes did not alter or massage the stories. Chapter 19 demonstrates that the female victim comes into the story as a concubine. Concubines were common addition to a rich man's household. Men purchased concubines for pleasure and for child bearing in order to build up their tribe. In other words, they were a possession. The KJV calls her a concubine, a wife and then a whore. This unnamed woman enters the story as the concubine of a Levite who lived in a remote part of the hill country of Ephraim. Like many of the Biblical heroines she had a strong spirit. She made her own decisions but was still subservient to male superiority. After some time she became angry. (We can only surmise what living conditions would have been for a high-spirited piece of property.) Leaving the man, she returned to her father's home in Bethlehem. I suspect that it took a long time for the man to find out where she had gone as it took four months for the Levite to come for her.

Arriving at the concubine's home, the father convinces the Levite to stay for three days. Probably to rest from the journey. Scripture does not reveal any negotiations. This tells me that the Levite paid for the woman. She is his property. On the fourth day the Levite prepares to leave with his concubine but the father convinces him to nourish himself for the journey. After eating and drinking, it became too late to leave. This happened repeatedly until the Levite finally departed. Later that afternoon, the Levite's servant suggested spending the night in a town of the Jebusites. The Levite would not stay in a strange town. Jebusites were foreigners and not part of Israel.

As sunset was upon them, they entered Gibeah, which belonged to the tribe of Benjamin. They sat in the city square waiting for someone to extend hospitality to travelers but it did not happen.

At nightfall, an old man who had been labouring in the field was returning to his home. After making inquiry, the old man invited them to stay in his home. In the dark of night the perverse men of the town came pounding on the door demanding the Levite be sent out so they "could have intercourse" with him (Judges 19:22). The old man pleaded with "the sons of Belial" (worthless good for nothings) but to no avail. (In the Middle East, when a host offers you food or water, he is responsible for your well being.) This is where male chauvinism gives way to cowardice. Men were to be the protectors of the household. When the perverted men of the town came to rape the Levite, the old man offered his virgin daughter and the concubine to the men to wantonly ravish. At this point, the Levite grabbed his concubine and threw her out to the men who raped her and abused her all night. After a good night's sleep, the Levite opened the door to find his concubine grasping the threshold.

The significance of grabbing the threshold is that the woman was making a statement that she was to have been afforded protection. She was claiming her right as a child of God. With no sign of remorse, the Levite looked down in disgust and said, "get up, we are going" (Judges 19:28). Receiving no answer the Levite threw her over the donkey and went to his home. The story becomes more revolting as the first act of the Levite was to cut the concubine into twelve pieces. Ironically, the Levite sent the pieces of concubine to the twelve tribes demanding retribution for his loss. To a western mind this story is detestable. To an eastern mind it is acceptable as it maintains man's authority over women. This perverted male bias is still practiced and seeks acceptance in the Christian world.

Note!

Heather Gurd explained to me that there might be some strange relationship to the Osiris the father of the Egyptian god Horus. Osiris was killed by his brother Set in order to get his throne. Isis found all the body parts with the exception of the phallus so she made a golden phallus to bring Osiris back to life in order for her to get pregnant and bear her son Horus. Mythology has many strange stories.

In Chapter 20, as the story continues, the Levite tells the council of tribes that the concubine was his wife. The story told to the council is not exactly what happened as he conveniently left out the part of his responsibility. The council decided to punish the men of Gibeah so they sent the tribe of Judah. The Benjamites responded by killing twenty two thousand men of Judah. The next day the men of Israel went up against Gibeah and lost eighteen thousand men in battle. On the third day, Israel lost thirty thousand men. Then, lured out of the city be a fake retreat, the men of Gibeah charged out and into an ambush. They lost twenty five thousand men. As the army left the city, ten thousand Israelites rushed into the city slaughtering everyone within. Again, notice the absence of God in these stories. Once again, the numbers are far too large for people who lived in a village.

The council then decided to curse anyone who gave a wife to a Benjamite. Then Israel had compassion upon Benjamin giving them back the women they had kept as slaves from Jabesh-gilead. Remember, a soldier could kill a woman or take her home as a servant or concubine. With very few women left in Benjamin Israel did not want to see the extinction of the tribe of Benjamin so they further devised a plan to get around the curse instituted on those giving a wife to a Benjamin. They said to the Benjamites, "the yearly festival to the Lord is taking place at Shiloh… go lie in wait in the vineyards and watch: when the young women of Shiloh come out to dance… carry them off… if there fathers complain say to them be generous and allow us to keep them." Again, this is reminiscent of the cult practices of Dionysus, the Greek god of the grape harvest; of wine, women and song. Remember Judeo/Christian morals are still a thousand years away. This practice may have been subjective but it was fun.

Having read this story numerous times, it never ceases to amaze me as to the purpose. First, why was it included in scripture? Second, what meaning did Israel derive from its inclusion? Possibly the resulting action explains how the Benjamites came to be massacred. Possibly, the story reinforces a man's right to do with a woman as he pleases; to treat her as personal property. Possibly, the meaning of the story for the civilized world is that it graphically illustrates that women were never meant to be personal property. Women, named and unnamed, have rights. Civilized societies need to execute with extreme prejudice the punishment of those who kidnap and buy women for use in prostitution. Members of religious sects who advocate Sharia Law or still adhere to the belief that woman are property, subject to the whims of a husband or father, will not be tolerated and forcibly removed from civilized societies. Many years ago, Edmund Burke, a British statesman, said, "all that is necessary for the triumph of evil is that good men do nothing."

I hope you can see that the Book of Judges is not only fascinating but also equally bizarre, incomprehensible and distinctly revolting. Imagine yourself in 423 BC when the rabbinical council decided to close the canon (the written works of scripture) without adding or subtracting one dot or iota. The decision to keep these stories must have been difficult considering the fact that there were dozen of books rejected for their lack of credibility. The same was true when the Christian canon closed. I extend my gratitude to the council for not trying to polish the variety stories from the various traditions. When human stories are too squeaky clean, too identical, too supportive of an individual agenda, investigators know something is wrong.

The date of writing scripture, who wrote scripture, and who determined the various canons of the Old and New Testament have occupied scholarly debate for centuries. The debate rages today as Roman Catholic and Protestant canons differ, as do Jewish canons. This work does not deal with these disagreements. It deals with what the words say, not what they taught you in Sunday school and certainly not what denominational dogma want the words to say. When in a scholarly discussion the quickest way to spot false man made doctrine is in the use of the phrase "we take this to mean." The phrase means, the Bible says one thing but we want it to mean something else. This book deals with the male bias in Biblical stories by pointing out how the opening statement may say one thing but the ensuing actions reveal the opposite.

## Ruth

The Book of Ruth is a women's story, as is Esther. In seminary, Dorcas told the class to pay attention to women's stories. They had something to say. Woman's stories are an important part of the Hebrew Oral Tradition. Passed down from generation to generation they too came to be included in the Hebrew canon. Two oral stories, believed to be the oldest writings of the Hebrew people, are The Song of Miriam and the Song of Deborah. Through a beautiful combination of poetic devices these songs reveal the joy and gratefulness of the people God has chosen. In the same way, the voice of the storyteller exposes Naomi's pain in the death of her husband and two sons. Ruth's dedication to her mother-in-law has become a universal example of women from two different cultures bonding together. It is a family story of destitution, poverty, heartbreak and death. Even more, it is story told in the context of a male dominated culture. Two lone women fight for justice as they are about to fall victim to the greed of a close relative.

The story is a familiar one of a family down on their luck. Famine caused them to move to a foreign land. Elimelech (my God is king) and Naomi (my delight) packed up and moved with their children Mahlon (sick) and Chilion (pining) to Moab. Elimelech died and Mahlon and Chilion took Moabite wives whose names were Orpah (gazelle) and Ruth (friendship). Ten years later both Mahlon and Chilion were dead and Naomi, feeling as low as a mother could feel, decided to return to her clan. Her daughters-in-law tried to go with her but Naomi told them she cannot have any more children. In that culture, a widow (Orpah or Ruth) would have waited for Naomi's boys to grow to the age of maturity in order to be impregnated by them so the male child could reestablish the family line. Orpah decided to return to her clan in Moab. She kissed Naomi goodbye and returned to her family. Ruth however refused to leave Naomi. Her song has been carried down through the ages, "where you go, I will go; where you lodge, I will lodge; your people shall be my people, and your God my God" (Ruth 1:16). Arriving home at the beginning of the barley harvest, Naomi said to the women of Bethlehem "call me no longer Naomi (my delight), call me Mara (bitterness) for the Almighty has dealt bitterly with me."

Chapter 2 gives the reader insight into the man Boaz. At the onset of the harvest, Boaz greeted his farm hands with words that have been incorporated into the liturgy of many denominations. The words are, "the Lord be with you" (Ruth 2:4). The men replied, "the Lord bless you." We now say, "and also with you." The following dialogue demonstrates that Boaz was immediately attracted to Ruth. He gave specific instruction for the workmen not to molest her. The men were to purposely leave grain in the field for Ruth. Boaz told Ruth not to go to any other field to glean but to remain in his field. If she was thirsty, go to the vessels set out for the men and drink. When Ruth inquired about his generosity, Boaz told her it was because of her kindness to Naomi. Boaz even invited her to partake of the bread, wine and parched grain with him and the workers. Throughout the harvest, Ruth stayed in the fields of Boaz as she would have suffered molestation from workers in other fields. Again, this victimization demonstrates the non-existent rights of a woman in a chauvinistic culture. It also reinforces the subjection of women when Boaz inquired, "to whom does this woman belong?"

With age comes wisdom. Naomi recognized the acts of kindness shown to Ruth by Boaz as acts of admiration (he had the hots for her) with affectionate overtones. Men in every age have always gone out of their way for a beautiful woman. Naomi instructed Ruth to wash, anoint herself and put on her best clothes. Naomi told Ruth to go down to the threshing floor and wait until the men had finished eating and drinking and then take note of where Boaz lay down. She followed Naomi's instructions. When Boaz lay down, Ruth stealthily "uncovered his feet" and lay down beside him. Boaz could feel someone beside him so he asked, "who are you?" Ruth answered "I am Ruth your servant; spread your cloak over your servant for you are next-of-kin" (Ruth 3:9). In the dialogue that follows, Boaz extols her virtues. He commends her for not chasing after the younger men and informs her that there is one other next-of-kin closer to her than him. In the English translations, Chapter 3 gives the appearance of an upright encounter. Clergy often preach upon the virtues of Ruth and Boaz. However, the motive for going and the actions of the story dictate otherwise. Here was a woman on a mission. She was washed, perfumed, and had her best clothes on, as well as a cloak and quietly lying down beside a man who had been drinking. In order for Naomi to take back her inheritance Ruth must get pregnant by a kinsman. In Hebrew, all the words in this part of the story have sexual connotations. There is no mistaking Ruth's action.

If you have ever been a woman on a mission, you will know how Ruth completed her objective. Men, if you have ever had a few drinks and had an attractive woman snuggle up beside you then you will know Boaz would never say, "go away, I want to sleep." This is not conjecture or opinion on my part. One of the beauties of the Hebrew language is that it is specific, as is the Greek. The best example is how English translates the Greek words Agape (spiritual), Eros (lust), Philae (brotherly), Storge (family), Charis (grace) and Eunoia (teacher/student) into the single word "love." The problem arises when a euphemism is used which was common in Hebrew. The Hebrew term, "uncover his feet," is a euphemism for sleeping with, or more bluntly speaking, having sexual intercourse. In the morning, Ruth told Naomi what had happened and Naomi knew it was out her hands. They had done all they could.

Understanding God's jubilee is essential to understanding what happens in Chapter 4. The reason for the sexual intercourse the night before surfaces; one other kinsman had the right to Elimelech's property. If a kinsman fathers a child in Ruth, the child, along with Elimelech's property, becomes the child's. If the kinsman takes Ruth to wife and does not consummate the marriage, the kinsman keeps the property as there never will be a living relative to inherit the land. Now, think back to the night before. Ruth, all dressed up in her finest clothes, goes to the threshing floor at night, sleeps with Boaz, returns with a cloak full of grain, and the translators want us to believe no-one saw her or they did not engage in sexual intercourse.

The next day, when Boaz offered the right of redemption, the kinsman refused to exercise his right. The kinsman refused to redeem the parcel of land belonging to Elimelech because he could not chance that Naomi was already pregnant. If the boy were actually the child of Boaz, then all his property would pass over to the line of Boaz. This was unthinkable. To find proof of the above listen to the words of the kinsman, "I cannot redeem it for myself without damaging my own inheritance. Take my right of redemption yourself, for I cannot redeem it" (Ruth 4:6). If Ruth were not pregnant, his inheritance would not have been damaged. Covering up the actions of Ruth is an example of how the Christian Church has tried to clean up the word of God.

Noteworthy is the mention of building up the house of Elimelech "like the house of Perez, who Tamar bore to Judah." Back in the Book of Genesis, Chapter 38, Tamar was in the same situation as Naomi. Promised a husband to keep the family line and inheritance in tact, Judah purposely kept from delivering that promise. Tamar took matters into her own hand. She dressed as a harlot and tricked Judah into having sexual intercourse with her. In both situations, "you gotta love a woman who knows how to get the job done" (Will Willomon).

In addition, the last verse of the Book of Ruth ends with the genealogy of David. Salmon married the prostitute Rahab and bore the child Boaz. Boaz and Ruth had a son and named him Obed. Jesse was the son of Obed and David was the son of Jesse. In these genealogies the name of the mother is not listed as were the many generations it would have taken as the time lapse from Salmon to

David was about 423 years. It is a physical impossibility to have four generations, from Boaz to David, pass in over four hundred years. By the time Israel crossed the Jordan male longevity was 53 years, tops. Only the important names have been documented.

# 1 Samuel

Proper names such as Samuel necessitate the asking of an important question, "did the Yahwist dominate the writing of scripture?" I say that because the name Samuel (Shemuw'el, sehm-oo-ale') means, "his name is El." Definitely, the use of LORD (Yahweh) dominates the Old Testament but the switch back to El (God) is puzzling, as they are two separate ways of naming the creator. Sometimes the Yahwist designation "Lord God" is used. Other verses use only the Elohists name (El) for the creator, "God." Nevertheless, Samuel was instrumental in calling Israel to turn away from the worship of Baal and return to Yahweh and yet his name upholds El, the ancient name of God. I would maintain that two traditions have been kept in scripture and part of the evidence is in the names of the prophets. Their names are not simply proper nouns but statements.

Samuel (sehm-oo-ale) means, "his name is El." Elijah or Eliyah (ay-lee-yaw) means "my God is Yehovah" or "Yah(u) is God." Please understand that the Yahwist and Elohists are not arguing about two different Gods. The argument is a disagreement over the name by which to call God.

Looking back to the story of Jacob, we see that he purchased a plot of land from Hamor outside of Shechem. Jacob "erected there an altar, and called it Elelohe-Israel," (ale el-o-hay' yis-raw-ale') meaning the mighty God of Israel (Genesis 33:20). What is of interest is the fact that Hebrew proper nouns are very specific. El (ruler) is the ancient name of God. Yahu (the beloved) was the only begotten of El. The tension exists in the name by which they called God. To give some background on the struggle for identity, Abram was to move the people away from the sacrificial practices of the followers of the Canaanite god Baal, who is also called El. I will quote the findings of Bishop Katia.

"Don't be dismayed by the bad things the Canaanite version of El was said to have done. Canaanite and Phoenician society was depraved (child sacrifice, sex slavery, vicious torture and execution methods)... so they made their gods and goddesses as violent and sexually perverse as themselves. The true El later became or merged with the Hebrew God. He was a noble, fatherly, kingly figure. Contrary to modern fiction and fantasy, the societies of the past were not full of romantic noble savages. We moderns must resist the urge to think wistfully, that religion was so much better, so much purer back then. No! It wasn't".

Samuel

Hannah's choice of the name Samuel for her infant made a definite statement. Hannah was barren, a common occurrence in the Old Testament especially among women who played an important role in Israel's development. Barrenness is an interesting Bible Study topic as the barrenness theme involves God taking something or someone who is barren and bringing life out of darkness. Hannah is a perfect example of how God answers prayer beyond our wildest imaginations. After Samuel's weaning Hannah dedicated him as one of the Nazarites, holy unto the Lord. Eli (ascension) was the priest and his two sons Hophni (pugilist) and Phinehas (mouth of brass) were wicked. A man of God told Eli that both his boys would die on the same day (1 Samuel 2:34). It came true. (Notice how the boys Pugilist and Mouth of Brass add insight to the story).

Eli raised Samuel. Samuel 2:26 states that, the boy "grew in stature and in favour with the Lord and with the people." Samuel was a respected judge and at the time, there was no king in Israel. Finally, the people went to Samuel demanding he anoint a king over them (1 Samuel 8:6). It raises the question, "why do humans need a tangible king as evidence of nationality?" God's only desire was to live in their hearts. Governments live in your wallet. The people's choice to abandon God displeased Samuel so he prayed. God answered, [anoint a king over them so they can be like everyone else.] God tried to comfort Samuel saying, "they have rejected me from being king over them" from the time in Egypt until now. Patricia's favourite saying, "kings will do the things kings will do" summarizes Chapter 8. God's prophesy was correct. [Israel's sons he will conscript into the king's army. He will take your daughters into the king's bedroom and kitchen. Kings take the best vineyards and orchards. Kings take, take, take and take some more.] Read Chapter 8 and ask yourself if anything has changed from the time of Samuel until now. Ironically, had God said to Moses, [build me a statue in the image of a supreme donkey] there would not have been any backsliding. Israel was to have evolved into a holy priesthood to serve God but Israel preferred to worship a Baal. Israel was to have revered God as their king but Israel preferred to revere a human king.

A King for Israel

The time had come to find a king. The irony of the first king named Saul (desired) was that he was a Benjamite from the despised town of Gibeah. He was a handsome man, standing a head taller than all other men. From all external appearances he was a good choice. Saul was a perfect example of how people make a choice. He looked good on the outside. From this point forward, when trouble came to Israel, the king would have to lead, not God. Not long after choosing Saul, King Nahash (serpent) laid siege to Jabesh-Gilead. The town's people tried to make a treaty with Nahash but the king insisted on a condition. The condition was that his soldiers "gouge out everyone's right eye, and thus put disgrace upon Israel" (1 Samuel 11:2). (This was also a hideous way of marking a man as a slave.) Messengers came to Saul asking for deliverance. Saul cut oxen in pieces and sent the pieces to the tribes with the warning that [if they did not come to help fight against King Nahash, Saul would slaughter them like the oxen].

When the people in Jabesh heard Saul was coming, they sent word to King Nahash that they would give themselves up and submit to his demand in the morning. In an early morning attack, the unsuspecting King Nahash was defeated and his men scattered. We do not know Saul's age when he became king. Damage to that part of the scroll has obliterated the number. In addition, there is an ongoing debate over the large numbers in scripture. As an example, when scripture notes that forty and two thousand men attacked a city, scholars are not sure if it means 42,000 or the smaller amount, 40 and 2000 (2040) men. Frankly, I side with the lower numbers as it is impossible to comprehend the food and water problems, as well as the waist disposal problems inherent with such a large force. The towns Israel attacked when they crossed into the Promised Land were small towns, villages. Remember, Simeon and Levi killed a total of 26 men in Shechem.

King Saul continued to fight the Philistines with his son Jonathan. In preparation to battle the Philistines, Saul sent for the elderly Samuel to offer burnt sacrifices to God. After seven days, Samuel had not yet arrived so Saul went ahead and personally made the offering. This displeased Samuel. It is also noteworthy to mention that Chapter 13 states that Israel did not have any weapons – swords or spears. Nor, did they have a smith to make or sharpen weapons. Saul's army carried plowshares, mattocks, axes and sickles for weapons. Please note the fact that Israel did not have any chariots and neither did David. When you get to Solomon ask yourself "where did all the chariots come from."

Saul's Downfall

Lost in the rhetoric of war, idolatry and unfaithfulness is the concept of peace. Yes, Israel must of necessity conquer the Promised Land by violence but once accomplished the north south corridor between Babylon and Egypt would be comprised of farms and villages. No self respecting king would think to conquer farmers. Kings attack kings. Kings attack capital cities. Kings need a prize to satisfy their vanity. Consider if you will, God's plan for an ideal society. In this context, God's plan for the chosen people becomes apparent. The reader needs to understand that Israel was to be the nucleus of peace. They were not to have an army. They were not to have a king, except God. Israel's God lived in the heart. No idols to capture. No temple to sack.

Through the Book of Judges God had provided a deliverer in times of trouble. Now, as Saul tries to build an army he finds that he does not have any chariots, horses, or weapons of war. Nonetheless, God is going to help Saul destroy the Amalekites for what they did to the Israelites when they came out of Egypt. However, Samuel had delivered very specific instructions to Saul. The instructions are repugnant to us today, but certainly understandable. The 3,000 year old history of war in the Middle East has always revolved around past atrocities one tribe committed against another in the past. Past atrocities have always been the justification for revenge, as survivors build an army and take revenge.

Upon defeating the Amalekites, Saul was to kill king Agag, and all the men, women, children, babies, oxen, sheep, camels and donkeys. This command was repulsive, but understandable. Saul did the things that kings will do. He took Agag captive for a kingly ransom. He also took the best sheep and cattle. The reader needs to realize that God is the provider for Israel. Once settled in the Promised Land God's people were never to make war for the purpose of gain. Samuel was furious with what Saul had done. He went to Saul, took his sword, had Agag brought to him, and then hacked Agag into pieces in front of Saul. Samuel then fled from Saul to Ramah for fear of his life after telling Saul that God was going to ripe the kingdom away from him in a like manner. The movie *King David* starring Richard Gere, 1985, is a good depiction of the lives of Saul and David. The movies does not "clean up" the Bible story.

Kings have always endeavoured to make themselves like gods. They do this by creating a "line." People have always accepted the propaganda of "entitlement because of birth" as being appropriate. The rich have always enforced this belief as it helps keep the rabble in their place. As a child of the 60s, I can attest to the struggle of individuals trying to rise above their station in life. Consider the impact of this philosophy throughout the ages. The 60s were an amazing time to be alive as the youth of America changed the way people looked at many issues such as war and slavery. When the children of the 60s became parents, they started to encourage their children to pursue their dreams freed from the encumbrances of racial prejudice and bias. Inter-racial marriages produce beautiful intelligent people with Godly gifts to offer society. Intra-tribal marriages create fanatics such as those produced by Nazism and Islam.

## David

Transition does not always happen quickly. Saul continued to reign as king even though God commanded Samuel to anoint a new king over Israel. Consider for a moment what was about to happen. Saul was a big man, rich, strong and handsome, skilled in war. David was the youngest son of Jesse, the one charged with tending the sheep. Solomon was the spoiled son of King David. He was raised in luxury, educated, and lived in a time of peace. The first three kings were completely different types of people, with three different kinds of life experiences. Yet, each earthly king fell short of what God required of a leader. God did not require a king for the chosen people. God required a shepherd. In fact, David should have understood this more than anyone.

David was a shepherd tending the flocks of his father Jesse. Unbeknown to Jesse Samuel arrived with the intent to anoint one of his sons. Naturally, Jesse felt Samuel would choose Abinadab, as he was the oldest. Jesse called seven sons in order of birth. Rejecting each one, Samuel asked if there were any more sons. The answer was yes, the youngest that was tending the flock. In obedience to his father's command, David arrived and Samuel beheld a red headed boy with blue eyes. Immediately, Samuel anointed David as king of Israel but David would have to wait for the right time to take power.

The story of David and Goliath is one of the most familiar stories in the Old Testament. David was not only skillful with the sling but also with music and song; songs which soothed Saul's troubled mind.

While Saul and the army were enduring insults from the Philistines, David came forward and offered to battle Goliath. With a single stone from David's sling, Goliath came crashing to the ground. David ran up, took Goliath's sword and cut off the Philistine's head. The enemy, now in complete disarray, scattered in fear with the army of Israel in hot pursuit. David's acclaim continued to grow as Saul's admiration for him diminished. The people began singing of David's victories. Notwithstanding David's popularity, Saul's son Jonathan (Yehovah has given) became a kindred spirit with David. This friendship was later honoured when David spared the life of Jonathan's son Mephibosheth (exterminating the idol). This was a huge gesture of friendship as the killing of anyone who had a right to the throne by inheritance was the acceptable custom of the time.

David had many opportunities to kill Saul but did not. Saul died in battle, not by the arrow that struck him but by the sword. Here is where the two traditions differ again.

Having been wounded by an arrow, 1 Samuel 31:4 records Saul asking his armour bearer to kill him, "lest the Philistines find him alive and make a spectacle of him." The armor bearer would not kill the king so Saul fell on his own sword. The armour bearer then fell upon his sword and died as well. 1 Chronicles 10:4 records the identical story.

2 Samuel 1 tells a completely different story. Impaled by a spear, Saul called out to a passing soldier, who was an Amalekite, ordering the soldier to kill him. The soldier did as commanded and then took Saul's crown and bracelet. David however was enraged that a commoner had the audacity to kill a king. For the indiscretion he killed the soldier. David had additional motive to slay the man, as the Amalekite spoils would have been evident throughout the camp as David had just come from slaughtering the Amalekites, which

fact the soldier was unaware. This precedence of only a king killing a rival king has carried down over the ages. It is an unwritten law which accords royal privilege. It is still present in society today when politicians will not punish other politicians for fear of being punished themselves when they are caught committing a criminal offence. Whether or not people live in a kingdom, a republic, or a democracy, there is a privilege the hierarchy of society enjoy. Politicians maintain this privilege so that they will not have to suffer the same consequences accorded to commoners for their illegal actions.

For all the fundamentalists who think God dictated these stories, please read the words scripture has recorded and ask yourself "why would God not know the details of these stories?" The word of God is in the stories told by the two traditions. Saul did not listen to God from the time of his anointing as king until his death. Please realize that God does not sit on a throne zapping people with bolts of lightning when they are disobedient. God leaves people to their own devices. The point of the story is God's removal of protection allowing Saul to pay the ultimate price for the sin of disobedience.

David's wives

While David was in hiding from Saul, he started to collect wives. Abigail (my father is joy) was beautiful and the wife of a cruel and evil man named Nabal (fool). David did have an eye for beautiful women. The story goes that Nabal refused to share food with David and his men. David set out to kill the rich man but Abigail interceded. A short while later we are told that God killed Nabal and David took Abigail as his wife (1 Samuel 25:38). How God killed Nabal is not known, but in the story of Bathsheba, David has Uriah killed. The question is, "why would God kill Nabal and not kill Uriah for David?" Learn to read scripture as a detective!

David had decided to make Jerusalem his capital. The Jebusites who inhabited the city believed Jerusalem to be impregnable. They said that "even a blind man could defend the city." David needed a way to infiltrate the city so he said, "whosoever goes up to the gutter, (human waste gutter) and kills the Jebusites... shall be chief and captain" (2 Samuel 5:8). Jerusalem had its own source of water supply and a sewer to carry waste away from the city. The soldiers did not enter the city via the aqua duct as some translations say, but crawled through the human feces to get inside the city walls. The city gates were opened and David took the city without a great deal of bloodshed.

# 2 Samuel

A nation is not a nation unless it has a past, a god and a temple. David's first order of business was to bring the Ark of the Covenant to Jerusalem. Next order of business was to build a temple to house the Ark which was the judgment seat of God. In the ancient cultures, a bull was often representative of the deity. The bull however was not the deity. The bull was the seat upon which the deity sat when visiting the temple. Such was the nature of the Ark of the Covenant. The spread wings of the Cherubim were God's seat of authority in the temple. When David revealed his plans for a temple, the prophet Nathan told him to go ahead with the building. That night the word of the Lord came to Nathan saying, "go and tell my servant David... are you the one to build me a house to live in?" God's statement is repeated in 1 Chronicles 17:6. David was not to be the one to build God's house. In Chapter 7 the reader learns how God has never required nor wanted a house in which to live, not from the time they left Egypt until now. God has always desired to live in the human heart. The desire to live in the human heart is uncharacteristic of every other god in Baal's pantheon. Also notice how David revealed "his" plans for the temple.

God knew that human kings want to build temples; they need an edifice, an image as evidence. David wanted to build a temple so God instructed Nathan to inform David that one of his sons was to be the builder. God is explicit in telling David what the temple is to be used for; that is, "for my name" (2 Samuel 7:13). Passed down from the time of Moses until now, the temple would serve as the only place the priest could speak God's name aloud. Loud noises were to muffle the vocalization of the ineffable name, the Shemhamphorash. The YHVH is the Tetragrammaton, the four-letter name of God. The scriptural story is that God would not allow David to build the temple as war still plagued Israel. In reality, a temple was going to be built whether God wanted a temple or not.

Bathsheba

The army of Israel was endeavouring to lay siege to the Ammonite city of Rabbah. David however remained in Jerusalem. One evening he looked down from his balcony to see a beautiful woman bathing on her rooftop. Her name was Bathsheba and she was the wife of Uriah the Hittite. He sent for her and slept with her. Fearing that she was pregnant, David sent for her husband Uriah in an attempt to have him sleep with Bathsheba in order to conceal his adultery. It did not work. Uriah would not go in unto his wife while the troops were fighting in Rabbah. Failing in this attempted deceit, David sent Uriah back to the fighting with a note to deliver to Joab, the commander of the army. The note instructed Joab to keep Uriah at the forefront of the battle until he died at the hand of the enemy. When the allotted period for mourning was over David brought

Bathsheba to his house as another wife and she bore him a son who died a short time later. After the child's death David went in unto Bathsheba, she conceived another son whom they named Solomon (Peace).

David's adultery displeased God so God sent Nathan to tell David a story. Nathan said there was a man who had plenty and when a visitor came to his home he desired to serve the visitor a good meal. To do this, the rich man went out and confiscated the only lamb of a poor servant. David replied in a rage, "this man deserves to die" (2 Samuel 12:5). Nathan replied to David, "you are the man." In this adulterous and murderous act, David had despised God. From that day forth until his death, David never knew internal peace. His son revolted in an attempt to take the kingdom. Over the course of history, many sons have killed their fathers and brothers to attain the kingly crown. It is difficult to assess if Bathsheba had any real say in the adultery or marriage. I doubt that she did. Some clergy have gone as far as to blame Bathsheba. (Wouldn't you know it was the woman's fault). Given the nature of the chauvinistic culture, I feel Bathsheba did not have any choice. She was a woman and women did not have the same rights as men.

David had a collection of many wives who gave him many children. It seems that David made a habit of marrying the daughters of defeated kings. David's son Absalom of Maacah had a sister named Tamar who was very beautiful. Now Amnon, the son of David and Ahinoam, fell in love with Tamar. On advise from a friend, Amnon played sick and had David send Tamar to attend to him and cook for him. Sending everyone from his room Amnon called Tamar to his bed where he took her by force. She told Amnon that she would marry him if he asked David but Amnon did not listen and raped her. It took two years but Absalom finally took revenge on Amnon by having him killed. Absalom also tried to take the kingdom from his father but did not succeed. Attempting to escape from Joab, Absalom rode into the out hanging branches of an oak tree. Joab found Absalom hanging in the branches and stabbed him three times in the heart. David lamented when he heard of Absalom's death crying, "would to God I had died for thee, O Absalom, my son my son" (2Samuel 18:33). From a kingly and community perspective, when Israel disregarded the blessings God had showered upon them, God withdrew the cloak of protection covering the people.

These stories, demonstrate the dichotomous nature of faith. From an individual perspective, God had blessed David but when he became king he surrendered to the temptations of power and lost his personal relationship with God. Not only does a believer have to express a belief in God, their actions throughout life must be living proof of the faith expressed. These stories also demonstrate the opposite. When your words are only words made in the emotion of the moment, humans fall victim to the results of their ungodly actions. This is what happened to Saul and to David. Two men, from different backgrounds, became victims to the lust of kingship. It is true that God is the only one who can take constant praise and adoration without changing. One only has to look at the myriad of instantly famous people to see the dramatic dichotomous change. When people receive too much praise, they develop a divine complex. Downfall comes when they believe superior stature in society justifies their foolish, lustful, illegal and indignant actions. Celebrities are prime examples even from small towns like Stratford.

David's repentance and subsequent forgiveness provide an example of the most powerful love of all, the love of God. If David is truly representative of the Hebrew people then David becomes a living example of the length, depth, and breadth of God's love for the chosen people and for humanity. In the past, God sent a flood to destroy a sinful and perverse people. Sexual immorality caused God to destroy Sodom (burning) and Gomorrah (submersion). In the desert, Moses had to talk God out of destroying the backsliding people. In David, we see God's promise to Abram fulfilled. This fulfillment was not how God had desired but Israel was now a nation. As the nation continued to prove to be unfaithful, God prepared to provide a Messiah to ensure the rescue of a sinful creation. Messiah in Hebrew means anointed one.

In a sense, the baptism of Jesus was his anointing. Christos is the Greek word for anointed. Translators have made the name Christ read as a proper name rather than a modifier as in Jesus the Christ. In Hebrew, all Messianic references are to an individual from the line of David. The gospels and the Apostle Paul identify Christ as the Messiah. Unfortunately, the church could not tolerate a Jew as the Messiah so the name Yeshua was changed to Jesus by St. Jerome. The Greeks had translated Yeshua to Iesous (ee-ay-sooce), from which St. Jerome changed to "Jesus."

Three Choices

As I have said, the Masoretes did not change conflicting stories, they recorded both traditions. One such conflicting story is found in 2 Samuel 24:1. To begin, David is the second king of Israel. The kingdom did not split until after the death of Solomon when a taxation dispute arose between Solomon's son Rehoboam and Jeroboam. Chapter 24 speaks of the split before it happened. Secondly, verse 24:1 states that the Lord told David to "go count the people of Israel and Judah." David's commander Joab questioned the decision but David ordered him to take the census. After the census God was angry and prepared to inflict punishment upon David for numbering the people. The grief stricken David asked God to take away his guilt for having numbered the people. God offered David three choices as punishment. One, three years of famine; two, David will have to flee from his enemies for three months; and three, to endure three days of punishment upon the land. David chose the three days of pestilence in which seventy thousand people died. Notice in the chapter that God is no longer speaking directly to David, but is speaking through intermediaries such as Gad. 2 Samuel closes with David purchasing the threshing floor of Araunah to erect an altar of uncut stone upon which to make a burnt offering to God. In 1 Chronicles 21:1 we learn that "Satan stood up against Israel and provoked David to number Israel." I will discuss this in 1 Chronicles. Suffice to say, it is a contradiction.

The Books of Samuel brings the reader from the time of Judges to Saul, the first king of Israel. He was rich in flocks, land and servants. Surely, he would know how to lead God's people. Before our eyes, Saul's first thought was a kingly one of wealth and power. His desire was a house (line) named after him. Next, Samuel anointed a shepherd boy. As a young man tending his father's flocks, David developed a friendship and a love for God. Blessed with the gifts of music and lyric, as well as a natural ability to lead, we watch as fame and power corrupt a man with a heart for the Lord. Now a third person stands in line for the crown of Israel. Thanks to his father, Solomon lived in a time of peace. The question comes to mind, "will Solomon learn from the hard lessons of the past?" However, before he could ascend the royal throne he needed the prophet Nathan to anoint him.

# 1 Kings

As David lay on his deathbed, he could not get warm. The solution, find the youngest, most beautiful virgin in the land to snuggle up next to him and keep him warm. Her name was Abishag (my father is a wanderer.) This practice would certainly be a lucrative one for our modern day retirement home industry. While David was suffering in bed, his son Adonijah (my Lord is Yehovah) made his move to drum up support and name himself king. Adonijah was the older brother of Solomon and the son of Haggith who was more than likely the daughter of Talmai king of Geshur.

Hearing the news of this palace power play the prophet Nathan and Bathsheba moved quickly to have David summon the priest Zadok and instruct him to anoint Solomon as king. David's commander Joab had sided with Adonijah and killed two other army commanders named Abner and Amasa. Even though Joab took refuge in the tent of the Lord, the act of grasping the horns of the altar for protection did not save his life. After this brief threat, Solomon sat unchallenged in the capital city of Jerusalem. As a prelude to the building of the temple, scripture establishes his wisdom with the familiar story of the two prostitutes. One baby died and both prostitutes claimed the other child as their own. Solomon said, "take a sword and cut the surviving baby in half." The real mother begged for the life of the child while the other said, "divide the baby in two." Solomon gave the living child the compassionate mother.

One of the most talked about, written about, theorized endeavors is now about to take place; the building of the temple at Jerusalem. On the world stage, the Hebrew people were insignificant. Yet, through this amazing story, they share the stage with the wonders of Egypt, Babylon, Nineveh, Greece and Rome. Bear in mind that God did not want a human king for Israel and God did not want a temple. The utterance of the name of God was supposedly its purpose. One of the reasons God did not want a temple was the burden such an endeavour would place on the people for the sake of a few people with big egos. Solomon knew God did not want any structure erected that was of human craft and design. Every monument and altar thus far in scripture had been a pile of uncut rocks. However, humans are shrewd, much like the serpent in Genesis 3:1. Solomon devised that all stones were to be cut in the quarry and carried to Jerusalem (1 Kings 6:7) so that "no sound of metal could be heard."

The cost of the temple was horrendous. To put it into perspective it would be the modern day equivalent of what the United States military spends on making war in every country that has oil, coupled with the added burden of the numerous police forces created in America to insure the safety of its citizens. This warring madness has left the United States of America without the ability to provide roads without tolls so the people can travel to work to earn the money to pay taxes for war. This warring madness has left the United States without the kind of healthcare people should expect in a civilized country. On the bright side, companies who service the military by making the arms and ammunition have gained untold wealth from workers who have no choice. Considering the fact that common people pay the taxes to go to war, all it cost the government is the lives of tens of thousands of young Americans. I know this is a radical idea, but would it not make sense to make the companies who profit on war responsible for paying for the healthcare of the veterans?

In a similar manner, the temple was built from the sweat and blood of the people. Scripture has always portrayed Solomon as wise. He told the people that God had given Israel rest from warfare so he could build the temple. 1 Kings 4:26 tell us that Solomon had forty thousand stalls of horses for his chariots and twelve thousand horsemen. Solomon used his military to enforce taxation and maintain a food supply from among the tribes. Each month one tribe was responsible to supply the king's table. That included the military. Solomon made a deal with Hiram, king of Tyre for the cedars of Lebanon. He conscripted a labour force of thirty thousand men sending ten thousand of them to Lebanon a month in three shifts. Rotating shifts of one month in Lebanon and two months at home was a routine enforced by the military. The Bible also records Solomon's work force to be seventy thousand labourers and eighty thousand stone cutters. The forced labourers had three thousand three hundred supervisors over them. Never forget, there is a beneficial fear factor to having a temple. That is, the temple is the recipient of all tithes and offerings. If you cheat on your offering, you cheat God. In addition, if you choose to rob the king's treasure, you must rob the temple and risk God's curse on your life. Having a temple also ascribes a level of divinity to the king.

The church has always looked at the result, the temple. God looks at the cost. God did not want a temple as the glory of man made structures belongs to the people who built the structure. Throughout the temple building chapters, the dialogue has God's voice giving the instructions. However, we get a glimpse of Solomon's ego in 1 Kings 8:12 when he says, "the Lord has said he would dwell in thick darkness. I have built you and exalted house, a place for you to dwell in forever." (Notice how Solomon's word choice was "I have built you." He then went on to establish that God's will was to have the house of David sit on the throne forever. When you read the 1 Kings account of the building of the temple ask yourself, "is this the same God who was jealous of crudely carved personal idols in the time of Moses?" Ask yourself, "is this the same God who would not allow any form of hand crafted altar or monument to be built?" Ask yourself, "is this the same God who only required the occasional burnt offering?" The only place God has ever wanted to dwell is in the hearts of creation, you and me. It is the same today; God simply wants to live in your heart. If humanity opened their hearts to God, it would show in our daily living. It would show in the way we treat each another, not just in our immediate families or community, but also the world. To me, the message of scripture is simply, "love thy neighbour." The way we demonstrate that we love God is to love our neighbour. I doubt very much that God gave the temple plans to David or Solomon. It was more like, "God, you are going to have a temple whether you like it or not."

Note!

In the past, churches and cathedrals have been built facing East. This is so those in prayer face the temple in Jerusalem. It has to do with the prayer of Solomon with regards to the future of God's people. Solomon's prayer is essentially saying, [if thy people should be scattered over the face of the earth and turn (repent) from their sinful ways and pray facing the east (the temple) then please forgive them] (1 Kings 8: 38-50). Churches are now built to accommodate the property, but even Christians should remember to pray facing the east.

Solomon's women

If you thought that David loved too many women, then hold onto your hat because Solomon loved more women than my mind can comprehend. 1 Kings 11:3 states that Solomon had more than one thousand wives. Wow! These chapters illustrate a Biblical ego trip beyond imagination. It is a three thousand year old rag to riches story beginning with Abram and culminating with Saul, David and Solomon. Almost overnight Israel went from a people struggling to become a nation to a nation rich beyond imagination. The amount of horses, chariots, soldiers, gold and silver purportedly heaped upon Solomon makes one suspect. The passages read as if Israel had become the greatest, wealthiest and most admired of all kingdoms that had ever existed. Personally, I read the passages and wonder how the third king of Israel came to be so wealthy. Other scholars believe Chapters 5 - 11 to be a gross over exaggeration. You will have to make your own decision. This is also a good time to think about the term "Word of God" in terms of whom it was that actually dictated and recorded scripture.

As Solomon entered his kingship, he demonstrated his ability for creative thinking. Scripture calls it wisdom. The first ten chapters record Solomon's back and forth dialogue with God over the building of the temple and of course, his personal luxurious home. I'm sure God would not want a personal representative living as a common Israelite. Chapter 11 is a record of a king who is above reproach, someone who feels they can do whatever they please. As an educated man, alleged to be wise, and who experienced a personal relationship with God, why does Solomon now follow Astarte, the goddess of the Sidonians? Why does he build altars to Chemosh, Molech and the gods of his many foreign wives? These were the very gods Israel was to reject. Chemosh required the Moabites to sacrifice human beings. Molech required a virgin sacrifice and the Ammonites burnt children in the sacrificial fire. I have always wondered, "why the virgin?" Why not an overweight, unattractive woman, unmarried and not well liked? When you think about religions that honour their god with the murder of other humans, maybe they are worshiping a fraudulent, man-made god. Also, do not forget that the children of Abraham broke the practice of human sacrifice. It was an abomination to Yahweh then, as it is now, for human beings to offer the creator's children back to the creator. Those who kill in the name of their god will rot in hell.

The story of Solomon is a prime example of words trying to convince the reader that Solomon was the epitome of kingly perfection. The words say Solomon:

- had a direct speaking relationship with God;
- was the wisest of all men;
- the richest of all kings;
- authored pearls of wisdom for all ages.

The actions demonstrate Solomon:

- married many foreign women to form international alliances;
- had thousands more horses and chariots than Pharaoh;
- conscripted labourers by force (slavery);
- disciplined the people with whips;
- evoked the burden of high taxation;
- did everything God despised;
- had to maintain hundreds of wives and concubines at the people's expense;
- raised a child spoiled even more than himself; and
- was the last king of a united Israel.

The Kingdom Cracks

Israel had enjoyed a relative peace throughout Solomon's reign but now the kingdom was about to crack. Solomon's son Rehoboam was crowned king in Shechem. His first kingly decision changed the nation of Israel forever. The people had lived under conscription, forced labour, over taxation and heavy tithes in order to sustain the construction, the workers, the royal family and all the upper class parasites. Never forget that once you establish a royal line it excludes all others from kingship. The tribe of Judah was the chosen line. Now Jeroboam, son of Nebat had to flee to Egypt but when Solomon died, he returned. The outcast Jeroboam, speaking for the people, came to Rehoboam complaining that the burden Solomon had laid upon the people was too heavy. The people wanted the burden lifted. Rehoboam said, I will think about it (1 Kings 12:6). Rehoboam took counsel with the older men who had advised Solomon. The older men told him to remove the burden saying, [if you remove the burden, they will remain in your service forever]. Rehoboam was not looking for that advice so he approached the young men with whom he had grown up with asking them the same question. Their answer was consistent with spoiled children who believe their birthright somehow endorses their entitlement. They told the king to say to the people "my little finger is thicker than my father's loins" (1 Kings 12:10). Translated to English it would be [my narcissism is much greater than my father's egotism]. Disregarding the advice of the older advisors Rehoboam called the people together and said, "my father made your yoke heavy, but I will add to your yoke; my father disciplined you with whips, but I will discipline you with scorpions" (1 Kings 12:14). This is the voice of a despotic ruler. It is not the way to win friends and influence enemies.

Pause for a moment. Go back and read what he said to the people. "My father disciplined you with whips". Think about the words of Rehoboam and the court parasites. In consideration of the fact that the name Solomon has become synonymous with the virtues of goodness and wisdom, how do these negative actions relate to the positive words in the beginning of Solomon's story? The fact is, they do not. The response of Jeroboam was not as Rehoboam had hoped. Speaking as the voice of the people, Jeroboam said, "what share do we have in David?... to your tents, O Israel! Look now to your own house O David." In other words, "we are out of here, we have had enough of this kingly vanity" and the kingdom people wanted was rent asunder.

Kingly entitlement and parasitic greed divided the kingdom. The tribes of Judah and Benjamin remained in the capital city of Jerusalem. Jeroboam was anointed King of Israel and made his capital in Samaria. (The Samaritans of the New Testament were comprised of the ten tribes of Israel mixed with people from other nations). From now on the name Israel refers to the ten tribes. Mount Gerizim was chosen as their high place of worship. God had commanded Israel to put a blessing upon Mount Gerizim after they came to possess the Promised Land (Deuteronomy 11:29). From here on, scripture records the exploits of two kings and two kingdoms as they never did kiss and make up.

## Elijah

Elijah was God's prophet in Israel (Samaria) when Ahab was the king. One hundred years had past when Ahab became king. In that time, apostasy had claimed most of God's prophets. Elijah means, "my God is Yehovah," whereas Samuel means, "his name is El." Two of the most revered prophets have strikingly different names. In this time, faithful followers of God had all but disappeared, only Elijah and a small group remained (1 Kings 18:22). King Ahab of Israel had married Jezebel (Baal exalts), daughter of Ethbaal (with Baal) the Phoenician king. The reason Elijah was still alive was that he had been in hiding from Queen Jezebel while she had been killing the prophets of YHVH. Elijah sent for Ahab and challenged him to bring all the prophets that ate at Jezebel's table. The number was greater than all the bishops and cardinals living in the Vatican. There were four hundred and fifty prophets of Baal, and the four hundred prophets of Asherah summoned to Mount Carmel. Ahab was to summon the people to attend in order to witness the challenge issued to Jezebel's prophets. This is another prime story which exposes the real problem in the Old Testament; that is, the battle for supremacy between Baal and YHVH.

1 Kings 18: 23-46 is among the most time honoured miracle stories in scripture. Elijah ordered the building of two sacrificial piles of wood, each pile big enough to burn a bull. The Baal prophets chose the first bull cut it in pieces and placed it on the first pile of wood. Elijah did the same with the other bull. He said to the Baal prophets; now call upon the name of your god to ignite the wood to burn the sacrifice and I will do the same. The people said "well spoken." The prophets called upon Baal from morning until noon but nothing happened. Elijah then began mocking them by saying, [maybe your god is on the toilet or maybe your god is sleeping.] Their prayers became even more intense as the prophets started to cut themselves, raving on into the afternoon but there was no response.

Elijah then took twelve stones from an altar of the Lord that the Baal prophets had thrown down. (Notice that altars were still uncut stones). He placed wood and pieces of the bull on top. Then he had a deep trench cut around the altar. Turning to the people, he ordered them to fill their water jugs and pour the water over the bull and the wood. He did this a second time and a third until the wood was soaked and the trench filled with water. Elijah offered a short prayer unto God. Immediately, a fire fell from heaven consuming the offering. The fire was so hot it turned the stones to dust and evaporated the water in the surrounding trench. When the people saw this, they repeatedly shouted, "Yehovah is El, Yehovah is El." (Read the Schema). This is the crux of the ongoing battle over who is the one true living God, creator of heaven and earth. Even today, every Christian denomination believes their way is the right way of worshiping and the others are wrong. Every tribe believed that the name by which they called their god is the right name. This is why the Tetragrammaton does not have any vowel pointing, as Israel did not want anyone else enticing God to become their God. Tradition has it that the pronunciation of the ineffable name was lost in Babylon. The priests could only repeat the word in the holy of holies and when the temple was destroyed the pronunciation was lost.

Elijah must have known the right pronunciation as God answered immediately. With the people in a wild frenzy, Elijah ordered the slaughter of all false prophets. In response, Jezebel sent a message to Elijah telling him that he would be dead by the next day. What is incomprehensible is why Elijah ran away in fear for his life. Nonetheless, God did not abandon him. During his escape into the wilderness, the angel of God came to him with food and drink. After a forty-day journey to Mount Horeb, the mountain of God, he spent the night in a cave. This passage is a good example of Hebrew literature in that a story is told twice. First, the reader hears the shorter version and then the more detailed version. This dual telling confuses clergy who think Elijah was at the mouth of the cave when God sent the wind, fire and earthquake. He was not. After the fire, there was a "still small voice" (1 Kings 19:12). In Hebrew the words dem-aw-maw dak kole means "voice whisper gently". Scripture is explicit in stating it was after hearing the voice that Elijah wrapped his face in his mantle and went to the mouth of the cave. We do not know what the voice said; we can only surmise God was calling him gently as scripture does tell us the voice was a whisper. Implicit in the whisper was the voice of love. Even the question God asks is soft and compassionate, "what are you doing here, Elijah?" Repeat those words softly to yourself and feel God touch you.

Elijah bears his heart to God, retelling everything he had done in faith. He said that he was afraid because he was the only one left and Jezebel had put a price on his head. He is told to go to Damascus and anoint Hazael (one who sees God) as king over Aram; Jehu (Yehovah is He) as king over Israel and Elisha (God is salvation) as prophet in your place. Chapter 19 ends with the results of worshiping false gods. A terrible extermination takes place leaving only seven thousand who "have not bowed to Baal… and have not kissed him." Hazael started the killing. Jehu was to kill those who escaped Hazael and Elisha was to kill those who escaped Jehu. The battle between YHVH and Baal was fierce.

To find out what happened to Jezebel, you have to read 2 Kings 9:33. In short, Eunuchs threw the painted Jezebel out of her palace window splattering her body on the ground. Jehu's horse trampled her body into the ground. Elijah's prophesy "dogs shall eat the flesh of Jezebel, and the carcass of Jezebel shall be as dung upon the face of the field… so that they shall not say, this is Jezebel" came to pass. A similar fate was prophesied for King Ahab but when he repented, God relented. Unfortunately for Ahab, he was to suffer the most terrible curse of all, "the disaster on his house," which means kingship would pass from his line.

# 2 Kings

The story of Elijah is continued in 2 Kings as does the story of Israel's backsliding. In 1 Kings, Elijah enlists the help of Elisha (God is salvation) to slay the prophets who escaped execution on Mount Carmel. As Elijah neared the end of his life Elisha was anointed in his place. However, knowing the power of God, Elisha asked for a double share of Elijah's spirit. Elijah replied, "if you see me as I am being taken from you it will be granted." Note here the preeminence of the prophet Elijah as he is only the second man to be "taken" alive into heaven. (Enoch was the first). The Bible tells us that Elijah and Elisha were walking along when "a chariot of fire and horses of fire separated the two on them and Elijah ascended in a whirlwind into heaven" (2 Kings 2:11). As requested, a double share of Elijah's spirit rested upon Elisha. This is evinced in Chapter 4 as Elisha brings back to life the son of a Shunammite woman.

There is another women's story that has always caught my attention. It has to do with the healing of the leprous Naaman, the highly favoured commander of King Aram's army. Notwithstanding the miraculous healing, is the bravery of a young girl taken captive from the land of Israel. This young slave girl served Naaman's wife. Consider if you will the precarious position and the faith of this girl as she tells her mistress of Elisha, a prophet in Israel who can heal Naaman. Men of this stature were extremely proud. To submit themselves unto a captive people in order to be healed was beneath their dignity. Nevertheless, the dreaded disease of leprosy compelled him to seek out this cure. Elisha had Naaman submerge himself seven times in the Jordan River. Now think of what would have happened to the slave girl had Elisha not been able to heal Naaman. I fear the slave girl would have died a horrible death had Naaman not been healed. Again, an unnamed woman fades into the dust of history.

1 Kings recounted the story of the slaying of Baal's prophets from Elijah's perspective. 2 Kings tells the story with more detail given to King Jehu and King Hazael and the death of Jezebel. It gives an account of the kings of Israel and Judah as well as the constant wars with their neighbouring tribes. The people had demanded an earthly king, now they have to live with the ramifications thereof. The problem with people who are organized under a king is that they become the target of larger kingdoms. They become the target of human vanity. Throughout the history of humanity there has always been a king who has desired to rule the world at the people's expense. In retrospect, imagine Israel as a shining pearl, protected by God from the invasions of ruthless human powers.

The Assyrians, under King Shalmaneser, besieged Samaria for three years. Finally, the defeated Israelites were carried away to a number of Assyrian towns. People from other nations were settled in Samaria. This is why the Samaritans were detestable to Judah as they were a mixed breed of people from the Middle East. This was also a very practical and strategic move on the part of the Assyrians. By moving small blocks of people to different locations to mix in with other small blocks of people the victor need only provide a small police force in each location to keep the tribes from infighting. People will separate themselves into communities out of fear, and for friendship. The same is true today in any major city in North America.

During the reign of young King Josiah the Book of the Law was found in the dark recesses of the temple. On hearing the contents, Josiah responded to Judah's dilemma by bringing out of the temple "all the vessels made for Baal, for Asherah, and for all the hosts of heaven" burning them in the fields of Kidron (2 Kings 23:4). (This reoccurs in Ezekiel). We also learn in verse 21 that the Passover had not been kept since the days of the judges. For hundreds of years Israel had neglected to celebrate what God had done in the remembrance feast of Passover. Unfortunately, Josiah was mortally wounded by an arrow when he chose to fight against the Egyptian King Neco who came to take the city of Chemosh on the Euphrates. Nebuchadnezzar later defeated the Egyptians regaining the city. Patricia often said, "kings will do the things kings will do." She also meant that kings send young men to endure the carnage of war for their own vanity. Today, governments send women as well and we call them barbaric.

Faith

Faith in God is nebulous, indefinable. It can only be seen in actions as words are but hot air, short-lived as the light of an extinguished candle. Proof of God lasts but for a short while. The problem is, every generation demands its own proof. But alas, faith would not be faith if substantiated by physical evidence. It is by faith that the Biblical stories become humanities' evidence of God at work in the world. When you read the Bible you come to believe that God desires a personal relationship with each and every human. Or, one can choose to keep looking among the pantheon of gods which man has created to satisfy their own wants and desires. Never forget, any religion that sets brother against brother or sister against sister is not of the Creator. A true prophet of the creator of heaven and earth preaches words of love and reconciliation. When a false prophet comes, you will hear words that favour the prophet and his desires. Also, God does not subject women to the will of men. God does not condone the abuse of children. God does not permit murder or killing. God's desire is to have humanity "love one another."

# 1 Chronicles

The Book of Chronicles was originally a single book. At one time, Ezra was believed to have been the author but now scholars believe the author to be unknown. Beginning with a genealogical list, Chronicles is a repeat of material from Genesis to Kings. As mentioned earlier, Israel needed a history to have credibility as a nation. They needed a past in order to justify their presence on the land which gave them a right to a future. Thus, 1 Chronicles records eight chapters of genealogies. Not only did Israel need a history, they needed a god. The history of the chosen people has included an infusion of people from a variety of cultures and religious beliefs. This fact is often overlooked because of the exclusive nature of Israel's story. The children of Israel were not the only people to leave Goshen. The Exodus is where the battle of the gods begins to heat up.

Beyond the warring madness of human vanity and lust for power is the battle of the gods. In this battle, humans of their own want and desire, become pawns in the game of godly supremacy. In the past, God had spoken with Abram, Rebekah and Jacob but now the voice of the one true living God enters into conversation with the Hebrew people. All other gods have remained deaf and dumb. They are never seen and only heard through the voice of human oracles whose prophesies are nebulous at best. Those who claimed to be prophets of God must of necessity prophesy correctly or they were to be killed.

Research into the history of the ancient gods reveals a pantheon of goddesses such as Asherah, Astarte and gods such as Chemosh and Molech. However, all these gods appear to be subject to one central god figure, Baal. This revelation sheds light upon Yahweh's conversation with Abram. On one hand the request of Yahweh to have Abram sacrifice Isaac is repulsive. On the other hand, the point of the story is that Abram was sent away from his tribe to be alone with Isaac and God. This is the story which separates God from every other deity. The distinguishing characteristic of the gods of the Phoenicians, Babylonians, Egyptians and the Canaanite people is that they all practiced child sacrifice. The abolition of human sacrifice was revolutionary in the ancient world. Much the same as was the abolition of slavery in Britain and the United States. Consider for a moment, how, in an educated and enlightened new world society, time has not quenched the fiery resentment to emancipation in the hearts of the ungodly. Resistance to the abolition of child sacrifice was no different to the resistance to the abolition of slavery in America and civil rights for all. The people who had been incorporated into Israel still wanted to practice human sacrifice. This may help to explain to people who are abhorred by animal sacrifice why God substituted a lamb in Isaac's place. Animal sacrifice must be seen as part of the transition process for God's people.

People understood the need for an unblemished sacrificial offering. Kings never went to battle without a fitting sacrifice to their god. This sacrifice comforted the minds of the soldiers because they believed the gods would only be on their side if the sacrifice was appropriate. The significance was that the supremacy of the most powerful god would be revealed through the victorious king. It was important to have the most impressive, most official looking sacrifice as possible. Even Saul, the first king of Israel waited a week for the prophet Samuel before finally making the sacrifice himself. Sacrifice had always been an important part of obtaining a godly blessing. It is in this context that Yahweh replaced human sacrifice with animal sacrifice. Over the course of time, God's true desire was revealed, "for I desired mercy, and not sacrifice, and the knowledge of God more than burnt offerings" (Hosea 6:6). In this way, the Chosen People became unique.

Chapter 16 tells of David bringing the Ark of the Covenant to Jerusalem and how, after the animal sacrifice, fed the people. The chapter is divided between prose and poetry giving God worship and praise. Chapter 17 sets the stage for one of the greatest desires of any king; that is, to build a temple to his god. It begins with David saying, [now that I have my house, I will build one for God]. Notice the first person use of "I." Nathan encourages David to build the temple but later that night God recited to Nathan the history of the tabernacle, God's home. It is interesting to note that among the various verses which indicate that God was in favour of a temple, 1 Chronicles 17 tells how God does not want a stone temple but realized that one was going to be built whether God liked it or not. Further evidence is in the deceitful way in which the temple was built. We would call it a prefabricated temple as "the house, when it was in building, was built of stone made ready before it was brought thither: so that there was neither hammer nor axe nor any tool of iron heard in the house, while it was in building" (1 Kings 6:7). Remember, every altar that had ever been built was of uncut stones. You can see how actions sometimes contradict words.

The tabernacle (tent) in the wilderness was not a permanent structure as God never desired anything built with cut stones. A permanent structure, a temple, was detestable to God. Every other people built a temple to their god. They needed something visible, something tangible. Stone monuments can do nothing but demonstrate the human ability to craft and create. God desired to live in the hearts of all who will believe and follow. Think about this for a moment, "did Jesus request that his followers build anything?"

Or did Jesus desire "hearts of faith" to worship God? Actions have always enabled people to recognize true desire.

## Voices

There have always been two voices in the Roman Catholic Church. One voice professed poverty for clergy that their work of service among the poor would lead to repentance and salvation. The other voice professed the building of huge stone cathedrals, the cost of which was placed on the backs of the poor, just like Solomon's temple. Have you ever noticed how temples are named after people? The church of Christ started in homes, in quiet meadows, where the rich shared their food with the poor. Today, the poor give their food to bishops and cardinals living Solomon's life of luxury in a palace. In the middle ages, those who openly disagreed with the church screamed for mercy as their lives ended in the fires set ablaze by a pious Christian Church. The Romans only crucified people whereas the Catholic Church tied them to a post and burned them.

The life and kingship of David was about to end. Solomon, the second child of Bathsheba by David was about to build the temple. I believe that Chapter 28 records the truth of the matter. It tells how, "David gave his son Solomon the plan of the vestibule of the temple, and of its houses, its treasuries, its upper rooms, and its inner chamber, and of the room for the mercy seat and the plan of all that **he** had in mind" (1Chronicles 28:11). Notice how the rooms and the treasury come before the little room for the mercy seat. Had King Saul not been embroiled in war all his life, he would have built the temple. Saul was anointed king in 1043 BC. It was about this time that David was born. We are not sure of the time between Saul's anointing and David's anointing. But before moving on, consider how scripture says "David died in a good old age" (1 Chronicles 29:28).

Historical records indicate that David died in 971 BC at 70 years of age. His reign was forty years long. In this time 70 years of age was a very old age and not most people lived that long.

As the chapter comes to an end, we are informed that the acts of David are recorded in the writings of the seer Samuel, the prophet Nathan and the seer Gad. Nathan and Gad were not included in the Hebrew canon. There is a large collection of works not included in the Canon of the Old Testament as well as the New Testament. When you read through the books of Samuel, Chronicles and Kings, you are listening to a variety of voices and theological perspectives, all of course, "dictated by God." The Pentateuch was organized into its final form around 700 BC even though the Yahwist and Elohists version are presumed written during David's reign. Deuteronomy was written in the time of Hezekiah, 716 BC.

# 2 Chronicles

Solomon is regarded as the greatest king who ever ruled an earthly kingdom. His name so renowned it is used synonymously for wisdom. Scripture tells us that God appeared and said, "ask what I should give you" (2 Chronicles 1:7). Verse 1:10 records Solomon's answer as, "give me now wisdom and knowledge to go out and come in before this people, for who can rule this great people of yours?" Anyone who has ever heard of Solomon knows the story of the two harlots who came before Solomon both claiming to be the mothers of the same infant (1 Kings 3:16-24). Solomon said; bring me a sword so I may divide the child in half. The real mother said, "No!" please give the child to the other harlot. By her action Solomon knew she was the real mother.

Solomon is mentioned hundreds of times in the books of Kings and Chronicles as well as celebrated in nine other books. One of the reasons for this book is to expose the difference between words and actions. This was adequately demonstrated in the story of Dinah. Consistent throughout scripture is God's desire to live in the hearts of the chosen people who were to live in such a way as to inspire the surrounding nations to follow Yahweh. Creating a king who was bigger, better and more blessed than any king of the past gave Israel a sense of fulfilling God's promise to Abram of a great nation. Driven by a desire for credibility, the temple had to surpass all others. Even though the building of the temple was a magnificent undertaking, it did no more than satisfy the vanity of a king. Bear in mind the huge burden Solomon put on the backs of the people he was called to care for. When asked what he desired, Solomon asked God how he should come and go before the people (how to govern). The interesting aspect of Solomon's actions is that they were not consistent with God's plan for a chosen people. A centralized government and a temple had never been part of God's plan. A wealthy king and a temple treasury would soon make Jerusalem a target for the Babylonians. Remember also, that the first responsibility for the people of a country is to protect the government. It is the same today. Had Israel remained in God's kingdom there would not have been a need to protect a throne or a treasury.

Scripture informs us that two mighty pillars adorned the entrance of the temple. That on the right was named Jachin (he will establish) and that on the left Boaz (fleetness). Some scripture translations have in brackets "in it is strength" for the meaning of Boaz. The Bible does not detail any priestly participation at the dedication of the temple. Masonic folklore however, has it that Jachin was the assistant high priest who officiated at the temple dedication. I have always wondered where the high priest was on the occasion of the most important dedication in the history of Israel. Maybe he was not feeling well or his wife wanted him to take her shopping in Damascus, don't know. In Ezekiel I will discuss the possibility that the high priest was sacrificed the night before the dedication of the temple. Still, it seems strange to me that of all the names that could have been chosen for the adorning pillars of the temple that the name of David's great-grandfather Boaz and the name of the assistant priest Jachin were chosen.

Many scholars question the grandiose style in which the temple was constructed as well as the furnishings of the temple. It is not my desire to overly debate the magnitude of the project or the means by which expenses were paid. My focus is on (a) what was God's desire versus Solomon's claim that it was really God who wanted a temple. And (b), if Solomon's wisdom was through a personal relationship with God (the chapter one conversation) then why were Solomon's actions contrary to God's command "thou shalt have no other gods before me" (Exodus 20:3)? The following passage in Exodus 20:4 is explicit, "thou shalt not make unto thee any graven image, or any likeness of any thing this is in heaven above, or that is on the earth beneath, or that is in the water under the earth." The Hebrew word paw neem meaning face is the same Hebrew word meaning before. They are used in the context of being in front of God. Words used in the context of "in front of" begin with the Hebrew letter Peh which is in the shape of a human face. Not only does the Peh mean to be in the physical presence of God, it also means not to have any other gods or images in God's presence. When God said, "thou shalt not have any gods before me" it literally means "not in any way, shape or form and not in any thought or desire of the human heart.

Bear in mind that "king" in its original ancient context is one who has the authority over the people for the purposes of leadership, judgment and care. When Abram came into the new land, the various tribes all had a leader, a king. This kingship was originally likened to a shepherd. The whole connotation of the word shepherd will be discussed from the ancient perspective of Hammurabi and from the divine person of Christ. In order to set the stage for the revolt against Solomon's son Rehoboam, listen to what scripture says about Solomon. "Thus King Solomon excelled all the kings of the earth in riches and in wisdom. All the kings of the earth sought the presence of Solomon to hear his wisdom, which God had put into his mind. Everyone of them brought a present, objects of silver and gold, garments, weaponry, spices, horses and mules, so much year by year" (2 Chronicles 9:22-24).

Scripture tells us in 1 Kings that Solomon:

4:26    built 40,000 stalls for chariot horses and had 12,000 horsemen;

5:11    gave Hiram, King of Tyre, 20,000 measures of wheat, and 20,000 measures of pure olive oil a year;

5:13    imposed a levy (forced labour) on 30,000 men, these men were rotated 10,000 men a month on a 3 month cycle;

5:17    70,000 men to bare burdens (uncertain if they were conscripted); 80,000 hewers in the mountains of Lebanon (uncertain if they were conscripted);

7:8    built a lavish house for one of his wives (Pharaoh's daughter);

8:63    made a peace offering of 22,000 oxen;

9:26    built a navy on the shore of Red Sea;

9:28    used the navy to raid Ophir taking 420 talents of gold as plunder;

1 talent is equal to 120 lbs., troy weight or 3,000 shekels,

1 shekel equals ½ oz. troy weight, or $3000.00 per shekel; modern day equivalent is $9,000,000.00 per talent; the modern day equivalent of 420 talents of gold would be $3,780,000,000.00;

10:10    the queen of Sheba brought to Solomon another 120 talents of gold, spices and precious stones;

10:13    the weight of gold that came to Solomon in one year was 666 talents, this is approximately $5,994,000,000.00;

10:16    he had made 200 targets of gold – 600 shekels of gold per target;

10:18    a throne of ivory overlaid with gold with six steps to the throne platform; one cast lion on each side of each step and two lions behind the throne;

10:21    made gold drinking goblets;

10:26    bought 1,400 chariots and horses from Egypt;

10:28    for the royal household he bought linen from Egypt;

11:1    loved many foreign women;

11:3    Solomon had 700 wives and 300 concubines;

11:4    Solomon's wives caused him to sin.

(We should know by now that women are the cause of male sinfulness.) Read about what Solomon built for himself and his wives in 1 Kings 7.

1 Kings 11:4-9 records all the detestable acts performed by Solomon. These dichotomous actions on the part of Solomon are confusing to say the least. On one hand, God had spoken directly

to Solomon twice (11:9). It is through this personal relationship with God that Solomon attains the glory ascribed to his name. On the other hand, we read of an unparalleled narcissistic ostentatious life style sustained by conscription, forced labour and high taxes. Obedience does not appear to be a distinguishing characteristic of any king, in any time and in any land. God had warned Solomon not to chase after foreign women because they would turn his heart to other gods (1 Kings 11:2). Solomon did not listen. The problem I have with the story is equating the word wisdom with the action of disobedience. Not listening to God is not wise. Did Solomon really write, "the fear of the Lord is the beginning of wisdom" (Proverbs 9:10)?

Have you been paying attention to the male dynamics in this passage in terms of blame? Women get the blame. Solomon's wives caused him to sin (11:4). Foreign women will turn your heart to their gods (11:2). Even the prophet Nehemiah (13:26) places the cause for Solomon's sin on women. The fact is, after direct dialogue with God, Solomon's human narcissism caused him to build altars to worship Ashtoreth, Molech, and Chemosh "and likewise did Solomon for all his strange (foreign) wives, who burnt incense and sacrificed unto their gods.

Scripture is fascinating in more ways than one. It contains statements such as "the wisdom of Solomon" juxtaposed by his narcissistic actions in suppressing Israel under the heaviest tax burden in the history of humanity. The record of his ostentatious life style, no matter how over exaggerated it may or may not be, enables the reader to understand the mind set of Solomon's son Rehoboam, who was raised in such opulent surroundings. The sad irony of history is that kings are rarely punished for their sins. Ordinary people are the ones who always suffer the consequences of kingly greed and vanity. Just ask Presidents Nixon and Bush!

Vanity is a trait easily passed on from generation to generation. Scripture is witness to the fact that the only qualification for kingship is birthright. It is the luck of being born into the right family. Merit plays no part in the royal line of monarchy. For this reason, democracy and education has always been the enemy of despotism. Despotism is not only found in government, but in religions and in families. Individuals and groups who have inherited power will fight to the death or kill anyone who is a threat to their position of wealth and privilege. In this context, Rehoboam represents the true outlook of those born into wealth and privilege. At the time of his father's death, Rehoboam had gathered around him young noble friends accustomed to the benefits of extreme wealth. He was also surrounded by Solomon's advisors. The temple was complete. Solomon's house was complete. It was time for the colossal tax burden to be lifted. Solomon's advisors said, "lift the tax burden." Rehoboam's advisors said, "No! we have grown too accustomed to living off the backs of the people, increase the tax burden." Narcissistic superiority split the kingdom.

It came to pass. The people had cried out, "we will have a king over us, that we may also be like all the nations" (1 Samuel 8: 19-20). In 1043 BC Saul became king and his reign of 32 years was plagued with war. When Saul died in 1011 David became king in Judah and united the kingdom in 1004. David died in 971 after reigning over a united kingdom for 33 years. Solomon reigned 40 years after David's death. The people cried out for a king so God allowed a well-established land owner and tribal leader (Saul) to reign. Then God had Samuel anoint David, a young boy who was a musician and shepherd. Following David's death, the temple priest

Zadok anointed Solomon to be king. He was a man who became known for his wisdom. Three completely different men, with three different life-styles had been king. Like all other kings before them, egotism became the distinguishing characteristic of their reign. This characteristic came to full blossom in Rehoboam.

Rehoboam

After 110 years of unity Rehoboam split the kingdom in his first kingly decision. Ten tribes united and made Jeroboam King of Israel. This left the tribes of Judah and Benjamin for Rehoboam to rule in Jerusalem. Obviously Solomon had not instilled any wisdom upon Rehoboam. Notice also, God does not speak to him. The only time God comes into the story is in Kings 12:23 where God instructed the prophet Shemaiah to tell Rehoboam (Judah) not to go to war against Jeroboam (Israel). Jeroboam was no longer interested in the God of Judah but feared that if Israel kept going to Jerusalem to present their sacrifices and tithes, his kingdom would fall apart. To circumvent that, "he made two calves of gold… [saying] behold thy gods, O Israel, which brought thee up out of the land of Egypt… and set one in Bethel and the other in Dan" (1Kings 12:28). This action combined with the intermarriage with other nations of captivity sheds light on the reason the Jews held the Samaritans in such contempt. The stories of Elijah, the fiery sacrifice, the Samaritan King Ahab with his wife Jezebel are all factors in Judah's disgust of the Samaritans.

Rehoboam's reign of 17 years was tenuous to say the least. Both Israel and Judah did evil in the sight of the God. As a matter of Biblical fact, murder, mayhem, perfidy and apostasy are the legacy of the next 208 years under the rule of 20 kings in Israel. In 723 BC Shalmaneser (fire-worshiper) the King of Assyria besieged Samaria for three years. The Persians and Assyrians were followers of Zoroaster who sacrificed children in the holy fire. The Assyrian captors broke the Samaritans into small groups and dispersed them among cities along the Gozan River and the cities of the Medes. As mentioned previously, this prevented a unity among the multi-national captives.

Hezekiah (Yehovah is my strength) became king in Judah in 716 BC. 2 Chronicles 30 recounts for us the story of a people returning to God. Hezekiah summoned the people to keep the Passover saying, "the Lord your God is gracious and merciful, and will not turn away his face from you, if you return to him" (2 Chronicles 30:9). The people came to Jerusalem bringing an abundance of tithes and offerings. Hezekiah re-organized the priests and Levites; he stopped all the springs around Jerusalem to cut off the water supply to the invading army of the Assyrian King Sennacherib. Disgraced by his inability to sack Jerusalem, Sennacherib returned to his own country. On entering the temple of his god "his own sons struck him down with the sword" (2 Chronicles 32:21). Notice how the enemies of Israel are somehow defeated when the people put their trust in God.

The people of Jerusalem did not repent after the Assyrians took the Samaritans captive. After 354 years and 20 kings in Judah, with the exception of Josiah and Hezekiah, idol worship was still being practiced. With all the wars that had gone on around Jerusalem, after Sennacherib had failed to destroy Jerusalem, the people really believed God would never allow the city, and especially the temple, to be sacked. Unfortunately, the people did not continue to honour God but retained to their old ways of polytheism. Too bad, so sad!

The example of Samaria did nothing to change the idol worshiping ways of the people in Jerusalem. Finally, and only after the treachery of Jehoiachin did Nebuchadnezzar besiege and destroy the city of Jerusalem. When we hear that the people of Jerusalem were taken captive to Babylon, the reality was Nebuchadnezzar "carried away all Jerusalem, and all the princes, and all the mighty men of valour... all the craftsmen and smiths: none remained, save the poorest sort of the people of the land. And he carried away Jehoiachin to Babylon, and the king's mother, and the king's wives, and his officers, and the mighty of the land... all the men of might, even seven thousand, and craftsmen, and smiths a thousand, all that were strong and apt for war" (2 Kings 24:11-16). Nebuchadnezzar left the uneducated rabble behind.

Historically, the events in Daniel (God is my judge) begin c. 607 BC. The prophet Ezekiel (God strengthens) begins to prophesy in Judah c. 592 BC. The inhabitants of Jerusalem were taken into Babylonian captivity in 586 BC. The people of Judah spent two generations in Babylon and grew accustomed to their new way of life. It is at this point that the Synagogue system of Yahweh worship began as the temple had been destroyed. The captivity also spawned something unique. After all these years of individual prayers in the temple, a serious of prayers were formulated and written on scrolls. Although it was a good idea at the time Jesus came to call repetitive prayers vain. Personally speaking, I think this is where left brain thinking individuals took control of religion. Nonetheless, Cyrus, the new Persian King, felt compelled to allow the captives to return to Jerusalem under the leadership of Zerubbabel (sown in Babylon) and rebuild the temple. The Babylonian exile lasted from 586 – 537 BC. Zerubbabel had to make a number of trips to Babylon in order to convince the exiles to return and help build the temple. He also had to seek the protection of Cyrus from those in the land that did not want to see the temple rebuilt and David's line re-established.

Rebuilding the temple began in 520 BC and was completed 516 BC. The story of Esther takes place in Persia in 480 BC demonstrating that there were still many Jews in Persia after the temple was reconstructed. Malachi, also the last book in the Canon, began to prophesy c 397 BC. Alexander the Great conquered Palestine in 333 BC; the Ptolemy's begin ruling in 323 BC; the Seleucids begin to rule in 198 BC; the Hasmoneans begin rule in 166 BC; the Romans, under Pompey conquered Palestine in 63 BC. Supported by Mark Anthony the Roman Senate made Herod the Great king in Judea in 37 BC. Later, Herod could see the tide turning in Palestine and switched allegiance from Mark Anthony to Octavian. Herod is also credited with murdering his own family. He died in 4 AD. Jesus is thought to have been born between 7 and 3 BC. I have always used 3 BC as his birth date as Jesus was crucified at 33 years of age in the year 30 AD. It is also worth noting that more blood has been shed in Palestine than anywhere else in the world. The people said "we will have king over us" (1 Samuel 8:19), and God cried.

## Ezra

The Book of Ezra takes place in the time of King Cyrus of Persia who had conquered Babylon in 539 BC. Through his liberal policies Cyrus allowed the Jews to return and start reconstruction of the temple in 536 BC. The Book of Ezra continues to record the genealogy of the exiles who returned to Jerusalem. He also records the intense opposition to the rebuilding of the temple from the inhabitants of the land surrounding Jerusalem. This opposition ended with the decree of King Darius who supported the rebuilding of the temple. Ezra also demonstrates a repugnance to racial intermarriage as the men were required to send away all the foreign women they had married along with all the children of those marriages (Ezra 10: 16-17,44). To this day, Orthodox Jews will only marry within their community.

Note!

Have you ever noticed how children of mixed racial marriages are strikingly handsome/beautiful, intelligent, of strong inner character and creative? Could this be "a God thing?" Consider also, the children of incest, or intra-tribal marriages. It makes one wonder. The research of Hal Herzog, Ph. D. states that "the problem with having sex with close relatives is that there is an astonishingly high chance that your offspring will be born with a serious birth defect. Take the results of a study of Czechoslovakian children whose fathers were first degree relatives. Fewer than half the children who were the product of incestuous unions were completely healthy. Forty two percent of them were born with severe birth defects or suffered early death and another eleven percent were mildly mentally impaired." In Leviticus 18 God spoke clearly against incest.

## Nehemiah

The Book of Nehemiah records similar events as recorded in Ezra. They are written from a priestly perspective and acknowledge the sin of the people. As in the Garden of Eden and the sin of Solomon, these prophets place the blame on women. Adam said, "the **woman** that **you** gave me;" David was lead astray by the beauty of Bathsheba; Solomon was beguiled by so many foreign women and now the way back to God is by casting away foreign women and children. This religious restriction on racial intermarriage was not necessarily about foreign women, it was about adopting their foreign gods. Personally, I think intermarriage is not only wonderful but healthy. As difficult as it is for racists to accept, an enlightened society will embrace a "melting pot" philosophy and not multiculturalism. Melting pot is a metaphor symbolizing the evolution of a heterogeneous society to a homogeneous society. Ethnic societies that enforce intra-cultural marriages are to be feared especially when enforcement is driven by religious authority.

This is true of our Bible. Listen how Nehemiah 13: 25-27 speaks to Jewish men concerning the intermarriage abomination. "And I contended with them, and cursed them, and smote certain of them, and plucked off their hair, and made them swear by God; ye shall not give your daughters unto their sons, nor take their daughters unto your sons, or for yourselves. Did not Solomon King of Israel sin by these things? Yet among many nations was there no king like him, who was beloved of his God and God made him, king over all Israel, nevertheless even him did outlandish women cause to sin. Shall we then hearken unto you to do all this great evil, to transgress against our God in marrying strange wives?" Israel failed in their mission to evangelize the world to God and the prophets put the blame on women. In a male dominated society, the finger of blame is rarely pointed at men. To say that male bias does not exist in scripture is to be closed minded.

Note!

The Babylonians place small groups of people in villages because they would not unite and pose a military threat. The practice of segregation is nothing more than the stronger culture trying to keep their race pure. If Jesus came that "all flesh shall see the salvation of God" then God does desire a homogeneous world family (Luke 3:6, Titus 2:11, Hebrews 5:9).

## Esther

In juxtaposition to the records of male prophets, the story of Esther is a "woman's story." Should you chose to read Esther, take some time to quickly read a few passages in Ezra, Nehemiah and the Solomon passages in 2 Chronicles. I say that because (a) the writing style, the syntax, is completely different. Syntax is how words are organized in a sentence and (b) the bias or lack thereof. Be mindful that bias is slightly different than prejudice. As in the Book of Ruth you should notice that the story is about a woman and how a woman was able to navigate in and around the customs of a male culture. Notice the dramatic difference in these stories as opposed to Dinah's story which is obviously told by men. The woman's voice in scripture is important. The woman's voice speaks for fairness and justice. Bear this in mind when reading the New Testament.

## Job

The Book of Job (hated) actually presents an interesting picture of heaven, albeit short. One needs to pay attention to the dialogue between Satan (adversary) and Yahweh (the existing one). Notice how Satan needs permission "to do," or "to inflict" acts of a physical nature. Remember, Satan is the adversary of God and the tempter of humankind. Over the centuries, the church has managed to manipulate the image of Satan into something comparable to the wildest creation of Hollywood. The first two chapters of Job make it clear that Yahweh is LORD (YHVH) and freewill exists in heaven. In this book we see a Yahwist snapshot of heaven surrounding the ancient Elohists story of Job. Two entities present themselves before YHVH. They were the Sons of God and Satan. The phrase "Sons of God" appears five times in scripture. It appears twice in Genesis and three times in Job. The Genesis story is interesting in that the immortal Sons of God come to have sex with mortal women and not to have a monogamous relationship. Throughout scripture there is not one single reference to a feminine deity in Yahweh's court. All angels in the Bible are masculine. Imagine yourself as a director blocking this scene out on stage. How would you present this scene to the audience?

As a student of scripture pay attention to the fact that the Yahwist tradition has taken an Elohists story (Job) and made it their own. The Yahwist tradition acts like bookends to an Elohists story. By that I mean, from the end of verse 2 until the beginning of verse 38, the word LORD is used once in Job 12:9. This is odd as there appears to be a change of syntax and if you remove it from verse 12:9 the story carries on uninterrupted. As I have stated, the Yahwist voice is dominant in the Bible. The word "Lord" is used 7,836 times. The word, "God" is used 4,444 times. The term, "Lord God" is used 2,339 times. If you subtract "God" from the conjoined phrase, it denotes the fact that the Yahwist name for the deity is used 7,836 times while the Elohists name for deity is used 2,105 times. In other words, 74% of the references to the deity are in the Yahwist form.

When the storyteller wants to indicate that Yahweh is speaking he uses the word "LORD." Throughout the dialogue between Job and his friends, (verses 2:8 – 38:1) the word LORD (Yahweh) and the word Lord (Adonai) are **not** used. Only El, the ancient form for the word God is used. Two things are evident. First, Job is an Elohists' story. Second, Job and his friends do not know the name Yehovah; they only know El as their deity.

The ancient story of Job takes place in the land of Ur. Some Biblical scholars believe the location of Ur to have been near Damascus.

Others speculate Ur to be closer to the Red Sea. Both opinions lend support to the desire to have Job as part of the line of Esau, Abraham's grandson. This desire also keeps Yahweh's relationship with the people in Palestine. God however is know in other lands as demonstrated by the 4,000 year old story of Job. The opinion that makes the most sense to me is that Job is in Mesopotamia, meaning, the land between the rivers (Tigris and Euphrates). Job did not live in a city and neither did Terah. It was God who called Terah (Abram's father) out of Ur of the Chaldees. Ur is located 365 km south of Bagdad, Iraq, near what is now the city of Nasiriyah. At the time Ur was in the heart of the Sumerian Empire. They worshiped the moon god Sin whom some believe is now called Allah. The study of ancient gods is not only interesting but demonstrates the migration of these gods from one civilization/culture to the next.

The Book of Job is the oldest written record in the Hebrew canon. The dialogue in the book demonstrates the insertion of a Yahwist tradition into an Elohists story. Verses 1:1-5 open in the Elohists voice, then verses 1:6 through 3:1 record a Yahwist dialogue between Yahweh and Satan. In this dialogue both terms (El and Yahweh) are used. From verse 2:8 through to verse 38:1 the ancient name of El is used exclusively for God. In verse 12:9 the name Yahweh mysteriously appears in the middle of a story about El. I doubt that it was part of the original story.

This book does not intend to discuss the allegorical interpretation of dialogue or the significance of the story. I will however, make some observations. The first observation is the power dynamic between Yahweh and Satan. In this dynamic free will is apparent but also divine authority. Satan (adversary – in both the Old Testament and New Testament) comes into the presence of Yahweh with "the sons of God" who present themselves before Yahweh. The essence of the dialogue in Chapter 1 is that Satan has witnessed only disobedience. God asks "have you considered my servant Job?" Satan retorts with the accusation that Yahweh "has built a fence around Job." This is important as Satan's accusation suggests that humans do not have the ability to resist sin and temptation without divine protection. If this is true, then Satan is pointing out to the heavenly host that Yahweh is flawed and creation is not good (Tov) of its own accord.

Secondly, and of prime importance is the fact that even Satan must have Yahweh's permission to do more than tempt. At this point Satan is given permission to cause events to happen around Job, but he must not touch Job. Note that the power of the Biblical Satan is limited to temptation. God then agreed to allow the Chaldeans to raid and destroy Job's family and possessions. Still Job does not curse God. The determined Satan bets that Job will curse Yahweh if Satan is allowed to infect Job with terrible sores. Satan is allowed to do this but must not take the life of Job. Notice how the celestial dialogue is between Satan and Yahweh and the terrestrial dialogue speaks only of Eloheem (God). Notice also how there is no mention of a temple or of an idol in Job.

God is the supreme authority. Satan's restriction is also demonstrated in the New Testament when Jesus overcame the three temptations in the wilderness. The way I read scripture is that the limit of Satan's power is temptation. There is not a cause and effect relationship between God and creation. The phrase, "the devil made me do it" was Bill Cosby's humorous way of pointing out that humans often use Satan to take the blame for something they did. Satan (adversary) does not make anyone do anything. You listen and then follow your heart's desire.

Having said this, I realize it is a direct contradiction to the nonsense the Roman church has professed over the centuries. The

Greek word devil (dee-ab-ol-os) in the New Testament means slanderer or false accuser. The devil has served the Roman church well over the years. A study of the devil will reveal an evolution in the grotesque. Early church images reveal humans suffering in a sea of burning sulfur. Contrary to the teaching of the Old Testament, the church created an individual capable of inflicting physical harm. The Satan of the Old Testament required God's permission to be the direct cause of harm. Instead of promoting a theology of "loving thy neighbour" the church has chosen to instill the fear of hell into the hearts of believers. The Roman Church's theology of a devil can be coupled with Dante's invention of purgatory. The church used this fantasy to sell indulgences to families so they could buy the release of loved ones from purgatory. This money built many cathedrals in Europe and Brittan. In the early part of the 14th century Dante wrote a divine comedy, a fictional allegory, and the Roman church sold it as theological. I will speak on church fiction later. For now, think about how the Book of Job demonstrates the faith God has in humanity. Never forget that the sacrifice of Jesus is the prime example of God's faith in humanity. God wants you, of your own free will and accord, to love and accept God as your heavenly father.

The Book of Job has God describing creation in a manner the ancient people could understand. We are told that heavenly angels traveled back and forth to earth which has been evinced by the story of Jacob's ladder (Genesis 28:12). We also get a glimpse of the "hand of God" so mysteriously present in human events. When the hand of God was upon Israel, no one could prevail against them. When the hand of God was withdrawn, Israel became victims to those who had succumbed to the same temptations Jesus had to endure in the wilderness.

Previously, I noted that the body of dialogue in Job was Elohists, using only the term "El." It is also noteworthy to mention that from Chapter 3 until Chapter 42, the last chapter, the dialogue is in the form of Hebrew poetry. This advanced form of writing predates Abraham. Poetry is a much easier form of literature to memorize. If you consider the beautiful song/poetry of Miriam it is not hard to imagine that Job may well have been passed down by women as well as men.

The names in any Hebrew story are also important. Job means hated but scripture does not note any parent or genealogical listing. Had Job been in the line of Abraham a genealogical reference would have been included. Eliphaz (my God is gold) is a Temanite (south). Bildad (confusing) is a Shuhite (wealth). Zophar (sparrow) is a Naamathite (pleasantness). Later in the story, Chapter 32, the young Elihu (he is my God) enters the story proclaiming God's justice (Elihu has no genealogical reference). Never forget that the Bible is the story of God's relationship with the Hebrew people, the chosen people. We are not told how God has worked, or tried to work, in other cultures or civilizations. Always remember, Melchizedek (my king is Sedek) knew of God before Abram.

Christians have developed a very narrow view of God's interaction with the people of the world. This exclusive view denies God's involvement with humanity in every age. Christians love to proclaim that God is at work in the world, but then take a very narrow-minded view that God is only at work through Christianity. Wrong! At the time of Abram God was determined to make a great nation of the lowliest people on earth. God's desire is to live in our hearts. We too have forgotten that the sanctuary of God is not a temple made of stone but a heart of faith.

# Psalms

The number of books written on the Psalms is enormous. Unfortunately, the man I knew (Dr. John Davis) who had made the Psalms a life long study developed Alzheimer's in his retirement. Had he not, his thoughts would most certainly be contained in this work. Suffice to say, the Psalms are counted among some of the most beautiful and inspiring works of Hebrew literature. The best known is Psalm 23. Because of its beauty it is a funeral favourite among those who know nothing about scripture or attend church. One can always tell when they are at the funeral of someone who did not attend church. The pastor reads Psalm 23 and the congregation sing "Amazing Grace." Prior to that, when David's heart was crying out because God had forsaken him, David wrote Psalm 22. Read it. Read how he moves from desperation to praise, to his eternal statement of faith in Psalm 23. Read then Psalm 24, David's instruction to those who would follow God. In the Presbyterian 1972 Book of Praise, hymn 9, "The Lord's my Shepherd" is followed by a hymn by Andrew M. Thomson, 1778 – 1831. "Ye gates, lift up your heads." It is based on verses 7-10 of Psalm 24.

David did not write all of the Psalms as some were written 300 years after his death. Psalm 79:1 in Book 3 is an example. David knows God as Yahweh but also used, Eloheem (God) and Adonay (Lord) as well. One form of "Lord" means an earthly superior. Psalm 150 is a closing song praising the LORD (YHVH). In verse 6 the Psalmist proclaims, "let everything that breathes praise the LORD." This statement essentially acknowledges Yahweh as the one true living God, creator of heaven and earth.

# Proverbs

The Book of Proverbs is ascribed to David's son Solomon. Chapter 1:7 states, "the fear of the Lord is the beginning of knowledge; fools despise wisdom and instruction." Proverbs teaches good morals as well as ethics while keeping the love of God at the forefront of those who value wisdom. It gives parental advice, even though following the guidelines in twenty first century North America would land a parent in jail for abuse. Instruction in the Book of Proverbs is from a male perspective. It describes the difference between a wise and foolish man. It also describes the difference between a wise and foolish woman but never lets us forget that woman is subject to man. The book affirms that women lead men astray. Chapter 2 tells how the prudent man will be saved from the way of evil. The way of evil is defined as, "the loose woman" and "the smooth words of foreign women."

Admittedly, 1 Kings 4:29-32 tells us that "God gave Solomon unparalleled wisdom and understanding exceeding the sand on the sea shore. Solomon's wisdom surpassed the wisdom of all the children of the east and all the wisdom of Egypt, "for he was wiser than all men… and his fame was in all nations round about" (1 Kings 4:31). He spoke three thousand proverbs and his songs were a thousand and five." Wow, I think whoever wrote that was truly inspired.

The problem I have with the Book of Proverbs is not the wisdom it imparts, rather in believing that Solomon was the author. The whole of the book is written in Hebrew poetry/song which would necessitate a gifted writer. First, with all the glory and honour constantly being heaped upon Solomon and the tending to the needs of a thousand or more wives, when did he find the time to write? Second, the teaching is from someone who not only had a personal relationship with God but understood how obedience to Godly wisdom enables one to live a just and upright life. Are we to understand that the man who wrote "the fear of the Lord is hatred of evil" is also the man who did so much evil in the sight of the God he professed to follow (Proverbs 8:13)? The previous chapters record a vain and lavish life style. Yes, some of scripture tells how God ordained the building of the temple; tells how God drew up the plans for David to give to Solomon. The problem with these verses is that they contradict our historical understanding that humans are not to construct anything to symbolize or represent the creator of heaven and earth. God's logic is "what can creation possibly make to represent or honour the creator of all things?" Speaking to God Jeremiah said "shall a man make gods unto himself" (Jeremiah 16:20)? Transliterated from the Hebrew the passage reads: Aw-dawm Asah Eloheem; then translated to English, "can Adam fashion God?" The modern day translation is, "and man made God in his own image." This insolence reverses the Genesis story. In the Genesis text Adam means "earth", the clay from which God fashioned Adam. Therefore, it is impossible for someone to fashion the creator God from material which God has created.

It is now necessary to pause for a moment to clarify our understanding of Biblical names, terminology and words that are gender specific.

| God | Elohiym | (El o heem) | masculine | Pre-Moses |
|-----|---------|-------------|-----------|-----------|
| LORD | Yehovah | (Yeh ho vaw) | masculine | Post-Moses |
| Yahweh | YHVH | ineffable | masculine | Post-Moses |
| Lord | Adonay | (Ad o noy) | masculine | Pre-Moses |
| lord | adown | (aw done) | masculine | Pre-Moses |
| Spirit | Ruwach | (roo akh) | feminine | |
| Soul | Nephesh | (neh fesh) | Incorporeal immortal life | |

| Wisdom | hokmah | (khok maw) | feminine |
| Understanding | tabuwn | (taw boon) | feminine |

You will have noticed from the above the masculine nature of God. You will also notice that wisdom and understanding are feminine terms. It is believed that wisdom is the feminine aspect of God. One of the beautiful features of the Hebrew language is that every proper noun has a specific meaning and can denote gender. The reasons for pointing this out will soon become apparent. Please take a few minutes to read Proverbs 8:22-36. Notice that the voice is feminine. Notice that the actions in the passage are feminine. In Hebrew literature wisdom rejoices and dances. This passage is the story of creation from the feminine perspective and like a mother, "her delights were in the sons of men" (Proverbs 8:31). This is an important passage to consider when reading the opening of the Gospel of John. I have heard John 1:1-4 preached many times but I have never heard clergy preach on Proverbs 8:31.

Inasmuch as I have challenged the common propaganda of "who wrote scripture" I do believe that an individual who follows Biblical instruction will gain wisdom. Not necessarily in the same way a fundamentalist will find reinforcement but in a way which is liberating. The Book of Proverbs is one of those books in which the feminine aspect of God reaches into the soul and touches the heart that desires knowledge. The following are a few examples from Chapter 22 which hold "the wisdom of Solomon" in juxtaposition to the actions of Solomon. Ask yourself, "do these pearls of wisdom sound like a man who enforced slave labour?

| Verse 2 | The rich and poor have this in common; the Lord is maker of them all. |
| Verse 8 | Whoever sows injustice will reap calamity. |
| Verse 9 | Those who are generous are blessed; they share their bread with the poor. |
| Verse 16 | Oppressing the poor in order to enrich oneself... will lead only to loss. |
| Verse 22 | Do not rob the poor because they are poor. |
| Verse 23 | The Lord will plead their case. |

The Book of Proverbs sounds as if it had been written by a social reformer, not a king who imposed conscription, decreed the poor to forced labour, used whips to keep the people in line and taxed the people to the breaking point so that he could live a life of luxury beyond the imagination of any human being. As I have said, you can read the words but you must also scrutinize the actions. Do they match?

The Temple

When the temple was finally completed, it was not large. Modern diagrams of the temple show the design was for religious purposes. When Jerusalem was sacked a fabulous amount of treasure was taken. This was because ancient kings used their temples like we use a bank vault. The cost of the building of the temple pales in comparison to the cost of Solomon's house. Think about it. The temple was not lavish. It was a simple stone building with individual chambers (bank vaults) and a small room to house the Ark.

Now think about lavishness of a king's house, especially a king who had the best of everything imaginable. Think about the value of all those talents of gold given to him and gained by pillaging. By today's standards, the estimated value of that gold would be in excess of ten billion dollars. Four thousand years ago it was a fabulous amount of money. I will close with words ascribed to Solomon, "remove far from me vanity and lies; give me neither poverty nor riches; feed me with the food that I need" (Proverbs 30:8). Do the above words correspond with Solomon's actions? The words of scripture say Solomon was wise. The actions demonstrate he was despotic, vain and lustful. Huge Hefner would be jealous of Solomon's sex life. It saddened God's heart to be rejected as King of Israel. God had said, "kings will do the things kings will do." Saul, David and Solomon were three completely different types of individuals. Not one of them governed with the fear of the Lord in his heart.

## Ecclesiastes

The Book of Ecclesiastes is said to have been written by the "Preacher," (Qoheleth) the son of David. Qoheleth is Hebrew for "public speaker," or one who speaks in the assembly. In the past it was supposed that Solomon wrote this book. However, the writer of Ecclesiastes understood toil and pain; Solomon did not. The writer understood reality, especially the reality of the common citizen during the reign of a despotic king. The book opens with "vanity of vanities, says the Preacher, vanity of vanities; all is vanity. What do people gain from all the toil at which they toil under the sun" (Ecclesiastes 1:2-3)? It is difficult to imagine that Solomon, a man consumed by vanity, gold and foreign women, lots of foreign women, knew anything about pain and toil except of course in the bedroom.

Personally, I suspect the writer was someone within the royal palace. Someone who could observe what was happening (something like Ebenezer Scrooge on Christmas Eve) and wrote in first person omniscient. This person had empathy for those who felt the pain of suppression brought on by vanity, desire and greed. This is not mere speculation as Solomon did have male and female singers; people who were well skilled in the arts. To think Solomon could take this much time to write in the midst of his continual delusions of grandeur is not realistic. Modern scholars realize that many of the books of the Bible were not written by the person whose name appears on the book. There are five Books in Psalm. There are three authors in the Book of Isaiah. Not all of the letters originally credited to the Apostle Paul were written by Paul. To think that with all the glory and honour being heaped upon Solomon, the administration required in running such a huge empire, and the time needed to satisfy his lust for every woman he ever laid eyes on, makes one wonder when Solomon had time to let his mind go that quiet place to contemplate and write.

Many scholars believe these illusions of grandeur to be hyperbole attributed to Solomon to demonstrate the Godly shroud covering the chosen people. At the time of writing, the chapters of Ecclesiastes are the ultimate rags to riches' story. The book is the human interpretation of the fulfillment of God's promise to Abraham to make of his seed a great nation. It is important to see the desires of man's heart as opposed to God's heart. God never did desire a human king to reign over the chosen people. The reality of Biblical hyperbole is that material possessions and human glory become the subjects of Israel's history. Isaiah wrote about the power of the moth and worm as well as the power of love. That which is lasting is love, God's love. Those who live for self at the expense of others eventually crash and burn. That is exactly what happened to Rehoboam after Solomon's death.

While Chapter 2 speaks of all Solomon's possessions Chapter 3 is a return to reality. It was written far from the posh surroundings of a royal court. Listen to the heart felt reflection of someone who has experienced the other side of wealth and privilege. My generation will remember these words as sung by the Momma's and the Poppa's. The words were taken from the following verses of Ecclesiastes 3:1-8.

To every thing there is a season, and a time to every purpose under the heaven:

> A time to be born, and a time to die; a time to plant, and a time to pluck up that which is planted;
> A time to kill, and a time to heal; a time to break down, and a time to build up;
> A time to weep, and a time to laugh; a time to mourn, and a time to dance;
> A time to cast away stones and a time to gather stones together;
> a time to embrace, and a time to refrain from embracing;
> A time to get, and a time to lose; a time to keep, and a time to cast away;
> A time to rend, and a time to sew; a time to keep silence, and a time to speak;
> A time to love, and a time to hate; a time of war, and a time of peace.

In a sense, the passage is saying "what will be, will be." When one looks back on life, they can see how the events of life have unfolded. Unfortunately, there is no balance or equality as some are blessed with the joys of life, while others suffer in pain and anguish. There is no divine reason for it except that most people make their own bed, so to speak, while others learn to leave the past in the past. God does not bless some people with pleasure or inflict other people with pain for the pleasure of the heavenly host. The phrase, "God is doing this to teach me to _ _ _ _ _" (you fill in the blank) is complete rubbish.

Any theology that puts the blame or praise on God for an event is either justifying the blessing or absolving one's self of responsibility for their actions. Preachers who tell their television congregations that God wants to bless them with riches beyond imagination must have graduated from the Solomon School of Theology.

Chapter 12 was certainly not written by Solomon for his son Rehoboam. It begins with a reminder to remember God before it is too late. Happy clappy clergy who preach redemption for everyone, no matter what, very rarely preach on the not so popular words of Jesus who said, "whosoever therefore shall confess me before men, him will I confess also before my Father which is in heaven. But whosoever shall deny me before men, him will I also deny before my Father which is in heaven" (Matthew 10: 32-33). Like the Book of Proverbs, Ecclesiastes is a book of instruction for the wise. Rich in metaphorical imagery it concludes with an admonition; "fear God, and keep his commandments; for that is the whole duty of man, for God will bring every deed into judgment, including every secret thing, whether good or evil" (Ecclesiastes 12: 13-14).

A present day reality that would have been impossible to imagine until the 21st century was the power of computers. Computers are like the human brain. As a forensic investigator can look inside a computer and see every place you have been, every message you have ever written, every image you have viewed, so can God look into a human being and view the same. The analogy makes it easy to see how God will be able to determine every motive, for every act a person has committed as well as why they did not do the things they should have.

## Song of Solomon

The reader will find biblical eroticism at its finest contained within the eight chapters of the Song of Solomon. It is partially a song in praise of women. More particularly, her physical attributes. The genre in Ecclesiastes is primarily left brain logical instruction. The whole of the genre of Song of Solomon is right brain creative song/poetry. It is difficult to believe they are products of the same author. In all likelihood it was written about Solomon. Chapters four and five are reminiscent of the patriarchs, Abraham, Isaac and Jacob, who also married their sisters. It also notes the very young age that women were given to men in marriage. Looking forward to the day of her betrothal the writer states, "we have a little sister, and she has no breasts" (Solomon 8:8).

The erotic imagery almost kept this book out of the canon. Thankfully it was included as we have another view of what life was like for those in the palace, especially Solomon's. As in most kingdoms, the inner recesses of the palace are off limits to the moral eye of the commoner. Nudity, sexual promiscuity, drugs and alcohol have always been part of the lifestyle of those in the inner circle. Wine, women and song are still the order of the day, even in a democracy. Speaking of her beloved, the book opens with the desire for his kiss; "let him kiss me with the kisses of his mouth, for your love is better than wine" (Solomon 1:1). The book closes with Dionysus type overtones from Greek mythology reflecting the desire for intimate love when she calls to her lover, "come away, my lover, and be like a gazelle or like a young stag on the spice-laden mountains" (Solomon 8:14). Drama students will recognize the parallels. The Song of Solomon also helps us to understand why Rehoboam and his royal friends were not willing to give up this opulent lifestyle.

# Isaiah

Isaiah (the Lord saves) is commonly referred to as the greatest of the writing prophets. While Amos and Micah are prophesying in Israel in the early part of the 7th century Isaiah begins to prophesy in Judah c. 755. He is a court prophet as opposed to a peripheral prophet. A court prophet enjoyed the comforts of the royal palace and the temple. A peripheral prophet was on the outside looking in, often ranting and raving about the sinfulness of both commoner and royalty; somewhat like John the Baptist. It is apparent, by the unsurpassed literary quality, that Isaiah was well educated. His sole authorship has been disputed but there are a number of arguments for a single authorship; those being his expression for God as "the Holy One of Israel" and the use of "fiery punishment." God gave Israel plenty of warning through the prophet Isaiah but they would not listen. More than 150 years later Jerusalem fell and Judah was carried into Babylonian captivity in 586 BC.

Tom Long, on speaking of the beauty of Isaiah used, as a glowing example, the Isaiah 52:7 passage; "how beautiful upon the mountains are the feet of the messenger who announces peace, who brings good news, who announces salvation; who says to Zion, Your God reigns!" Not only did Isaiah's prophesy come true it demonstrated the patient forgiveness of God in allowing creation time to return to the source of their salvation. To demonstrate God's patience Dr. Long used one of the most beautifully written soul-searching passages in scripture.

"For he grew up before him like a young plant,
and like a root out of dry ground; he had no form
or majesty that we should look at him, nothing in
his appearance that we should desire him. He was

despised and rejected by others; a man of suffering and acquainted with infirmity; and as one from whom others hide their faces he was despised and we held him of no account. Surely he has borne our infirmities and carried our diseases; yet we accounted him stricken, struck down by God, and afflicted. But he was wounded for our transgressions, crushed for our iniquities; upon him was the punishment that made us whole, and by his bruises we are healed" (Isaiah 53:2-5).

Oft times a reader can feel the writer's pain but do they hear the beauty. Listen to the following example as Isaiah cries aloud for Yahweh to come down. Feel his pain, feel the depth of his faith and feel his profound assurance in God's almighty power.

"O that you would tear open the heavens and come down, so that the mountains would quake at your presence - as when fire kindles brushwood and the fire causes water to boil - to make your name known to your adversaries, so that the nations might tremble at your presence! When you did awesome deeds that we did not expect, you came down; the mountains quaked at your presence. From ages past no one has heard, no ear has perceived, no eye has seen any God besides you, who works for those who wait for him" (Isaiah 64:1-4).

The Bible Story

The Bible is more than disobedience and punishment; it is more than rules and regulations; it is the story of a relationship between a creator God and creation. It is not told through the eyes of a perfect people but it is told by a chosen people. Human characteristics such as pain, suffering, joy and happiness are evident in the divine voice of God past down to us by those who recorded the stories of both traditions. Whether you want to admit it or not, male bias permeates the Biblical stories. At times, disobedience feels like the main theme in scripture but never let it cloud your belief that redemption, for those who are redeemable, is the hope humanity can cherish in good faith. Understanding how God is speaking to you is of prime importance and in the words of the writer of Hebrews, "faith is the substance of things hoped for, the evidence of things not seen" (Hebrews 11:1). Humanistic elements intertwined with the divine enhance credibility. Fundamentalists need to believe God dictated the words in order for the truth of God's word to shine through. However, I have already pointed out several contradictions pointing to human authorship while still acknowledging the light of love and forgiveness. Unfortunately, the Bible is a book of faith, not evidence. The Bible promotes love, not hate. Only fanatics take their holy book and use it for an excuse to kill. When a so called holy man promotes war and says, "God wills it," then people need to silence him with extreme prejudice. Think logically about the nature of the two basic kinds of god theology.

First, the ancient Middle Eastern people worshiped a household god who became a community or tribal god. People built individual shrines in their homes to offer prayers and to burn incense to a hand-made effigy of a god. These were the clay idols Rachel stole from Laban (Genesis 31:34). As families grew into tribes then into expanded communities, they needed a central god who was superior and more powerful than the individual family god. The size and elaborate surrounding equated to prominence. The power and prominence of the king were in direct relationship to his god. One needs to keep this philosophy in mind when thinking of the prominence of Solomon. As in the game of chess, the object of one king has always been to capture the other king and his god, proving that he and his god were superior. Egypt, Babylon, and Assyria are examples of human kings paralleling themselves to godliness. All cultures had their own god and some of these gods were simply called by a different name but the characteristics were the same. As nations grew, so did their god.

Secondly, we believe that God is at work in the world and God has been at work from the creation of the world and will be at work in the generations to come. All major Middle Eastern nations have a creation story and a flood story. The Hebrew flood story demonstrates God's desire to save humanity. This can be challenged as an ironic statement considering the fact that a portion of humanity had been annihilated in the flood. What it demonstrates is the power of sin and its ability to separate creation from God. Possibly, it is an example of the fate of those whose sin is not redeemable. Quite simply, sin is human disobedience to God's will for creation. God's work in the world is to gather those whose sin is redeemable, which is the purpose of God's Messiah. The story of God at work in the world continues in Christ Jesus. It continues to evolve day by day testifying to the fact that God holds out an immense faith in creation and an enormous hope for our salvation. I have always found it reassuring that God continues to have faith in creation and hope for my salvation.

151

Darwin felt strongly that humans evolved over millions of years. However, the scientific discovery of the individual DNA building block has demonstrated a process of creation. Something as complex as DNA did not simply evolve, it was created. Professor Ovey Mohammed pointed out that this necessitates two imperatives. One, a creator/God exists. Two, the creator/God is the maker of the DNA building block. Most major religions believe there is life beyond our earthly existence. This belief, coupled with direct instructions from creator God, helps humans to establish moral and ethical codes of conduct. Simply, we learn as children the things that are right and the things that are wrong. Of prime importance is the knowledge that murder is wrong and the forfeiture of one's own life is the punishment.

It is this belief in a heavenly life which should compel thinking individuals to scrutinize the instructions passed down from their god. Simply put, is the god you worship credible? Does the god you worship value human life? Or, is the god you worship an egotistical maniac who rejoices when humans destroy each other? Simple questions can help explain the mind set behind the creation of various religious beliefs. By that I mean, gods who have been created to serve individual desires will not have any regard for the people beyond that individual faith group. In other words, it is permissible for those of one religious club to mindlessly go out and kill people who belong to a different club? (Club is my brother-in-law Nick's name for denominations). Does it sound logical for the creator of humanity to promise afterlife rewards for the zealous of the faith that die in the mindless destruction of other human beings? The problem with this kind of philosophy is that it demonstrates the human characteristics of the family idols worshiped in the ancient Middle East. This narrow minded view supposes that a creator god wants some of the creation to kill others in creation. You can say what you want about your religion, but your actions will either demonstrate a belief in creator God or a belief in a man-made god.

Inversely, a faith group who proclaims their god to be the creator God must of necessity acknowledge that there is only one creator and that all people, of every tribe and nation, are children of that one creator. To claim that the creator God has instructed or given permission for one group from within creation to kill the others of creation is absurd. It would be like the father of a large family saying to the fifth born son, "you go ahead and kill your brothers and sisters; I will enjoy watching the carnage." If the words of instruction in your book of faith appear to reflect human characteristics and a desire to destroy, then it is my opinion that those words were written by a human, for a human. If the words happen to parallel the wants, needs and desires of the writer, then those words were not from God. When you read the biography of Mohammed, you will notice that all of the sera's from Allah happen to coincide with Mohammed's specific needs of the moment. A book with a single perspective makes me suspect. That is why there are very few words of love in the Quran as Mohammad was always in conflict. If the words are too focused on proving a point, they are not from God. If the words are too focused on a myriad of rules open to human interpretation, they were created by a human. This is the main shortcoming of the Hebrew/Christian scripture, the 632 Leviticus Laws. These laws evolved because the people tried to find loopholes in the simplicity of the Ten Commandments. The Commandments evolved because the people needed a further clarification of Deuteronomy 6:14 and Leviticus 19:18.

Likewise, Christians have not been immune to the need for clarification as there is a great discrepancy in the New Testament created by Christians. This discrepancy is centered on how to obtain salvation. While it is true that none come unto the Father except through the Son, it is not true that this occurs through baptism or professing the name Jesus while you roll down the isle in awe and wonder that all you had to do was to know how to spell the Saviour's name. The salvation story is tied to actions, not words, much to the mortification of fundamentalists. This will be discussed further in the Letter of James.

Note!

Anything you see in scripture that is in brackets has been added in by the copyists over the course of time. For centuries monks copied scripture from other scriptures. Sometimes they made mistakes. Sometimes they felt something had been left out so they wrote a margin note that later came to be included in scripture when another copyist thought the previous copyist left it out.

# Jeremiah

Like many other major prophets such as Isaiah and Samuel, Jeremiah (whom Yehovah has appointed) received his commission directly from God. His prophetic career was the longest, spanning 41 years from 627 until the Babylonian captivity in 586 BC. In short, with impending doom and destruction literally facing Jerusalem, king and people did not recant. They had an arrogant belief that God would not allow the holy city to be destroyed. Jeremiah's call was to announce the pending destruction. His prophesies were relentless, so much so, he suffered many indignities when thrown into the dungeon, then into the cistern, but his prophesies were to come true. Under King Zedekiah Jerusalem fell to the Babylonian King Nebuchadnezzar.

It has been said that more blood has been shed in Palestine than any other land in the world. In terms of world powers, the tribes and people of Palestine were insignificant. The real powers were Babylon, Egypt, and Assyria. A quick look at a map will show that in order to get from the Persian Gulf to the Red Sea was a huge undertaking as the trek from east to west across the Arabian Desert was approximately 500 miles. The Persians traveled north up the Euphrates River, then south through Damascus, west across the Jezreel Valley, south along the Mediterranean coast to the Nile in Egypt. In order for the Egyptians to attack Babylon, they had to take the same route in reverse. Unfortunately, their armies often met along the Mediterranean coast. The beginning of the end for Jerusalem took place in the time of Jeremiah when Nebuchadnezzar defeated Pharaoh Neco II in 605 BC at Carchemish. King Josiah sided with the Babylonians and was mortally wounded by an Egyptian arrow.

In the Book of Jeremiah God's exasperation is revealed. From creation, through a Biblically silent era where God had been at work with other people, to a final attempt in the children of Abraham, God finally admits creation is flawed. In the beginning God had said everything was good, (*Tov*) not perfect, just good. Sodom and Gomorrah were an attempt to rid creation of immorality. The twelve tribes would have perished in the desert had it not been for Moses' ability to change the mind of God. For hundreds of years, miracle after miracle had saved Israel from destruction. The people knew that had it not been for God other kingdoms would have taken them into slavery long ago. Now, in the time of Jeremiah, God uses the analogy of a potter and clay to explain the past and warn humanity of the future. God said, "cannot I do with you, O House of Israel, just as this potter has done? Just like the clay in the potter's hand, so are you in my hand, O House of Israel" (Jeremiah 18:5-6).

The frustration God has endured continued to be expressed through the prophets. In the era of captivity apocalyptic literature appears in the form of the Book of Daniel. Admittedly, I am not well versed in this form of literature and therefore not able to offer an educated opinion. Suffice to say that the divine miracles recounted in Daniel should have been sufficient to evoke a loyal worship of God the Father almighty, creator of heaven and earth. But alas, it was not to be.

Husband is a theme in Jeremiah, but more so is the theme adultery. God is portrayed as the loyal husband and Israel the adulterous wife. It is an analogy. Unfortunately, the use of these relationship terms continues to send a bias message that women are the adulterers and not men. I doubt that God or Jeremiah meant it this way but it is easy to see how the constant use of this sort of analogy will leave a long-lasting impression in the minds of the people.

## Lamentations

Traditionally, the Book of Lamentations was credited to the prophet Jeremiah as he was an eyewitness to the Babylonian destruction of the temple in 586 BC. The writer however remains anonymous. The literary form of Jeremiah is primarily prose whereas the entire Book of Lamentation is written in Hebrew poetry. Students of literature might want to study the form and layout of the book for the sake of beauty alone. As the title suggests there is weeping and gnashing of teeth over the doom which has fallen upon Jerusalem. Yet, there is a glimmer of hope in the promise of God. Chapter 5 opens with a plea for God to remember Israel and a cry to God that the chosen people have now been disgraced. Also, as if negotiating, a reminder that their inheritance has been turned over to aliens. In order to elicit sympathy, the writer uses an analogy of his own, saying, "we have become orphans and fatherless; our mother's like widows" (Lamentations 5:3).

The last few verses of Chapter 5 support the argument that the book was written in exile c. 575 BC. Verse 18 speaks of Mount Zion lying desolate. Then, after a short verse of praise the reader will note the change from a plea to accusation. Yes, accusations can be found throughout the Old Testament. In verse 20 the writer complains, "why do you always forget us," as if to say, "ok, we have been punished enough." Following the complaint is the writer's remedy, a call to restoration, "just like the good old days." The chapter ends with the question, "unless you have utterly rejected us?" This accusation is the same as saying "are you going to break your promise to Abraham?"

Calling the Almighty to offer a defense is not a major theme in the Old Testament but it is a theme nonetheless. The following are a few of those verses.

Exodus 5:22   Then Moses turned again to the Lord and said, "O Lord, why have you mistreated this people? Why did you ever send me?" Then Moses went on to complain how God allowed the people to be mistreated by Pharaoh.

Habakkuk 1:2   O Lord, how long shall I cry for help and you will not listen? Or cry to you "Violence," and you will not save? Why do you make me see wrongdoing and look at trouble?

Jeremiah 20:7   O Lord, you have deceived me, and I was deceived; you have overpowered me, and you have prevailed. I have become a laughingstock all day long; everyone mocks me. For whenever I speak, I must cry out, I must shout, "Violence and destruction!" For the word of the Lord has become for me a reproach and derision all day long.

Job 24:1   Why are times not kept by the Almighty and why do those who know him never see his days?

God's answer came to Job, "and the Lord said to Job, shall a faultfinder contend with the Almighty" (Job 40:1). The Bible never offers a defense for God's actions.

People throughout history have accused or questioned God for disastrous events. When children die, or a family member is killed in a tragic accident, we ask why? When despots or terrorists senselessly murder thousands of innocent people, we ask why? The reverse is also true as well. When fortune falls upon people, they thank God for the blessing. Blame and credit are nothing more than a theology of evidence. Then there is the most bizarre statement one can make, that is; "God is doing this to me to teach me to (insert own lesson)." Can you imagine that God would kill, maim, or inflicted loss on someone to teach you a lesson? Clergy who preach this theology should be shot. As Tom Long has said, "God is in the world as promise, not evidence."

The promise of a good life is true. Obey the only two commands in the Bible that really matter.

1) The command to love God in Deuteronomy 6:5;
2) The command to love your neighbour in Leviticus 19:18.

The other 632 commands, rules and laws are for the people who try to find loopholes in the law. The way we demonstrate that we love God is to love our neighbour. In case no one has noticed, God stopped responding to demands for evidence about 2,000 years ago. The atrocities that have happened over the centuries are no different than those that happened to Israel when the people were left to their own devices. When people of one faith or nationality think they have the right to subjugate other people, atrocities happen. When the male bias is allowed to subjugate women, atrocities happen. Calling God to account for human disaster is fine, but you have to be willing to listen to God's response. The problem is, people never really want the answer; they just want to complain.

## Ezekiel

Ezekiel (God strengthens) was a major prophet who lived during the Babylonian captivity by the River Chebar, (far off) which was near the royal canal of Nebuchadnezzar. He was also one of the prophets to whom God spoke in a vision. Chapter 1 uses imagery that would rival the creative mind of Steven Spielberg. It is reminiscent of Elisha's record of Isaiah's ascension into heaven. The Book of Isaiah is the book that gives us the clearest picture of what drove God to use such a drastic measure of punishment as the captivity. From time to time we read about the images of the Baals, the Asherah pole, Tammuz, Molech and other detestable images brought into the temple. The chosen people were to have been a monotheistic people but we must never forget the constant pressure upon Israel to be polytheistic. This pressure is part of reason why the Pharisees in the New Testament were so averse to change. Jesus brought a new way of thinking and if you have been part of the change dilemma in a Christian church you will know that the old guard would love to kill those who bring change. Christians will only embrace change if the result is that everything remains the same.

Patricia taught that Israel was to have been an influence upon the nations/people/lands they came to possess. There was never to have been a temple, but David simply told God, [you are going to get a temple, like it or not]. The paradox of the scriptural story is that it presents an almighty, omnipotent, ethereal God who has time and again demonstrated a miraculous presence in the affairs of humanity and yet the people kept turning to idols made of stone. To my knowledge, there has never been any stone or wooden effigies perform one miracle throughout history. There are many stories as to what these gods can do but there is no evidence. Many charlatans have returned from the mountain with a word from god. Unfortunately, people have only their word. The Bible is the only book to demonstrate what God can do, will do, and has done. The story of Elijah's challenge to the prophets of Baal is one such example. The Bible is a witness.

The imagery in Ezekiel is as astonishing as God's prophesies that have been delivered through the prophet. So too is the abomination of abominations in Chapter 8. Thus far in scripture the reader is only aware that Israel sinned by worshiping other deities. Prior to Chapter 8, the Book of Ezekiel describes the detestable worship which drove God to inflict the disasters which befell Israel. Now we will look at the objects of detestable worship which caused God to "pour out my wrath upon you" (Ezekiel 7:8).

First, there was Chemosh, the god of the Moabites. He was the male counterpart of Ashtar whose symbol was the Ashtoreth pole. With the exception of Yahweh, these other gods indulged in amorous male and female relationships. (To my knowledge there were not any male to male relationships). Chemosh (subdue) and Ashtar (star) were two of the gods in the Phoenician pantheon under the supreme god Baal (lord). Like Baal, they demanded human sacrifice.

Second, was the god Tammuz (sprout of life) who was the Sumerian god Dumuzu who represented life, death and rebirth. Rebirth and reincarnation were ancient beliefs. After all, what is the point of a god if faithful worship will not inherit life eternal? These beliefs of rebirth and reincarnation were at the heart of many ancient celebrations which we have come to term "orgies." I will discuss the Apostle Paul's aversion to orgies later in this work but suffice to say that he was the advocate of monotonous Christian marriages. Tammuz was the fertility god and is recognized in various cultures by the phallic symbol. Many cultures built pillars in the shape of the human phallus in or near their temples. According to scholars the Church of the Nativity was built over the shrine to Tammuz and Adonis.

Abominations

Ezekiel was sitting in his house by the River Chebar when, through a Godly vision, was transported to Jerusalem. Directed to look north of the altar gate he saw the image of jealousy which was more than likely an image of Ashtoreth. Ezekiel was then told that he will see still greater abominations. Moving through the gate into the court of the temple he saw a hole in the wall. Instructed to dig through the hole Ezekiel emerged and found an entrance to a chamber through which he was directed to go. In this chamber Ezekiel saw frescos of many creeping things, loathsome animals and all the idols of the house of Israel. Idol (Baal) worship was the sin Israel continued to commit. They were never punished for double parking their camels.

161

Next, Ezekiel saw seventy of the elders of the house of Israel with Jaazaniah (Yehovah hears) son of Shaphan (rock badger) standing among them. What happened next is difficult to understand from a simple reading of a translation. Verse 11 records seventy elders in accordance with God's command to Moses to appoint this number of elders to attend the tabernacle (Numbers 11:24). Jaazaniah was also an elder and the assistant high priest. He was the son of the high priest Shaphan. The reader should take note that the New Testament uses the plural term "high priests" which is incorrect. There was only ever one high priest. The priesthood was not like the Optimist's club or the Rotary, where there is a different president every year. The Roman church adopted this model for the Pope. There is only one Pope. The assembly is the College of Cardinals, not the College of Popes. A new Pope is only elected after the death of the incumbent Pope. For much of its early history the papal court was comprised of 72. The temple priesthood was comprised of 72 elders/priests, under the leadership of the high priest. The interesting part of this passage is that the high priest, Shaphan, is not mentioned.

Following the elder's atrocity, Ezekiel is shown a greater abomination of women weeping for Tammuz. These women carried cakes of bread baked in the shape of the phallus. I am not sure why the women were weeping but it will have something to do with fertility or lack thereof. It is interesting to note that it appears to be a part of the ritual appointed to the women as Jeremiah 7:18 tells of the women kneading the dough and making phallus shaped cakes to the queen of heaven (Ashtoreth). Now the story gets really interesting; 25 men are lying prostrate, facing the east, waiting for sunrise. It is unclear whether or not the 25 men or the 71 elders are putting the branch of acacias to their nose. Putting the sprig of acacias to the nose has a funerary symbolism signifying the resurrection to immortality. So just what is going on in the temple built unto the name of YHVH?

First of all, it is night so they think God cannot see them. Second, if the branch is being held to the nose then someone has died and a ceremony of resurrection is taking place. My understanding of the passage with the presence of idols and other godly images is that Shaphan, the high priest, has been sacrificed. Israel wanted out from the suppression of Babylon. That is why there is only mention of 71 elders; the high priest had been sacrificed. The women weeping for Tammuz represent prayers for a rebirth at the beginning of the day as the sun, the life-giving force of God, was about to rise in the east. The modern day practice at a Masonic funeral is to symbolically face the east and place a sprig of acacias upon the apron of the deceased brother as a symbol of the resurrection to eternal life.

A story taken from 1 Kings has a Biblical and Masonic significance. At the building of Solomon's temple two pillars were placed at the entrance. That on the left was named Boaz (God will establish) and that on the right was named Jachin (in strength) (1 Kings 7:21). Jachin was the assistant high priest. It is highly unlikely that the high priest was on vacation at the time or had a head cold preventing him from officiating at the dedication. I believe he was sacrificed the night before and that is why the assistant high priest had to officiate at the temple dedication. That is also why Jaazaniah, the assistant high priest, is mentioned in Ezekiel and not Shaphan. The elders expected the dead body of Shaphan to rise with the sun. I also find it interesting that in this cult-like ceremony the elders were each swinging smoking censors. Jeremiah 44:19 tells us that burning incense is an abomination to God. If the burning of incense to the queen of heaven is an abomination to God, then why is this practice of swinging a smoldering censor still carried out in many Episcopal denominations? If you want to know what is really going on in scripture you will have to read it yourself and not count on the Sunday school mentality of clergy who have not studied scripture in the Biblical languages. Ezekiel is a powerful voice in scripture. Jeremiah speaks of the final days before the captivity and the opportunities placed before Israel to repent. Ezekiel reflects upon the depths of deprivation to which Israel had sunk. A close reading of scripture will most definitely open your eyes.

Chapter 9:3 talks about how the glory of the Lord had gone up from the cherub on which it sat. The Ark of the Covenant was to have been the throne of God. The outstretched wings of the cherubim represented the actual seat. Some cultures built a representation of their deity. Other cultures provided a throne upon which the deity sat to direct or judge the people. In Baal worship, the bull was not the Baal. The bull was the judgment seat of Baal. Israel adopted the same model; hence, the arc of the covenant became the judgment seat of God. But alas, the glory of God would no longer reside in the temple. Chapter 11 ends with the vision of impending doom and Ezekiel telling the exiles in Chaldea of "all the things the Lord has shown me."

The Bible is partially a record of the back and forth battles between good and evil, of God's grace and human sin, and of the hope God holds out for humanity. Christians are always told to have hope in God but are rarely told of God's hope for a creation that has the potential for good. In the past, Christians have been taught that they are now God's people, as if this designation were singular. Nazism tried to exterminate the chosen people while the Roman Church buried its head in the sand. Unfortunately, for the simple minded, God has never given instructions, with the exception of King Saul, for this kind of thinking. A rational deduction would determine that if God's covenant with the chosen people can be broken, then so can Jesus' promise. The Apostle Paul understood the covenant to now include all who believe and obey God. He taught that everyone who believed could find salvation in the redemptive blood of the Messiah. I will speak more on this subject later, but for now, the Apostle Paul does not understand Jesus to be God. To Paul, Jesus is the Son of God, the Lamb of God. Paul would have agreed with Bishop Arius. There are 48 mentions of the phrase "Son of God" and with the exception of one mention in the Book of Daniel, the rest are all in the New Testament.

Gathering

Chapter 20 of the Exodus recounts God's frustration with Israel in the Egyptian wilderness. Clear instructions were given not to make or worship idols. The ten commandants clearly define their relationship with God and with each other. The Decalogue simply defines the command of how to love God and to love each other. Yet, even though the people continued to reject God, the promise of "gathering" was held out to those who would accept. Gathering is a huge Biblical theme. Jesus used the analogy of a hen gathering her chicks to express his desire to bring the people back to God (Matthew 23:37). But you must remember that Jesus came to redeem sinners, not the unredeemable. This is a theological perspective the Christian church fails to teach. Redemption is preached in such a way as to cloak the requirement of turning, of repenting. Restoration will come to Israel and it will come to everyone who turns to God and obeys. Read of the redemption promise in 1 Kings 8:48.

The Book of Ezekiel foreshadows the person of Christ in that the Lamb of God is also the Shepherd of Israel. Chapter 34:11-13 speaks of the extent God will go to gather the scattered flock. Verse 16 speaks of those who will be gathered and those who will be destroyed. The Messiah was not sent to nullify the promises humanity does not like. The Messiah came to redeem the redeemable, to save all "that might be saved." When you read scripture, particularly the passages of promise, forgiveness and salvation, pay attention to modifiers like "might" and "if" used within the statements. Let me ask, "have you ever heard a minister **not** preach hope in salvation at a funeral?"

Once again, I would urge you to read the Book of Ezekiel to gain a better understanding of the heart and mind of God. Humanity was created in the image and likeness of God. Do not be afraid to enter into a relationship with God. Scripture is not just meant to be read. Scripture should evoke dialogue with God, much like the dialogue between a loving parent and a child. For centuries the church has treated people like mushrooms; kept them in the dark and covered them with manure.

## Daniel

Any attempt on my part to write intelligently on apocalyptic literature would reveal how much in the dark I am with regards to my understanding of this genre. I will leave apocalyptic interpretation to those of my colleagues who have spent a lifetime researching its meaning. It is worth noting however that the one use of the phrase Son of God occurs in Daniel 3:25. Nebuchadnezzar had Shadrach, Meshach and Abednego thrown into the furnace but when he looked inside there was a fourth; the Son of God.

# Hosea

Hosea (salvation) is the first of the minor, or peripheral, prophets. Peripheral means they did not have a place in the palace or were supported by the palace treasury. The Minor Prophets directed their rage towards Israel's leaders as well as the people. To give her students a sense of their veracity and rage with which they shouted "co aw mar Adonay" (thus sayeth the Lord), Patricia would often use a comparative analogy. She would say, "what is the difference between a lunatic and a peripheral prophet?" The silent students would anxiously await the answer, "the lunatic did not have anyone to record his words on a scroll." The statement was not meant to be disrespectful but rather convey the force and volume of voice used as these John the Baptist prototypes hurled their incriminating accusations towards people and royalty alike. When the preface "co aw mar Adonay" (thus sayeth the Lord) is used in the Old Testament it is used to indicate that the following words are from God and not the prophet. It was a statement that sent shivers up the spine of those who heard the words. That preface denoted the verbatim word of God.

Erotic analogies saturate this book. The irony of the Book of Hosea is that it speaks the word of God in a language the people were all too familiar with. It clearly demonstrates God's frustration with the people called to be holy. Previous prophets had been called to ingest the word of God. Hosea is told to "go marry a whore." After Hosea lay with Gomer (complete) she conceived and bore Hosea a son whom he named Jezreel (God sows). Gomer conceived again and bore a girl who was named Lo-ruhamah (no mercy). Once more she conceived and bore a son who was named Lo-ammi (not my people).

As future generations listened to these words in the synagogue the analogies would be painfully clear.

The dilemma that has always faced God is to fulfill the promise to Abraham that "the number of the people of Israel shall be like the sand of the sea" (Hosea 1:10). In a biting analogy to Israel's whoredom, Hosea tells his children that Gomer is not his wife. He pleads with his children to tell Gomer to quit her whoring and remove her adulterous ways from her breasts or he will strip her naked and expose her. During these gutter snipe accusations the age-old culprit is revealed; the supreme Canaanite deity Baal, God's arch nemesis. In the midst of God's rage Chapters 3 and 4 hold out a glimmer of hope in salvation. God is determined that Baal will not win the battle for humanity and that one day God will declare of Abram's children "you are my people" and the people will gratefully declare "you are my God" (Hosea 2:23). Hosea is then instructed to marry another adulteress but not to have sex with her to symbolize the barren time period before Israel's return to God. I was just thinking that with all the so-called "reality programs" on television the Hosea version could be called "I married a whore."

Oft times people will say, "if I were God" in an attempt to make things right or to make sense of a tragedy. Humans who think that way cannot begin to comprehend the complex dynamics of our heavenly relationship. Hosea alludes to past events in humanities' relationship with God. In Chapter 6 he reminds the reader that, "God desires steadfast love and not sacrifice." Do not think about this solely in terms animal sacrifice but of human sacrifice, child sacrifice. Reflect upon what Jesus said about harming children ever remembering there is no redemption for sin unto death. Clergy can walk with a condemned prisoner to the death chamber, but unless that individual has made his own peace beforehand, a last minute confession is useless. It would be like telling a police officer you were sorry for going twice the speed limit in a school zone in hopes you will not get a ticket.

Hosea's writings truly reflect the dilemma of God. The book closes with a prime example of God's *hesed* (loving kindness). Hosea's voice softens in Chapter 14 as he calls to the human heart with the plea "return, O Israel, to the Lord your God." Then God's voice is heard through the prophet saying, "they shall again live beneath my shadow; they shall flourish as a garden; they shall blossom like the vine; their fragrance shall be like the wine of Lebanon." For those who think that God's chosen people are "out" and Christians are "in," please read your Bible again. This time, listen. Think also of how God wanted to be Israel's king. It was an invitation back to the garden in Eden. Think again about "they shall again live beneath my shadow" and how I have saying that when God's protective had is over Israel no harm can come to them!

Notice the change of language from Chapter 1. Notice the change in the analogies for people who will turn and repent. Notice how the strenuous voice softens to one of love, compassion and promise for those who truly repent. God requires two things of creation that need be repeated often. The first is to love God. The second is to love your neighbour. People demonstrate their love for God "by loving their neighbour." God truly has hope in our salvation.

# Joel

Joel's analogies give us a definite sense of disgust and condemnation. As with all the prophets there is a call to repentance as well as a call for prayer. It is important to realize that prayer is the means by which we listen for God's word in our lives. God is not a divine Santa Claus whose function it is to give spoiled children everything their hearts' desires or to bail people out of every self induced mess. Prayer actually consists of two parts. The first is to empty the heart of burdens and desires, remembering that desires are not defined as needs. The second is to listen in silence, remembering Elijah in the cave. God is not like a slot machine that when the lever is pulled the results appear immediately. God waits until your heart is ready to receive direction.

The Book of Joel provided God's response to the promises made to the children of creation. When you read scripture, you must always be mindful that, from start to finish, the context of the writing is to agrarian people. Joel also reveals another side of God's nature. With Moses we see God's love responding to the prayers of the people. The continual backsliding of Israel drove God to reconsider the promise made to Abraham. The Babylonian captivity revealed God's ability to make stern judgment. In Joel, God's jealousy is revealed. Each Godly emotion expressed in scripture is also a human quality. There is one quality however humans do not often use but possess. That quality is forgiveness.

When I think back over my ministry and recall the faithful people who came and sat religiously in their pew every Sunday, it makes me wonder if they ever really heard God speaking in the sermons. When people have been wronged, they would sooner take their petty grudges to the grave rather than forgive. Ironically, people will forgive a heinous criminal before they will forgive the neighbour who broke their faulty lawn mower. Maybe, just maybe, when humanity learns to forgive, as the author of forgiveness has forgiven, then God's children will once again feel like sons and daughters of God.

I should say at this time that one of the most important aspects of forgiveness is the freedom it gives one's soul in that forgiveness gives the wrong up to God. God is the only one capable of honest judgment, rightful punishment or forgiveness. Forgiveness unburdens a heart full of hate. Bear in mind that you cannot forgive someone for an atrocity committed against another individual. If someone close to you is murdered for instance, you cannot forgive that person of murder. All you can do is give the hate you bear in your heart to God. In this way, you neutralize the acid that will erode your soul.

## Amos

Another voice cries out in scripture but this time it is speaking to Israel's neighbours. Amos (burden) is the only book that uses the phrase "for three transgressions of… and for four, I will not revoke the punishment." The formula is used eight times and a transgression is a simile for rebellion or for war. In Amos the surrounding nations will suffer God's wrath as well as Israel as those nations continue to reject correction. The need to reaffirm God as creator is evident in Chapter 5. In the well known plumb line passage (7:7) God says, "I will not pass by them anymore". In Hebrew it is *yaw-saf aw-bar* which means "to add or to take away." It can also be translated "to increase or to pass over." The act of passing over signifies the saving grace of God upon those who truly believe.

It is at times like this we need to remember one of the most profound stories told by Jesus. I know that Christian theology teaches that Jesus is the way; it teaches that one must profess the name of Jesus; it teaches that everyone is forgiven no matter what they have done. This theology is incorrect. Professing is not the way. Actions are the way. I say this because the story is a direct quote from the mouth of Jesus. Read the story of the sheep and goats in Matthew 25: 32-46 and try to figure out another way to obtain salvation. In

Jesus' own words he reaffirms the Amos 8:4-7 condemnation against those who do not love their neighbour.

Amos, as many of the other prophets, ends his book on a positive note. Verses 9:13-15 reassure Israel that the land will once again flow with milk and honey; the fortunes of the people will be restored and the people will never be sent into exile again.

## Obadiah

Obadiah (servant of Yehovah) is the shortest book in the Old Testament with only 21 verses. His vision is directed against a proud Edom (red) prophesying that the wise will be brought low. The book closes with the promise that those who have been saved will possess to the land.

## Jonah

Most everyone is familiar with the story of Jonah (dove) and the whale. After God had directed Jonah to travel to Nineveh (abode of Ninus), Jonah disobeyed God and boarded a ship to Tarshish in an attempt to get as far away from Nineveh as possible. When a high wind threatened the ship, everyone started praying to their god, all except Jonah who was found sleeping in the hold. The sailors decide that Jonah was the one who had caused this abnormal storm so they throw him overboard where he was swallowed by a whale. For three days and three nights Jonah was in the belly of Scheol (hell) before he prayed. The King James Version has translated the Hebrew word Scheol to the English word hell. Although Scheol can mean "underworld," it typically means "grave" or "pit." The ancient world believed that the souls of the dead arrived at the shore of the

River Styx where a ferry carried them across the water to Hades, the place of the dead. (Hades was a Greek god but over time people came to call the place Hades). As in the Trojan funerary practice, Priam placed two coins on the eyes of his slain son Hector to enable him to pay the boatman called Charon. It was believed that the dead who arrived without coins to pay the boatman were doomed to wander on the shore of the River Styx for 100 years. This is where Dante Alighieri likely got his idea for his Divine Comedy, *Inferno*. Purgatory (place of purging) was on the shore of the Styx River and deemed to be the place between heaven and hell. The Roman church made good despotic use of Dante's fiction.

Jonah however, found himself in his own hell, yet, when he turned to God in prayer, his prayer was answered. The whale spewed him up on the shore. Jonah had not wanted to go to Nineveh because he hated the Ninevites and he feared that if he called the Ninevites to repentance, they would repent. This they did and were spared. Analogy, figurative speech, allegory, or actual happening is not within the compass of my discernment of Jonahs' experience. Suffice to say that when the word of God is preached people can and will change.

# Micah

Micah (who is like God) is the sixth of the twelve Minor Prophets. The theme of a shepherd gathering the flock is part of the promise of restoration. His prophesy of the Messiah being born in Bethlehem came true (Micah 5:2). The book ends with Micah's statement of faith that God will be faithful to the promises sworn to Abraham.

## Nahum

Nahum's (comfort) message is different in that he prophesies the inevitable destruction of a foreign power, Nineveh the Assyrian stronghold. This is good news for Judah as it will end the Assyrian domination.

## Habakkuk

Habakkuk (embrace) cries out against the wicked in Judah. He reiterates what God has tried to explain to the people. Verses 2:18-20 asks, "what use is an idol once its maker has shaped it? It is a cast image, a teacher of lies? For its maker trusts in what has been made, though the product is only an idol that cannot speak! Alas for you who say to the wood, wake up! to silent stone, rouse yourself, can it teach?" See, it is gold and silver plated, and there is no breath in it at all." Always remember, the Bible is more than a book recording the historic relationship between the creator and the creature, it is a witness to the fact that the God we worship has spoken "face to face" with many people in the past.

## Zephaniah

Zephaniah (Yehovah has treasured) records the ongoing struggle for godly supremacy between God and Baal. It may seem strange to hear it said that way but the reality of scripture is that Baal is the arch-rival of God, not Satan. Israel had continually succumbed to the temptation of worshiping man-made idols. Zephaniah also reaffirms God's desire to be Israel's king. Verse 3:15 proclaims "the king of Israel, the Lord, is in your midst; you shall fear disaster no more." Had Israel remained faithful to God, had not chosen an earthly king and had not continued to worship idols, I believe they would not have suffered the disasters inflicted upon them by surrounding nations.

The book closes with a confirmation of God's desire for Israel; "at that time I will bring you home, at that time when I gather you; for I will make you renowned and praised among all the peoples of the earth, when I restore your fortunes before your eyes, says the Lord (Zephaniah 3: 20).

# Haggai

Haggai (festive) is one of the prophets who lived in the time of King Darius (lord) during the Babylonian captivity. Zerubbabel (sown in Babylon) had been appointed as governor of Judah over those who had not been taken to Babylon. The captives had become comfortable in their new surroundings but now God is telling Haggai, "its time for my people to come home." It took a long time and not all returned.

# Zechariah

Zechariah (Yehovah remembers) relates the story of God sending Zerubbabel to King Darius and the subsequent release of the captives to rebuild the city of Jerusalem and her temple. When Moses went to Pharaoh, it was by deceit and the mighty hand of God that Israel gained her freedom. In Zechariah we hear how God through Zerubbabel brought about their freedom; "not by might, nor by power, by my spirit says the Lord of hosts" shall my people return to Jerusalem (Zechariah 3:6). The heavenly host (tsaw-bah) is the heavenly army.

The Book of Zechariah also prophesies the coming Messiah. The Messiah was the anointed one whom the people of Jerusalem were waiting. As David came to the emerging nation of Israel, so this prophesy proclaims how the Messiah will come to Jerusalem; "rejoice greatly, O daughter Zion! Shout aloud, O daughter Jerusalem! Lo, your king comes to you; triumphant and victorious is he, humble and riding on a donkey" (Zechariah 9:9). A prophet's mode of transportation was a donkey, just like the prophet Samuel. It symbolized service on the part of the prophet, not servitude. Those who expect servitude on the part of the people are not servants of God.

Chapter 10 gives the reader a glimpse of the ancient meaning of the designation shepherd. There is a reason the leaders of God's people were called shepherds. This was the reason Jesus needed to dawn the mantle of a shepherd. It has to do with a Godly understanding of government and those who govern. The shepherd's designation goes back to the laws of Hammurabi. This will be discussed in the context of Jesus as the shepherd of his people.

The second temple era began with its rebuilding in 520 BC and ended in 70 AD with its destruction when the Romans, in their frustration with the people, tore down the temple, the walls and burnt the city.

## Malachi

Malachi (my messenger) began his prophesies in 397 BC and his is the last book in the Hebrew canon. It contains short but interesting prophesies. Beginning with God's declaration of love, Chapter 2 moves to God's promise to curse the priests. Whether we are priests or pastors it is the nature of our calling that the word, all of the word, is to be preached with integrity lest we face a special kind of judgment. Malachi uses simple deductive logic in his statement, "have we not all one father? Has not one God created us? Why then are we faithless to one another" (Malachi 2:10).

It took 400 years for Malachi's prophesy to come to pass but it explains the expectations of the Pharisees. God had said, "see, I am sending my messenger to prepare the way before me, and the Lord whom you seek will suddenly come to his temple" (Malachi 3:1). The book ends with a final admonition, "remember the teaching of my servant Moses, the statues and ordinances that I commanded him at Horeb for all Israel. Lo, I will send you the prophet Elijah before the great and terrible day of the Lord comes. He will turn the hearts of the parents to their children and the hearts of the children to their parents, so that I will not come and strike the land with a curse" (Malachi 4:4-5).

It is worth noting that at every Passover, God's chosen people prepare the Passover meal and leave the door open for Elijah to enter. There is always an extra seat placed at the head of the table so that Elijah might come and take his place as God's Holy prophet. Christians and Jews wait in anxious anticipation for the fulfillment of God's promise.

# CHAPTER TWO

## The New Testament

### Introduction

The New Testament begins the third part of the greatest four part story ever told. The first part of the story is termed pre-history as it begins with creation and ends with the Terah leaving Mesopotamia (land between two rivers) and travailing up the Euphrates into Anatolia (now Turkey). Terah named the settlement after his deceased son Haran. It is from Haran, near the head waters of the Euphrates, that Abram migrated south past Damascus. In this part of the story, humanity exercises their freewill powers in the catastrophic decision to listen to temptation rather than obey God.

The decision in the garden and subsequent expulsion did not turn creation back to God. In fact, sin became so rampant that the great flood destroyed, with the exception of Noah and his family, all the people living in the western part of the Fertile Crescent (Palestine). The Fertile Crescent extends from the Persian Gulf, north along the Euphrates and Tigris Rivers into Turkey, then south along the coast of the Great Sea and into the fertile lands of the Nile River in Egypt.

Considering that the Roman Church had people believing creation had existed for only 5,000 years, modern evidence indicates this to be incorrect. The ancient village Hasankeyf, Turkey, near the head waters of the Tigris River is riddled with hundreds of caves cut into the mountains. This evidence indicates an ancient cave dwelling civilization going back as far as 12,500 years was in existence more than 6,000 years before the great pyramid of Giza, Egypt. Terah would have settled at or near the caves at Hasankeyf.

The second part of the story can be said to begin with the personal relationship God cultivated with Abram. With the exception of Job, scholars are not aware of God's (El) presence in the lives of any other ancient people. The span of 2,000 plus years from Abram until the coming of the Messiah may seem like a long time but in God's reality, it is not. Consider the multitude of ways God spoke and interacted with humanity. Sometimes face to face (paw neem - paw neem) as with Moses (Exodus 33:11) or in visions, dreams and direct communication with Abram, Samuel, Elijah and Ezekiel. In this period of time God's emotions parallel the broad spectrum of emotions experienced by humanity. However, God's most predominate emotion is love; a love so amazing it gave birth to the quality of forgiveness. The backsliding which was at the heart of Israel's sin is Baal worship. The full dynamic of this war between the people of God and the people of Baal is never fully developed in scripture. The people in and around the Promised Land were in one way, shape or form, worshipers of Baal. Israel was to have shed light on, and lead all people to, a personal relationship with the one true living God. Personally speaking, there is only one LORD. All other gods are a human creation.

After more than 2,000 years of failed relationships God devised another plan for the redemption of humanity. The plan is the partial gift of God's self in the form of a Messiah maw-shee'-akh (anointed one). I say partial gift as this is the Hebrew understanding of the anointed one. Considering the fact that Jesus never referred to himself as God I will demonstrate that scripture only supports the claim that Jesus is the son of God. While fundamentalists are choking on their indignation ask yourself the question, "what difference does it make to God's grand design if Jesus is the Messiah and not God?" In my opinion, none! When my time comes I know there will be a redeemer to stand beside me before God's throne of grace. Who knows, maybe I am related to Bishop Arius.

Jesus is the third part of the story; the son of God sent to live among humans. He experienced first hand human emotions, sorrows and joys. Christians have developed many self interest theories and dogmas with regard to the person of Jesus. The fact is, about 70 years after the birth of Jesus the Romans destroyed Jerusalem and sent the chosen people into a 2,000 year exile. The problem with much of Christian belief is that it excludes the redemption of the Hebrew people even though the Apostle Paul affirms that God's covenant with Israel will never be broken. In the words of Yogi Berra, "it ain't over till [God says] it's over." We are still living in the third part of the story. The forth part of the story is yet to come.

The Return

Following World War II a boat carrying Jewish immigrants landed in Palestine and by May of 1948 the United Nations allowed the creation of the State of Israel. Having survived indignation and attempted genocide by both Christians and non-Christians, the remnant of God's chosen people returned to the city and temple God never wanted built in the first place. If there is one thing that should be evident by now is that God has learned to live with human stubbornness and desire. Christians believe that Jesus will return bringing with him a millennium of peace and love. It should also be evident by now that humans are incapable of bringing this about on their own.

The Gospels

Two types of gospels exist. They are the synoptic gospels and the gospel of John. Synoptic means "seen as the same" in terms of literary genre. Mark, Matthew and Luke are seen as witness gospels. (Syn - together and Optic - view) There primary purpose is to present the stories of those who witnessed the life of Jesus. The Gospel of John is an inspirational gospel. Written at a much later date it is not a witness gospel as such, but a creation of what the writer wants the reader to believe about Jesus. John's purpose was to prove the divinity of Jesus.

Trying to explain the order of the writing of the gospels and source of information has plagued theologians forever. The most widely accepted theory is that Mark is the original surviving gospel. The possible sources for Mark's gospel were the Apostle Peter and Quelle. Scholars believe that Q (from the German Quelle meaning source) was in existence before Mark and was copied in part by the writer of Mark. Both Matthew and Luke copied from Q and Mark. Personally, Mark reads as a stand alone gospel with its own unique writing style. The Greek language is not as demanding as the English language allowing a variety of ways to express statements in a sentence (syntax). Scholars believe that when sentence syntax is identical in scripture, copying has taken place. One of the best ways to study the similarities in the synoptic gospels is by reading *Gospel Parallels* by Burton H. Throckmorton Jr. I will use Burton's work in many of the following parallels. There have been many hypothesis put forward as to the date of writing, authorship and sources. Throckmorton's work will help you make your own decisions. Most widely accepted is the hypothesis that the order of witness is Mark, Matthew then Luke.

# Mark

Discussion will open with the Gospel of Mark. Mark has always been my favourite gospel. Precise and succinct, Mark is a straightforward witness account. Mark's attitude is simple; "here is the story, believe it and you will live; believe it not and you will die, the decision is up to you." His writing style has been criticized from a grammatical perspective but I will demonstrate one particular literary technique not often observed. It is called a chiasm. Mark's abridged gospel opens with an adult Jesus whose coming is heralded by a messenger, John the Baptist. John is identified as the figurative representation of the prophet Elijah who was to herald the arrival of the Messiah. Throughout the synoptic gospels listen to the language used to identify Jesus and for the language Jesus used about himself and his father. Also understand that there were many stories circulating with regards to Jesus' reappearance. Mark believed as the disciples and the Apostle Paul, that Jesus would return before those who were witnesses died. Therefore, he did not feel the need for a birth story, or an ending. Mark's gospel actually ends at verse 16:8. The two endings in modern translations were later additions appended to the gospel.

Mark's story begins with the Baptist's call to repentance. This is a call to adults. In the Hebrew culture children could not make that decision and baptism in the early church was an adult decision. Jesus confirms this when he said, "I have not come to call the righteous, but sinners to repentance" (Matthew 9:13). I will discuss infant baptism later in this work. Jesus' ministry starts with baptism to signify a believer's first visible step and public act of repentance. As we believe Jesus did not have any reason to repent, it signifies for us a beginning, not an ending. Baptism is the willing acceptance of God as king in our lives and the turning (repentance) from all ungodly thoughts and actions. Baptism is not something that can be done for you. Baptism is a public event and is never to be done in private.

Jesus' baptism also makes a relational statement; "as he was coming up out of the water, he saw heaven torn apart and the Spirit descending like a dove on him. A voice came from heaven, 'you are my Son the Beloved; with you I am well pleased.'" Three things need to be noted. First, the voice of God is heard. Second, the Father is speaking to the Son. Third, God calls Jesus the Beloved. The name David in Hebrew means Beloved, the king chosen and ordained by God. In a sense God is saying, [if you want a human king, then that king will be my son.] History has proven that human governments excel at self preservation, war and taxes. God's idea of a king is one who will shepherd the people, not fleece the people. You will also notice that everything in the beginning of Mark happens fast. The over-use of the adverb "immediately" drives the story forward, giving the actions a sense of urgency. The use of immediately is a good literary device.

Next, "the Spirit immediately drove Jesus out into the wilderness" (Mark 1:12) to be tempted by Satan (one who opposes God). That's it, no temptation story. All we are told is that Jesus was tempted. Following the wilderness experience Jesus began his selection of disciples. First Simon (rock), then his brother Andrew (manly), followed by the sons of Zebedee (my gift), James (supplanter) and John (Yehovah is a gracious giver) fishermen all. Jesus promised to make them fishers of men. As you can see, the pace of the story matches the urgency of Jesus' ministry. By verse 21 four disciples have been called and Jesus now enters the synagogue in Capernaum to teach.

This brings about an interesting perspective on Jesus' earlier life. People do not arbitrarily walk into a church or synagogue, ascend into the pulpit and start to preach. Jesus was recognized as a religious figure; a teacher, a rabbi, or one of the Essenes. The Essenes were a peripheral order of Zodakite priests. It is in the synagogue that Jesus performed his first miracle but at this point they were all amazed even though it was the Sabbath (Saturday). The Biblical Sabbath is Saturday, the seventh day. Notice that no one got their nose out of joint with regard to the healing. Leaving the synagogue, Jesus went to the home of Simon and Andrew where he healed Simon's mother-in-law. Even though people were gathering around the home, Jesus waited until after sundown before healing anymore of the sick. After sundown the Sabbath was over and Sunday begins.

It has always intrigued me that the NRSV translates Mark 2:1as Jesus was at home in Capernaum. It dispels the notion that Jesus was like a vagabond without possession. Most people are familiar with the story of the paralytic man lowered through a hole cut in the roof of the home. Neither Jesus, nor anyone else is upset over people digging through his roof. The story also brings to our attention the first rumblings of the scribes and the age old question "who can forgive sin but God alone" (Mark 2:2)? When Jesus told the paralytic that his sins were forgiven the scribes immediately called it blasphemy.

It will be prudent to define certain terms used throughout the New Testament. Using Bible Works 7, I will define the following terms:

| | |
|---|---|
| Scribe | Hebrew caphar (saw-far) |
| | to number; take account of; public servant; secretary; interpreter; |
| | in the Bible, a man educated in the Mosaic law and in the sacred writings; |
| Scribe | Greek grammateus (gram-mat-yooce) |

|              | a clerk, scribe; a public servant, secretary, recorder, same duties as above. |
|--------------|-------------------------------------------------------------------------------|
| Sanhedrin    | The Sanhedrin was the supreme council, or court, in ancient Israel. It was comprised of 70 men, plus the high priest, who served as its president. The members came from the priests, scribes and elders, but there is no record on how they were chosen. |
| Sadducees    | Greek Saddoukaios (sad-doo-kah'-yos) a new religious party (350 BC - 70 AD) among the Jews, who denied that the oral law was a revelation of God to the Israelites, and who deemed the written law alone to be obligatory on the nation as the divine authority. They denied the following doctrines: the resurrection of the body; immortality of the soul; the existence of spirits and angels and divine predestination. They did however affirm free will. |
| Pharisees    | Greek Pharisaios (far-is-ah'-yos) They were a Jewish sect that started after the Jewish exile. In addition to Old Testament books the Pharisees recognized in oral tradition a standard of belief and life. They sought for distinction and praise by outward observance of external rites. They held strenuously to a belief in the existence of good and evil angels, and to the expectation of a Messiah. Pharisees and Sadducees are not to be found in the Old Testament. |
| Teacher      | Greek didaskalos (did-as'-kal-os) In the New Testament, one who teaches concerning the things of God, and the duties of man; |

| | to have discernment, insight, understanding, intelligence, and be discreet. |
|---|---|
| Rabbi | Hebrew (hrab-bee) |
| | Rabbi, a title used by the Jews to address their teachers, and also honour them when not addressing them. |
| Priest | Hebrew cohen (ko-hane') |
| | priest, principal officer; |
| | priest-kings such as Melchizedek and the Messiah; |

The titles by which the people referred to Jesus were more than honorific, they were literal titles.

Disciples

Mark is quite matter-of-fact about Jesus' actions. After healing the paralytic, Jesus observes Levi (joined) sitting in his tax booth and calls him to follow. Levi's name was somehow changed to Matthew (gift of Yehovah). It is worth noting that many of the Hebrew names in scripture have been changed to western names. There is a subtle dynamic set in place by changing the names of all the "good guys" in scripture to western names and leaving the "bad guys" with their Hebrew names. The funniest of all is the calling of Simon by the name of Simon called Peter and of Thomas called Didymus. Simon is Hebrew for rock. Peter/Petros is Greek for rock. I doubt very much that the man was called Rock Rock or even Petros Petros. Peter is an invention of the early Catholic Church (St. Jerome).

If you have a Bible that has been properly translated such as the NRSV, look at Mark 3:16. It reads, "so he appointed the twelve: Simon (to whom he gave the name Peter); James (to whom he gave the name Boanerges, that is, son of thunder) and Andrew and Philip and Bartholomew, and Matthew, and Thomas, and James, son of Alpheus and Thaddaeus and Simon the Canaanite, and Judas Iscariot, who betrayed him".

First of all, the parts of the above passage in brackets are not in the older manuscripts. The brackets indicate this information was added into scripture by scribes in or around the thirteenth century. Jesus did not give James the name of Boanerges (son of thunder) as Boanerges is a proper Greek name. He was Greek and not Hebrew.

The most humorous of all is the name Thomas "which is called Didymus." Thomas means twin. Didymus is Greek for twin. Scripture is saying that they called Thomas twin twin. The following is Mark's list of disciples:

Simon - Andrew - James son of Zebedee and John, all of whom were fishermen.

Levi a tax collector and supposedly renamed Matthew

Philip - Bartholomew - Thomas - James the son of Alphaeus - Thaddaeus - Simon the Canaanite and finally Judas Iscariot, who betrayed him. When Jesus finished appointing the twelve, "he went home" (Mark 3:19). Notice there are no name changes in Mark.

In the chapter which follows, Jesus is often found teaching by the sea. This was not simply to call the people in fishing villages to renew their faith in God but so that large numbers of people could hear. Have you ever been out on a lake unavoidably listening to the crystal clear conversation from a distant cottage? Water transmits sound. That is why Jesus was often in a boat (Mark 4:1). Jesus also spoke in parables (an understandable relational analogy). In verse 4:13 Jesus said, "do you not understand this parable?" Place yourself in the disciple's sandals. They were simple ordinary people, with a limited education, fishermen from small villages. Understand that humans have four levels of brain development. Without an educational system in place, people in tribal communities were lucky to develop past a second level of brain development.

An infant can watch a toy train go inside a tunnel then act surprised when the train appears at the other end. This reaction will happen over and over again as the child does not realize it is the same train. As a child continues to develop, they come to understand the physical. That is, if one puts their hand into a fire it burns. Third level development would be comparable to youth under twelve years of age understanding the basics of mathematics. Fourth level development enables an individual to understand abstract concepts and solve problems from conclusions drawn from observations. This thinking only develops in children from 12 to 15 years of age who have received some degree of education. Up until the twentieth century this level of education was only accorded the wealthy. The educated of the past could tell a person one story today and a contradictory story tomorrow using nonsense rational and the uneducated individual could not figure out what was wrong with the story. They could feel they were being cheated but could not verbalize their feeling with reasoning.

People in the time of Jesus were not stupid, they were uneducated. This is why Jesus tried to use relational stories which began "it is like leaven" or "it is like a mustard seed." The people understood how leaven made bread dough rise. Jesus was truly a teacher who tried to develop his disciple's ability to reason. Never listen to clergy who portray "Jesus as smart and disciples as stupid." Realize that the disciples were yearning for a higher level of understanding and Jesus took the time to teach them.

Chapter 5 is a prelude to the faith and confidence development of the disciples. It is also a prelude to faith healing as well as an example of Jewish leaders who put their trust in the Messiah. A synagogue leader came to Jesus because his daughter was dying. On the way to his home, Jesus took the time to heal a woman who had suffered from hemorrhages for twelve years. While this was happening, people came to tell the synagogue leader his daughter had died but Jesus pressed on to bring back to life the twelve-year-old girl.

Chapter 6 is fascinating. When Jesus returned to his hometown he was met with skepticism by everyone. His own words capture the disbelief, "prophets are not without honour, except in their hometown, and among their own kin, and in their own house... and he was amazed at their unbelief" (Mark 6: 4-6). What happened in his hometown bears directly on what happens next with his disciples. Verse 5 is explicit in that Jesus "**could not** do any deed of power there." Mark does not say Jesus "would not do" any deed of power, but "could not do" any deed of power. This demonstrates a direct relationship to faith and the power of faith.

Next is an event in Mark's story that is often overlooked by clergy. Preachers love to tell how Jesus sent out the disciples two by two giving them authority over unclean spirits. Verse 6:12 tells how they "went out and proclaimed that all should repent." Remember, Mark's gospel begins with a call to repentance. Now pay attention; in Jesus' absence the disciples cast out demons; anoint the sick with oil and cure them. Hallelujah! Praise the Lord! But all of a sudden, the story switches to the beheading of John the Baptist by Herod. The story is lengthy spanning fifteen verses from 6:14-29. The return of the disciples resumes at verse 30. Scholars feel Mark needed a place to put the beheading story so he used it as a break to indicate the many days/weeks the disciples were "among the villages teaching" (6:6).

As you begin to read at verse 30 realize that Mark's brevity does an enormous injustice to what happens next. It helps promote the idea of "good Jesus" and "inept disciples". Imagine that you were one of the disciples whom Jesus sent out. Your words call people to repentance. You cast out evil demons, anoint the sick and cure them with your prayers. On the disciples return, scripture makes it sound as if they were matter-of-fact with regards to their experiences. I would be bouncing off the wall. It would take six men to hold me down, contain me as I jumped for joy relating everything that happened while proclaiming God's word in Jesus' name. It is one of the reasons Jesus wanted to get away to a secluded area that his heart might be warmed by the accomplishments of his disciples. But alas, it was not to be. People were now coming from everywhere to meet the Messiah, Jesus of Nazareth. They were coming because the people wanted to meet the "Master," and find an answer for the question that had been burning in the hearts of the Hebrew people, namely, "could this be the Son of God?" This is the context in which the feeding of the five thousand takes place. As stories unfold in scripture, it is wise to look to previous events to understand context.

Please look at the story once again with new eyes, with new understanding. God's people were like sheep without a shepherd. The hour was getting late and understandably, the tired disciples just wanted them to go home. The disciples asked Jesus to send the people away so they too could get something to eat. The size of the crowd was overwhelming. Jesus replied to their request with "you give them something to eat." In light of the past success of the disciples, Jesus appears to be looking at this as a teaching moment. Unfortunately, this is where the story gets misinterpreted by clergy. The disciples bring five loaves of bread and two fish to Jesus. Jesus tells them to arrange the crowd in groups of fifty and hundreds. Try to imagine the area required to seat 50 groups of 100 or 100 groups of 50. Looking out over the people, Jesus raised the food to heaven and blessed the bread and fish, then gave it to his disciples.

Now the big question, "did the bread and fish continue to multiply because of the blessing of Jesus?" I believe it was the continued faith of the disciples that multiplied the blessed food? I believe it was a continuation of the disciples' growth and development. I believe they had just as much a part in the feeding as Jesus. They were not simply delivery boys running back and forth. Clergy who blindly accept the usual interpretation of the story, "good Jesus, inept disciples," justify the lame excuse that disciples can do nothing. I believe it is our faith in Jesus which allows us to be miracle workers in our own way and in our own time. Church pessimists have often squashed the ability of God's people to work miracles because of their own lack of faith.

The story also says that the disciples, like good little boys, went around and cleaned up the left over's and scraps. Nonsense! Their baskets were full from the distribution. The disciples were not environmentally conscious, nor would they be able to keep that much bread and fish from going bad. This story sounds good to the simple minded, but what was the point of collecting that much food? How would they keep it from going bad? This is one of the great miracle stories in the Bible. It is not just a story of what Jesus can do. It is a story of what you and I can do as disciples when we trust in God's only begotten son. The meaning of begotten is to have been brought forth, to have been fathered. The synoptic gospels are about how the Son of God, the Lamb of God, was able, of his own accord, to remain sinless. Having remained sinless, Jesus now sits on the right hand of God to be our heavenly advocate.

Before we continue, I would like you to look at a chiasm I discovered during my doctoral studies. It is from Mark and it is self-explanatory.

# Mark 6: 30-44 - Chiasm

30    Only the Apostles are gathered around Jesus.

31         Deserted place with nothing to eat.

32              Disciples come to be feed.

33                   Empty people have come to Jesus for a blessing.

34                        5000 scattered sheep without a shepherd.

35                             An empty deserted place.

36                                  Crowd has no food.

37                                  **You give them something to eat.**

38                                  Disciples have food.

39                             A crowded lush green place.

40                        Shepherds gather sheep in flocks of 50 & 100.

41                   Blessed food is set before an empty people.

42              All who came were feed.

43         Crowded place with plenty to eat.

44    Thousands are gathered around Jesus.

As you can see, the command in verse 37 is the turning point. This chiasm is not an accident or coincidence, it is designed to demonstrate what can happen when the followers of Jesus listen to Jesus and obey his commands. The story also dispels the notion that the disciples remained stupid and incompetent until the Holy Spirit said "shazzam, you are henceforth scholarly and capable." Never forget there is difference between being stupid and intellectually underdeveloped. Driving a wedge between stupid disciples and smart Jesus injects a great injustice to the scripture story.

In the chapters to come, Mark continues to witness the miracles and teachings of Jesus. Peter gets a bad rap when he responds to Jesus' foretelling of his death whereas the statement expresses love and devotion, which, in the end, Peter did demonstrate. Peter could not have possibly realized that Jesus was to be the sacrificial Lamb of God. To him, Jesus was the Messiah, the knight in shinning armour. Even after being rebuked, Peter was still present at the transfiguration.

Christians have their share or religious zealots. For the most part they use the Gospel of John to promote a Johannian brand of Christianity. I say that because I hear three different Christian voices speaking in scripture. The first is the synoptic gospel Christianity of Matthew, Mark and Luke. Then I hear Pauline Christianity. Lastly, I hear Johannian (Gospel of John) Christianity. John's gospel is what I call inspirational where the writer has a little information, then goes to a deserted place, smokes some really good stuff, and comes back with a divine revelation. There have been many who have perpetrated this hoodwink on humanity. The problem with believing these people is that Emmanuel means "God with us." Notice the plurality of "us," and not "God with an individual.

Events

Listen to the following dialogue; "John said to Jesus, teacher, we saw someone casting out demons in your name and we tried to stop him because he was not following us. But Jesus said "do not stop him; for no one who does a deed of power in my name will be able to soon afterward speak evil of me." Whoever is not against us is for us. For truly I tell you, whoever gives you a cup of water to drink because you bear the name of Christ will by not means lose the reward" Mark 9: 38-41). Pay attention to what Jesus is saying. A positive reward is gained by acts of kindness (love thy neighbour). Likewise there is a negative reward for evil (Proverbs 28:10). Verse 42 has Jesus saying, "if any of you put a stumbling block (to entice into sin) before one of these little ones who believe in me, it would be better for you if a great mill stone were hung around your neck and you were thrown into the sea." Remember, Jesus came to redeem sinners, not abolish "sin unto death" (1John 5:16). Trying to get a death row prisoner to spell the name of Jesus the day before execution is not Biblical (Ecclesiastes 12:1).

The next event has always seemed out of character to me. Scripture informs us that Jesus was hungry so he went to get some figs from a tree alongside the road. As it was not the season for figs, there were none on the tree so Jesus zapped the tree and it died. Surely, this has raised questions in your mind. Why would Jesus destroy a tree? It was not because it did not bear fruit but rather, the tree was destroyed to dispel the common belief in reincarnation. Many cultures believe in reincarnation as do people today. The belief in Palestine was that the soul of the dead person past through the ground to dwell in certain trees, such as a fig tree. It remained there waiting for the right moment when a pregnant woman past by so the soul could leave the tree and enter a developing fetus. Jesus' response was a definite "No" to reincarnation.

When Jesus observed the buyers and sellers in the temple court, he became indignant. Isaiah 57 speaks of God's adoption of anyone, from any nation who accepts God's covenant, as being welcome in the house of prayer. Notice, Isaiah did not say temple but "my house shall be called a house of prayer for all the nations". Jesus, knowing how to win friends and influence enemies said to the chief priest, "you have made it a den of robbers" (Mark 11:17). Again, to make it sound as if all the priests and officials were opposed to Jesus, translators pluralized (ar-khee-er-os) to read chief priests. If you read scripture in Greek or Hebrew, you will see the word is singular "Chief Priest."

Whereas, the word elders is plural as translated from the Greek Presbyters *(Pres boo ter os)*.

In Chapter 12, Mark captures the real essence of the conversation between a scribe and Jesus. The scribe had been listening to Jesus correct the mis-belief of the Sadducees with regards to life after death. The Sadducees believed humans died and that was it, no eternal life. Jesus responded by quoting God who was speaking to Moses saying, "I am the God of Abraham, the God of Isaac, and the God of Jacob." Jesus went on to say God, "is God not of the dead, but of the living; you are wrong" (Mark 12: 27). Clergy who treat the following story as a trick are wrong. Hebrew Midrash is a method of clarifying Biblical texts by means of a rational back and forth discussion. When the scribe asked Jesus "which commandment is the first of all," Jesus replied with the Schema, "Hear, O Israel: The Lord our God is one Lord: And thou shalt love the Lord thy God with all thine heart, and with all thy soul, and with all thy might" (Deuteronomy 6:4-6). Unfortunately, in the middle ages some copyist decided to give the Schema a little more impact and added "with all your mind" (Mark 12:30). It is highly doubtful that Jesus would have made that mistake, or that Jesus made an arbitrary change (Matthew 5:17). The Schema consists of only three – heart, soul, and might.

When Jesus answered the scribe, the scribe said, "you are right." The way of Rabbinical Midrash is, one does not simply say "you are right," but that you repeat what has been said. In this way there can be no equivocation, the audience hears the same words twice and can acknowledge the parties to be in agreement. If you do not know the Hebrew Jesus and the Hebrew culture, you cannot possibly preach the gospel of Christ. One does not need an education to preach the Jesus of the New Testament. Simply memorize a few key verses, preach salvation and forgiveness for terrorists and perverts and whenever in a discussion, go cherry picking. Cherry picking is my term for clergy who randomly pick the verses they need out of scripture to prove their point. As in Matthew 25, the gospel of Mark does not say it is as simple as knowing how to spell the name Jesus. Salvation is attained by obedience to God's first command. Jesus was saying that [we demonstrate our love for God by loving our neighbour.] Loving is an active verb, not passive. A backside molded to the shape of a pew is not the way to attain salvation.

In Chapter 13 Jesus prophesies the destruction of the temple which did take place forty years after his death and the destruction ended Judah's ability to worship in the Jerusalem temple as they were dispersed over the known world. Many families eventually ended up in what is now northern Europe. Following the Chapter 13 prophesy Jesus told his disciples, "this generation will not pass away until all these things have taken place" (Mark13: 30). Humans, being naturally inquisitive, have sought for centuries to figure out what Jesus meant. It has been an exercise in futility. Many books have been written and television charlatans still attempt to do what is not possible. All those who have made their life's work preaching end times prophesy have wasted their time and defrauded the fools who listen to them. Pay attention to the words of Jesus, "but about that day or hour no one knows, neither the angels in heaven, nor the Son, but only the Father. Beware, keep alert; for you do not know when the time will come... I say to all, keep awake" (Mark 13: 32-37). It does not get any clearer. The Apostle Paul knew Jesus said, "this generation will not pass away until all these things have taken place." So it was he began his ministry by preaching Jesus' imminent return. It must have been humiliating for "know it all Paul" to admit in his later letters that he did not know when Christ would return.

Jesus did come to his disciples after his crucifixion, when he will return a second time, only God knows.

Luke records, in the Acts of the Apostles, the appearances of Jesus and the manner of his ascension. Like many people over the centuries, Paul wanted to believe Jesus would return in his lifetime. It is not possible to determine the return of the Son of God. All who try are quacks, fakes and frauds. Please do not support those ministries with your money. Mainline churches that have foreign and domestic outreach programs will put your donations to work to the glory of God and not the financial gain of quacks and charitable organization that pay their CEO's millions of dollars to convince you to send them your money.

As Jesus and his disciples approached Jerusalem, Mark's sense of urgency waned. He stopped using "immediately" at verse 10:52. The word only appears once after that in Chapter 14:43 in relation to Judas' betrayal because the adverb immediately gives us a sense of how fast they wanted to put Jesus to death. Scripture makes it clear that Jesus was betrayed by Judas. However, the whole garden scene and nightly court scene at the time of the Passover make me suspect of the "Jews" collectively wanting Jesus dead. (Jew is a later term taken from the Hebrew word Yehudim used in the Book of Esther).

Luke 23:51 reveals that Joseph of Arimathaea was one of the leaders not invited to the clandestine meeting held to condemn Jesus. This type of meeting is contrary to Jewish Rabbinical Law. Also, consider the feeble reason for Judas' turn-coat action of betrayal. The Bible suggests that Judas moral integrity was as low as that of some of our Canadian double dipping senators. I would submit that Judas' betrayal of Jesus did not have a sinister purpose. His purpose was to force Jesus to reveal himself as the long awaited Messiah. The people had been praying for someone to lead the rebellion to drive out the Romans. Forensic investigation considers all the evidence and motives when investigating an event. Selling Jesus for 30 pieces of silver is just too weak. Have you ever noticed that all four gospels tell us that Judas (he shall be praised) betrayed Jesus, but none give any hint as to the reason for such an unprecedented betrayal, save a few piece of silver?

Prior to the betrayal we gain an understanding of the importance of Jesus' desire to celebrate the Passover with his disciples. This Passover is celebrated on the evening of the fifteenth day of Nisan (April). The day of Pentecost comes 50 days later and celebrates God's giving of the Torah to the chosen people and in gratitude for a bountiful harvest. Christians typically celebrate their Passover on Maundy Thursday and the death of Jesus on the cross on "Good Friday." This practice however creates a problem for clergy to explain how Jesus spent three nights in the grave. The problem comes with how we define "day and night." In the Bible, night comes before the day. "And the evening and the morning were the first day" (Genesis 1:5). The change of day occurs at sundown. Therefore, Wednesday night precedes Wednesday. We are out of sync folks by a half day.

In reality, the room for the Passover was prepared on Wednesday morning and afternoon. That evening, Thursday night, they held the Passover and later that night Jesus endured the clandestine trial. On Thursday morning Jesus was convicted and later crucified. He was taken from the cross and put into the tomb before Thursday afternoon turned to Friday night. This had to happen so that the women might not be ritually unclean for the day of preparation and the Sabbath. Jesus spent Friday night, Saturday night and Sunday night in the tomb and then was raised Sunday morning. Again, Christianity has shown a complete disregard for the Hebrew Messiah, the man we call the Son of God.

Mark's account of the Passover is brief. Jesus takes the bread, blesses it and gives it to his disciples saying that it represents his body. There is no break in Mark and Matthew to indicate that the wine came at the end of the meal as in Luke. The dramatic, overwhelming change that Jesus makes to this ancient tradition is that now, the blood of the Messiah, the life saving blood of the covenant is symbolized in the wine. (Not grape juice – wine, you holier than thou Baptists.) Wow! Amazing! This is the single most important piece of information in the gospels, the vicarious sacrifice of the Messiah. Even Jesus, in the end, did not really want to go through with it. His obedience was due to the power of prayer and love.

Prior to his death, Jesus spent time in the garden. This was a fitting place as humanity first sinned in the Garden of Eden and now, Judas' betrayal is perpetrated in the Garden of Gethsemane. As I have said, Mark's gospel is so short that the reader can miss the compelling poignant moment of prayer when the Son cries out to a Father. But alas, God does not answer. Jesus must do this without a protective shroud or a divine immunity to pain. God's absence is very noticeable in the garden as Jesus must of necessity do this without aid, without any morphine so to speak. The resurrection would have no meaning if Jesus were covered or protected with a heavenly shroud. This is the final test of ultimate trust. Jesus knew God could bring about salvation whatever way God wanted. In his prayer Jesus said, "Father, for you all things are possible; remove this cup from me; yet, not what I want, but what you want" Mark 14:36). The pain Jesus was about to endure would be real. Although Mark is written in third person omnipotent, it reads as if it is first person omnipotent. This story is coming from the mouth of a witness. What we need to remember is that the death of Jesus was ordained to come to pass in Jerusalem.

You know the rest of the story. Jesus endured a mock trial and was crucified. Did the "Jews" kill Jesus or just the priests in the inner circle? Did the Romans really kill Jesus or were they pawns in a political power struggle? One could argue that the story had to be told in such as way as to not alarm the Romans. The covert actions of the priest can be seen as a way to camouflage the truth that the Romans were quick to eliminate any threat of rebellion. Some people deny that Jesus died on the cross. They say he was taken down and revived. Then he and Mary Magdalene ran away with their child who became the father of all French monarchy. This helps explain the arrogance of the French. The fact is, if Jesus did not die, we have no faith. Jesus did die and was raised by the Father. Father and son are two separate entities in scripture.

Mark records that Jesus, before he died at three in the afternoon cried out, "Eloi, Eloi, lema sabachthani" which has been historically translated as "My God, my God, why have you forsaken me?" The trouble is, Jesus was Hebrew and would have cried out in Hebrew. The word El is Hebrew for God, not Eli. Mark's translation only makes sense if Jesus cried out in Aramaic. Eloi means "my God" in Aramaic. Unfortunately, I have never bought the argument that Jesus spoke Aramaic to Jews, especially in the synagogue and certainly not on the cross crying to God. In Hebrew, the word Eli is a proper noun which means ascension. Is it possible the cry sounded like this, [ascension, ascension, why have you forsaken me?] Nonetheless, it is food for thought as Matthew does not use the Aramaic Eloi, Eloi, but rather the Hebrew Eli, Eli, which means ascension. Also, in the next verse Mark calls Elijah "Elias." There seems to be much confusion in the passages recording the final moments of Jesus. I do not doubt the death and resurrection of Jesus but I wonder which of the stories is correct? Could it be that Jesus was really crying out for ascension?

Remember, the author of Matthew is thought to have been a Rabbi. Crying for ascension fits perfectly with the abandonment Jesus had to undergo in the garden and trial. Theologically, it fits perfectly with your doubt of the resurrection. Problem is, you must die to find God's promise.

Before I close the Gospel of Mark I will note the women recorded at the cross and at the tomb. This record differs in each gospel.

At the cross - Mark 15: 40-41

> There were also women looking on from a distance; among them were Mary Magdalene, and Mary, the mother of James the younger and Jose, and Salome. They used to follow him and provide for him when he was in Galilee and there were many other women who had come up with him to Jerusalem.

At the tomb - Mark 16:1

> When the Sabbath was over, Mary Magdalene, and Mary the mother of James, and Salome brought spices so they might anoint him.

Notice how the presence of numerous women comes to light at the cross but are not mentioned as being present at the Passover. Never think the Passover was as the circa 1498 painting by Da Vinci. There were more people at the last supper than Jesus and his twelve disciples. Matthew, Mark and Luke all make mention of women followers.

When the women arrive at the tomb, they were met by a young man in a white robe who told them Jesus had been raised. They are instructed to tell Peter and the disciples that Jesus will meet them in Galilee but they were so frightened they said nothing to anyone. Mark's story ends as it has begun, no fanfare, just facts. His gospel is a witness of facts. If you have ever seen the C D of *Mark's Gospel* as told by Max McLean you can appreciate how the witness' story might have been told to those seeking the Messiah. Mark's witness ends abruptly. He is essentially saying, "you have heard the story and now you have to make a choice. Believe it and live. Believe it not and die." Amen!

## Matthew

The Gospel of Matthew begins with a lineage that stretches back to Abraham. Next, the writer of Matthew described the birth events according to the law as well as Isaiah's (7:14) prophesy. The writer is also careful to use definite terms; Joseph is husband and Mary is his wife. This is important to remember as Luke states that the couple was only engaged when Jesus was born. The hometown of Joseph and Mary is Nazareth in Galilee.

The above is part of the age-old Christmas story. Most people have seen or been a part of the obligatory Christmas Pageant celebrated by Sunday Schools throughout the Christian Church. It is a wonderful story, and part of what makes it wonderful is the differing perspective of Matthew versus Luke. Matthew tells the story as matter of fact but clergy feel it is necessary to intentionally intertwine Matthew's story with Luke's. The fact is, they are significantly different. Bear in mind that I am not casting doubt on the virgin birth of the Messiah, simply noting that Matthew's story is a prime example of male bias. Matthew does not give Mary a voice. He does all the talking for her. Luke gives Elizabeth and Mary the voice to tell their story in words full of wonderment and awe.

Matthew tells us the engagement and marriage took place in the couple's hometown. Many virgins have been married who were just a little bit pregnant. The unabashed biased way in which Matthew tells the story is typically male. Mary, a woman, has no voice. After all, she is only the mother of the Messiah. Notice that it is Joseph to whom the angel reveals Mary's delicate situation. Next, the story jumps to Bethlehem, to Herod and to the Magi. We only know through Luke the how and why of the couples presence in Bethlehem and it makes sense. It is like a puzzle. Just put the pieces together. Joseph and Mary would both have had a difficult time in explaining a fully developed baby from a short term pregnancy. So, off they go to a house in Bethlehem where the folks do not know how long they have been married. We are not told of the census as the writer does not appear to know of the couple's personal struggles. He is only concerned with the fulfillment of the Messianic prophesy.

Historically and biblically we know that Herod was a vicious monster. Having heard of strangers from the East, Herod mustered his political cunning to support the Magi in their quest to find the child who is to be born King of the Jews. The Magi continue to follow the star and they find Jesus. Our Sunday school theology tells us that there were three Magi, but the reality is, we do not know how many, but only that Magi from the East brought three gifts to ascertain the child's destiny. Hence, the three gifts were representative of the destiny of the child. Eastern custom in determining the destiny of a child born under a heavenly sign was to bring gifts of gold, frankincense and myrrh. It was believed that the first gift touched determined the child's future calling. If the child touched the gold for instance, the child was to be a king, the frankincense a priest and the myrrh a prophet. Surprisingly, there is no record of how many of the gifts the infant Jesus touched or if he only touched one.

Dreams and visions are part of the gospel story and once again an angel appears to the Magi who then vanish from the story; Joseph is warned in another vision and escapes with Mary and Jesus to Egypt. Herod is left in the darkness of vanity and goes berserk when he learns that he has been disrespected. Ordering the slaughter of all infants two years old or younger, Jeremiah's prophesy of loud lamentations in Ramah is fulfilled. Notice in the story the two-year time frame. After Herod died the angel told Joseph that it was safe to return to Nazareth. Hosea's prophesy requiring the Messiah to be called out of Egypt is fulfilled in Matthew's story. Notice the similarity of Matthew's story, one of the most precious stories in Christianity, to the story of Dinah's defilement. Up until the point of birth, Mary is the most important character in the story. She is young, vulnerable, and obedient under the most adverse of circumstances and yet her voice is silent. Is it possible that the male bias has dominated one of the most beautiful "women's stories" in scripture? Examine Luke's magnificent record of Mary's experience and her own words in juxtaposition to Matthew's harsh story of obligatory obedience. Luke not only gives Mary a choice, he gives her a voice.

Matthew's Chapter 3 parallels Mark's Chapter 1. This is where Burton's works demonstrates the existence of Q material. Matthew 3:11 and Luke's 3:16 are believed to have been copied from Q. When the same story appears in all three gospels we were taught in seminary that the story has a high level of importance. Jesus' baptism by John is important. If you look at the passages in Gospel Parallels you will see how closely they were copied. You will notice that Matthew improves Mark's grammar and how Luke improves Matthew's grammar. It is noticeable that in Matthew, as in Mark, God's proclamation is heard only by Jesus, whereas in Luke, everyone hears, "you are my

Son, the Beloved, with whom I am well pleased." Also notice that the proclamation is identical in all three gospels.

Following the proclamation, Jesus is led into the wilderness to be tempted by the devil *dee ab ol os* (slanderer, false accuser). This is our first introduction to the devil. Notice again, the Biblical devil is not someone who arbitrarily has the power to inflict but only to tempt. Like Adam and Eve, each individual makes the choice to obey or disobey God. This is exactly how the tempter was reprimanded when Jesus said, "thou shalt worship the Lord your God" (4:10) and the tempter left him. Notice the words to the tempter "the Lord 'your' God." It is interesting that Matthew also tells us that Jesus "left Nazareth and made his home in Capernaum by the sea" (Matthew 4:12). Could it be that Jesus was not as poor and penniless as the church has taught? Ironically, the poverty preached for Christians was not meant for the pope and his disciples as high church officials have always lived as luxuriously as Solomon.

Following his sojourn in the wilderness, Jesus began the process of calling his disciples, Simon, Andrew, James and John. Having called four fishermen, Jesus went throughout Galilee teaching in the synagogues and healing people of a variety of diseases. Crowds from all parts of Palestine were following Jesus so he chose an adequate mountain setting to deliver his now famous beatitudes along with many other teachings. Matthew's rabbinical background prompts him to hear things the others do not. In Chapter 6 the writer begins with "beware of practicing your piety before others in order to be seen by them, for then you have no reward from your Father in heaven." This section is all about your personal relationship with God which brings us to the theological split with regards to what is termed "the Lord's prayer."

Please understand that there are some very opposing societal and theological differences between the Liberal Luke and the Rabbinic Matthew. The writer of Matthew knows that prayer is a personal experience between the individual and God, and only God. We are never to pray to the saints, the virgin or her rock band, Peter, Paul and Mary, not even to Jesus. Prayers are to God. Christian prayers are to God in the name of the redeemer Jesus. Listen now to what the writer of Matthew tells us concerning prayer. First he says, "use not vain repetitions, as the heathens do" (Matthew 6:7). Then we are given an outline, a guide, a template, from which to model prayer. I feel that by repeating the Lord's Prayer week after week Christians have turned something beautiful into vain, repetitious and meaningless words. Prayer should reflect our love for God and our desire to remain in a close relationship with our creator.

Matthew understands that love is the foundation of any relationship. So it is, he records one of the most difficult teachings of all, "love your enemy and pray for those who persecute you" (5:44). Next, Jesus tells us that, [when you do charitable deeds do not boast] "as the hypocrites do in the synagogues… do not let your left hand know what your right hand is doing" (6:2-4). Now comes the teaching most denominations and most clergy reject, that is, "whenever you pray, do not be like the hypocrites; for they love to stand and pray in the synagogues… that they may be seen by others… but whenever you pray, go into your room and shut the door and pray to your Father in secret." The church has chosen to listen to Liberal Luke who has turned the Lord's Prayer into a vain repetitious prayer. After all these years in the church I would not hesitate to be judgmental in that the Lord's prayer is the only time most Christians pray; with the exception of the "get me out of this jamb Lord," or "please let me win the lottery." Prayer in a church should be a time of personal introspection, of confession, of intercessory prayer, and most of all, after you have had your say, a time to listen as God touches your heart with an answer you may not want to hear. Those who deceive their flock into thinking that prayer is vain repetition need to go back to a seminary.

The gospel writer Luke recorded many wonderful things but Jesus did not teach vain repetition. Luke's phrase, "let us pray as our Lord Jesus has taught us," is just wrong. Bear in mind that what I have just said is a record of what Jesus has said and recorded by Rabbi Matthew. Recorded in Chapter 6 is a formula or outline for prayer, not a vain repetitious prayer. Jesus does not say, "pray this prayer," he said, "pray in this way" (6:9). It is a template for prayer. Read it, understand it, and do not just mindlessly repeat it every Sunday morning. If you could read the Greek manuscripts you would see that Luke's prayer is different than Matthew's prayer. Over time, the church made them read the same. Find an old Bible and read them.

The component parts of the Lord's Prayer acknowledges to whom you are praying. Further prayer is as the Spirit leads. The church has done the people a great disservice in teaching a vain repetitious prayer when prayer should be a means to free the soul and connect with the creator. You will also note that Luke's prayer is liberal in the sense that it suggests that everyone will be forgiven. Matthew however, does not put forth false hope as the prayer is followed with, "if you forgive men their trespasses, your heavenly Father will also forgive you. But if you forgive not men their trespasses, neither will your Father forgive your trespasses" (Matthew 6:14-15). It is easier for the faint of heart to preach Luke's gospel. You know who they are. When they shake your hand it feels like you are holding a dead fish.

Fasting was something done in ancient times. It is actually a very healthy practice intended to cleanse the system. Here again, religious leaders used their sour-faced suffering expressions of piety to elicit perceived admiration from the people. Jesus taught his disciples that doing pious acts in public for the sake of self gratification, bragging, acting like a drama queen, will produce a short term injection of grandeur into one's ego, at the expense of your everlasting heavenly reward. As you can see, Matthew's rabbinical recording of a code of conduct helps us to understand who he was as an individual. Like the other writers, the healing powers and the miracles of Jesus needed recording. What should become obvious is that Jesus did not discriminate between rich or poor, clergy or customer.

## Devil

The New Testament introduces the reader to a new word for "evil one." The word is devil. Three Greek words are all translated devil. They are:

| | | |
|---|---|---|
| daimonion | (dahee-mon'-ee-on) | a spirit inferior to God but superior to men; |
| diabolos | (dee-ab'-ol-os) | a false accuser, |
| daimonizomai | (dahee-mon-id'-zom-ahee) | to be under the power of a demon. |

It is important to note that the ancients did not know how to explain mental illness, convulsions or seizures. People could see that something was wrong inside an individual so they were taught to believe these individuals were possessed by a daimonizomai. The church used evil possession in order to promote fear. The Inquisition, in part, was nothing more than a power play to stop people from questioning the church's bastardization of scripture, their mis-use of power and its lust for money. It was financially lucrative for the church as they ended up with the wealth of those wrongly accused. Accused people were tortured to confess heresies which they had never committed. Witch hunts were nothing more than an exercise to maintain authority by fear and an excuse for perverted little men to spread the legs of women in order to "probe them for the mark of the devil." I have no idea how those perverts knew what the mark of the devil felt like and where to look. When listening to a story try thinking like a forensic investigator. Simply weigh the words to the results of their actions in order to formulate a motive. As a modern day example, think about what was not going to happen in Vietnam, in terms of US military involvement, with J F K in the oval office. Now ask yourself, "what happened immediately after Kennedy was assassinated?" What happened may well point to the motive for his death and the real devil behind the assassination.

Speaking of the devil, which up until now in scripture, does not have an association with, or a clear understanding of, Hades. Hades is the place of the dead. In the Hebrew culture Hades (hell) comes from the ancient Greek understanding of the subterranean region on the other side of the Styx River. In the Old Testament, translators used the word hell in place of sheh-ole. Scheol simply means the grave, the pit, or the place of the dead. Hades is ruled by a mythological King called Hades. It is this place which Jesus refers to when he said, "the gates of hell shall not prevail against" the rock upon which I build my church (Matthew 16:18). Notice the word rock. Jesus did not use the word temple or church, but simply the solid foundation upon which the word of God would once again rest, an uncut rock. Remember, all edifices are detestable to God. All Old Testament sacrifices were upon uncut rock. It is also interesting to note that Tyre means "rock." Tyre was a Phoenician city on the Mediterranean coast whose inhabitants worshipped Baal. Solomon brought Hiram the builder from this city.

In the New Testament, hell is most often translated from the Greek word Gehenna (gheh en nah). Gehenna was an actual place south of Jerusalem in the Valley of Hinnon where they burnt dead animals. It was also a place to burn the bodies of dead soldiers when great numbers of dead were impossible to bury properly. You must realize that large numbers of rotting bodies would cause disease of epidemic proportions. When Jesus was speaking critically to the scribes and Pharisees he said, "you generation of vipers, how can you escape the damnation of hell" the word hell is translated from the Greek Gehenna (Matthew 23:33). This insult meant their bodies would be buried with the rotting flesh on top of the smoldering embers.

There is one more Greek word translated as hell which is Tar-tar-oo. In Greek mythology it is a place reserved for the most detestable offenders at the furthest regions of Hades. In the Hebrew, it is the place beneath the rotting flesh and smoldering coals of Gehenna. Please understand that it did not take much effort for educated clergy to embellish the old beliefs and drive fear into the hearts of their uneducated sheep. I am sure the Greek god Hades will have a substantial royal court of bishops, cardinals and popes to help him rule over the most heinous of unredeemable monsters. What will hell be like? Will there be an eternal hell? I do not know. All I know is that the redeemed in Christ will live in the presence of God. It will not depend on an individual's religion but on whether or not they obeyed God's two commands - love God and love thy neighbour.

The next disciple to be called was Matthew (Levi), the tax collector. In that society the tax collector was the lowest of low on the social scale. They were even lower than a prostitute. At least one got kissed for his money. Both Mark and Luke name this individual as Levi. When one considers the level of the writer's Biblical knowledge, it is highly unlikely that Levi is the Matthew who authored the book that bears this name. It would be doubtful that a man who could stoop so low as to collect taxes for a foreign government would also be the same man who possessed a great deal of Biblical knowledge. Remember, these are the things governments do; they collect taxes to make war, they have a higher standard of living than an average citizen and they are less likely to be held accountable for illegal actions. Also, a government's first function is to protect those in government.

It is not until Chapter 10 that the reader learns the names of the twelve disciples. It is also at this point that Jesus sends out the disciples two by two. There is a very noticeable difference between Matthew's story and Mark's. Matthew's failure to document the success of the disciples makes it appear as if Jesus does not need anyone and that is not correct. Mark's story is much more revealing. The church was to be built on the countless thousands of disciples who had faith in Jesus. Matthew's failure to relate the success of the disciples diminishes their faith journey thus far, including the faith of Judas. Possibly, Jesus was fully aware of the zealous nature of Judas and this is why he was chosen. Jesus understood the nature of his own sojourn among God's children and that his inevitable fate could not be avoided. I do not deny the fact that Judas betrayed but I do not believe it was for money. I believe Judas thought it would speed the coming of the long awaited Messiah; the saviour mounted on a white stallion with sword in hand, ready to vanquish the Romans. It makes senses that when Judas realized that God's way was not his way and that he had made a horrible mistake, he killed himself.

Matthew's story is similar to that of Mark's. The difference is, Mark connects the previous sending story with the feeding story. The story of the feeding of the five thousand takes place in Mark's Chapter 6, whereas in Matthew it is Chapter 14. The two feeding stories are essentially the same, with one notable exception, Matthew has Jesus do everything. Matthew 14:19 has Jesus "order" the crowds to sit down. After blessing and breaking the loaves Jesus gave the bread and fish to the disciples and the disciples acted as banquet waiters. Read the two stories and you will see Matthew's preference for an omnipotent Jesus and inadequate disciples.

This kind of bias causes the stories of Jesus to be seen through a narrow lens. Consider if you will the Matthew 13 story of the weeds and the wheat. It is a straight-forward story demonstrating that not all will be saved. I would submit however, that the New Testament is about repentance and forgiveness. If weeds are burned and only wheat is raised to eternal life then what is the point repentance. If a repentant individual can attain eternal life then maybe one of the reasons that humanity has not been called to "pull the weeds" is that our calling is to live in such a way, to love our neighbours in such a way, as to allow the weeds to become wheat through repentance. Had Christianity been called to "pull the weeds" we would have become worse than Islamic terrorists. The one true living God does not call creation to kill one another. The weeds were allowed to grow, to be given time to repent. Repentance and hope in salvation go hand in hand with God's continual mercy shown to Israel.

A close reading of Mark's gospel reveals that the adverb "immediately" gives a sense of urgency and drives Jesus forward to the day of crucifixion. Matthew uses the noun "multitude" forty times to demonstrate the growing number of followers. The King James Version translated the Greek *ochlos* as multitude whereas modern translations use the more correct word "crowd." Biblical students may be interested in doing a study of Matthew's "crowd theme" to understand how this noun drives the story to its completion. You will also note the word *ochlos* is used in the singular and the plural form. Interestingly, the Matthew 14:22 story and the Mark 6:45 story are identical with both using the word immediately with regards to the story of Jesus walking on water. Matthew has Peter get out of the boat and try to walk to Jesus. Mark does not. Luke did not tell this story at all and it is known in scholarly circles as "Luke's great omission." As I have said, if a student of the Bible wants to get a sense of the nature of the individuals who wrote the three gospels, then Burton's *Gospel Parallels* is essential.

All three gospels repeat Peter's confession as recorded in Matthew 16:16, "you are the Messiah, the Son of the living God." In Greek it reads "the Khris-tos" meaning the anointed one. The church has turned Jesus the Christ into the name, Jesus Christ. As I have said, the writers of the synoptic gospels, the original witnesses, do not recognize Jesus as God. Matthew continues to witness to the divine healing power of Khristos, the son of God, as he makes his way to Jerusalem. Metaphors in Chapter 20 reveal Jesus' attempt to liken heaven to situations the people could understand. It also contains the self-interest story of the mother of James and John wanting positions of authority for her sons. This lends support to the idea that Judas was convinced that Jesus was to be a military leader. Twelve disciples, each with their own dream, anxiously await the revelation of the master's plan. Images of servant-hood turn to visions of grandeur as the Passover approaches. These illusions begin to dissipate as the triumphal entry is followed with the heart breaking view of the temple court as nothing more than a bazaar.

Amidst the growing hope of a new way of life Jesus reminded his disciples of God's way of life. Matthew tells the story of the greatest commandment, the Schema. Both Mark and Luke use heart, soul, mind and strength. The Schema dictates that we are to love God with all our heart, soul and might. Somehow confusion has crept in among the monks who copied the manuscripts. It is highly doubtful that Jesus would have made a mistake or differed from the Deuteronomy 6:5 instructions from Moses. One can see how the Hebrew word Meh-ode (might) when translated into the Greek dee-an-oy-ah (understanding) and came to be translated into Latin as "mind," meaning "strength of understanding." Nonetheless, the imperative is to "love God first and foremost."

Jerusalem was the seat of religious power, much the same as Vatican City is the seat of religious power for the Roman Catholic Church. Imagine driving into Vatican Square shouting through a microphone the words, "woe unto you Cardinals and Bishops, hypocrites!" This might enable you to feel the indignation of the religious leaders when Jesus shouted, "woe unto you, scribes and Pharisees, hypocrites" (Matthew 23:13). Again, the passion of Christ begins its dark journey to the cross. The journey is symbolic of the first Passover in Egypt. This time however, the blood of God's sacrificial lamb will be shed for God's children. Unaware of the pending doom, the disciples fell asleep while Jesus prayed in the garden of Gethsemane. Later, Judas appeared with an armed crowd sent by the high priest. He kissed Jesus in order to identify him in the dark of night; an unnamed disciple drew his sword and cut off the ear of one of the servants; Jesus was arrested, taken to the high priest and his disciples fled for their lives. Matthew identifies Caiaphas correctly as the high priest - singular.

By bringing common people and selected temple priests to the home of Caiaphas in the middle of the night Matthew indicates that this was a clandestine meeting at best. At this mock trial Jesus was convicted of blasphemy. This is a crime fundamentalists believe is punishable by death. But the Jews did not have the power to condemn anyone to death. That power belonged to the Pilate, the Roman governor. It was to become a busy day. At sunrise, Jesus was brought to Pilate who asked him if he was the "King of the Jews?" Jesus answered simply, "you say so." Quite frankly, anyone perceived by the Romans as a threat to an orderly peace would be deemed an enemy. Pilate did not care if Jesus called himself God or anyone else. Pilate did realize what was going on however, and how badly Jesus had annoyed the Pharisees so he offered the people a choice for execution, Jesus, or the notorious criminal Barabbas.

Barabbas is a Hebrew name which means "son of the father." Now ask yourself, "what exactly is being said?" The Messiah is the anointed one, the son of the father. The people are shouting, release the son of the father, but Pilate released the criminal and sent Jesus to the cross. Frankly, I really do not understand what is going on in this passage, especially when Pilate is saying, [what on earth has this man done wrong] (Matthew 27:23)? Some scholars believe the apostles had to have a means of telling the story in such a way that the soldiers would not clue into the fact the Romans were the ones being blamed for the death of Jesus. Pilate knew Jesus had the potential to cause insurrection. The clandestine late night meeting of the priests at the home of the high priest was preposterous. Having the Hebrew people shout, "son of the Father, son of the Father," indicates that the people wanted Jesus released. Two thousand years later, all we know is they shouted "Barabbas." Never forget, the Jews were an oppressed people.

The trial could not have taken long as the crucifixion took place Thursday morning. Onlookers mocked Jesus, challenged him to save himself as did one of the thieves who was crucified beside him (Matthew 27:44). Verse 45 states that from noon on "darkness came over the whole land until three in the afternoon… about three o'clock Jesus cried with a loud voice Eli, Eli, lema sabachthani [ascension ascension, why have you forsaken me]? A short while later, Jesus cried out again and breathed his last.

Matthew lists the women who witnessed the death of Jesus at the cross as:

Matthew 27:56
>Mary Magdalene;
>Mary, the mother of James and Joseph; and
>an unnamed woman.

Mark lists the women who witnessed the death of Jesus at the cross as:
Mark 15: 40-41
>Mary Magdalene;
>Mary, the mother of James the younger and Jose, and Salome;
>and many other women who came with him from Jerusalem.

That afternoon, before sunset, a disciple of Jesus, one Joseph of Arimathaea, went to Pilate to get consent to take the body of Jesus down from the cross. (We are still in Thursday. After the sun set, it would be Friday, the day of preparation). This meant that a devout Jew could not touch a corpse and be ritually clean for the day of preparation and for the Sabbath. This is why the body was put in Joseph's new tomb covered only with a linen burial cloth. To have one's own tomb suggests that Joseph was rich. Scripture tells us that he was a disciple, as was Nicodemus, indicating that educated people were also listening and following Jesus.

The time in the grave is verified by both the witness of the women and the Pharisees. Verse 27:64 has the Pharisees reminding Pilate that Jesus said he would rise after three days. The women, not wanting to clean and prepare the body on Friday night had to wait until the morning after the Sabbath, Sunday morning. As the sun was about to dawn Sunday morning, the women went to the tomb, no men, just women. They were:

> Matthew 28:1
>> Mary Magdalene;
>> the other Mary.
> The women in Mark's gospel are:
> Mark 16:1
>> Mary Magdalene;
>> Mary, the mother of James, and Salome.

Compared to Matthew's matter-of-fact birth account, his resurrection story is personal and touching, yet the women still do not have a voice. Re-read verses 28:1-10. Next is the conspiracy story. After you read it, ask a soldier what would have happened if on duty soldiers went to their commanding officer and said, "sorry Captain, we were tired and fell asleep." Here again, the story of soldiers accepting a bribe does not stand up to reality. Matthew has recorded the rumours being spread by those who wanted Jesus dead, but for me, they are not credible stories. Soldiers, plural, do not fall asleep at their post and they certainly would not have reported it.

Word choice is critical when translating from the Greek to English. When Jesus said, "all authority in heaven and on earth" the word "authority" was translated from the Greek *exousia* (ex-oo-see`-ah) meaning "power of choice" or the "liberty of doing as one pleases." The question I would ask is, "who gave him the power?" The means to human salvation is undoubtedly Jesus (Joshua or in Hebrew Yehowshu`a). The power of choice has been given to the redeemer, the sacrificial Lamb by God. When you stand with Jesus in judgment before God, will Jesus say to you, "welcome my child" or, "I do not know you"?

Also, "baptizing them in the name" was translated from the Greek *baptizo* (bap-tid`-zo) meaning "to immerse, to submerge." Baptism was never meant to be a cheap imitation of sprinkling a few drops of water on an infant's head. Baptism is an adult choice to follow Jesus.

This book is not about casting doubt on the existence of God; the virgin birth of God's son Jesus, or the miracles recorded in scripture, but a better understanding of what the Bible actually says and not what the church wants the Bible to say.

The names of the Apostles are:

| | |
|---|---|
| Simon (Peter) | Rock |
| Andrew | Manly |
| James, son of Zebedee | Supplanter |
| John | Yehovah is a gracious giver |
| Philip | Lover of horses |
| Bartholomew | Son of Tolmai |
| Thomas | Twin |
| Matthew | Gift of Yehovah |
| Levi | Joined |
| James son of Alphaeus | Supplanter |
| Thaddeous | Big hearted |
| Simon the Canaanite | The zealous rock |
| Judas | He shall be praised |

Notice how the proper nouns are not simply names but part of the story.

# Luke

The Gospel of Luke is, grammatically speaking, the best written gospel. It is laid out like a doctoral thesis with an opening statement, followed by the proof or body of work, and closes with a summation. Luke has done an admirable job of writing "an orderly account" of the life of Jesus as well as including a refreshing feminine voice. Yes, women finally get to take part in the story. They have dialogue and offer insight beyond that of the male bias.

If you have not already noticed in your theological studies, all angels in scripture are male. In the Old Testament, angel *mal'ak* (mal-awk') means messenger. It is derived from the word *melek* (meh'-lek) meaning king. The king was to have been God's shepherd on earth. If you care to remember your ancient history and the Code of Hammurabi, you will recall how Hammurabi was not a shepherd in the literal sense but figurative. He was one who understood that the responsibility of public office was to care for the people. Hammurabi lived in ancient Iraq c. 1772 BC and the stele recording his laws is on display in the Louvre. It is the oldest deciphered writing of its type in the world. The code, or laws of conduct, parallels many of the laws written in Leviticus. Scholars believe the Hebrew people copied Hammurabi. However, I believe that the similarities suggest that Hammurabi received the laws from God? He lived in the same era as Abram.

Luke does not know much of what is written in the Old Testament. He is a Greek who came to believe in Jesus, probably through the evangelistic efforts of the Apostle Paul. His purpose was "to write an orderly account… as handed on to us by eyewitnesses." Notice that the plural us denotes a group of followers. (For all you fundamentalists, who want to believe God dictated the Bible, read Luke's introduction. He points out that he and others have decided to record a narrative of events). The date of writing is not certain but it is known that Luke traveled with Paul and that some of the accounts in the Acts of the Apostles are recorded from first hand observation which would necessitate a date from 55 to 65 AD. No one is sure when Luke became associated with Paul but a change from third person omniscient to first person omniscient takes place in Acts 16:10, "and after he (Paul) had seen the vision, immediately **we** endeavoured to go into Macedonia." As Paul was not familiar with the gospels, much of the research would have been carried out after Paul's death. Luke's research includes personal interviews with eyewitnesses as well as access to the Gospel of Mark. These interviews reveal one of the most beautiful stories ever told. Without realizing it, Luke's story unfolds from an Elohists tradition of human equality as recorded in Genesis 1:27. Transliterated it reads, *Elohiym bara awdawm tselem, tselem Elohiym bara zakar nequbah bara*. "So God created man in his own image, in the image of God created he him; male and female created he them."

Luke's gospel is undisputed. The second chapter of his work is the Acts of the Apostles. The Gospel of Luke opens with a purpose statement, that is, to write an orderly eyewitness account of the life of Jesus specifically for a man named Theophilus (friend of God). As Theophilus is also an honorific title some scholars suggest that Luke's gospel is addressed to anyone who loves God. The reality is that it does not matter if Theophilus was an individual or general term for those who seek to know about the Son of God. What is important is that we have his well researched witness.

Luke is regarded as a Greek physician and the gospel student needs to bear his education and social upbringing in mind in an attempt to understand the context in which he writes. It should be noted that everyone writes with a bias, and, dare I say, an agenda. Bias can be said as writing from a belief. As a Christian I write from an innate belief in God and salvation. As a Christian, I write from a bias. Bias is not necessarily wrong. Men write with a male bias. Women write with a female bias. Understanding bias and agenda help the reader discern the truth or a slant the writer takes on any given topic.

First, you will note that Luke begins writing in third person omniscient; that is, "I have recorded the story as was told to me by an eyewitness." Later, in Acts 16 Luke's writing switches to first person omniscient, that is, I am recording what I have witnessed with my own eyes. This is the only gospel scholars believe to bear the name of the writer. The names that adorn the other gospels are pseudonyms (pen names). Writers of the time did not think it wrong to name their book in honour of an individual.

As Luke was a physician, so it is believed that the writer of Matthew was a Jewish Rabbi. Understanding Matthew from this perspective is helpful as he is well educated and the most knowledgeable with regard to the Old Testament, Hebrew law and tradition. I believe that he led worship in a synagogue of believers who recognized Jesus as the promised Messiah. For Matthew, everything must of necessity be according to the law. The church has done good job of promoting hate. Yes, some Jewish leaders did not accept Jesus because he was not in their club. (Club is a critical term for a religious group of believers.) As is the case throughout history, it only takes a small group to give the whole group a bad name. Current example, "not all Muslims are terrorists."

Bias and agenda will help explain some of the striking differences between Matthew and Luke. Matthew's gospel was placed at the beginning of the New Testament as it contained, of prime importance, a genealogy. Remember, people needed a credible past to be acknowledged as a nation. They needed a capital city and a temple, all the things God did not want for the children of Israel. God does not value what humans build with the material God created. God's desire is the substance of the human heart. In the movie *The Kingdom of Heaven*, God's truth is revealed when, in the middle of the siege, Sala as-Din Yusuf ibn Ayyub (Saladin) asked the knight Balian of Ibelin, "what is Jerusalem worth" Balian answered truthfully, "nothing?" If blood produced fertile soil, then Palestinian soil would have the richest on earth.

We are enormously thankful for Luke's academic background which enabled him to discover and record the story of Zechariah (Yehovah remembers) and Elizabeth (oath of God). I am sure that many stories existed but were never recorded. The reason we have the gospels is that people believed that Jesus' return was imminent. It was only when they realized that the time of return had been mis-understood that the gospel writers started to record the events of Jesus' life. The birth of John the Baptist is one of those stories. It reveals how the Baptist was the personification of Elijah. Verse 1:17 tells us "he (John) will go before him" (Messiah).

Zechariah was alone in the temple as it was his allotted time to serve when the angel Gabriel (man of God) came to deliver the good news. Zechariah's response was one of dis-belief. He replied, [how will I know... I am too old... my wife is too old]. Gabriel's response seems harsh, but the fact is, Zachariah's questions were full of doubt. Mary's question on the other hand, was one of inquiry as she was a virgin. Poor Zechariah was struck mute. This allowed Elizabeth to name the child and only when Zechariah concurred was he able to speak again. Hallelujah, we hear the voice of a woman speaking in obedience to God's will.

Elizabeth, being advanced in years, was very careful during her pregnancy and even at her age was full of joy for the disgrace of barrenness was about to be removed. Verse 1:26 begins the angel Gabriel's visit to Mary, a virgin betrothed to a carpenter named Joseph (Yehovah has added) of the line of David. Gabriel visited Mary in the sixth month of Elizabeth's pregnancy. Possibly, Gabriel is providing a hint of prophetic proof to Mary. Nonetheless, Mary makes preparation and journeys to be with Elizabeth. Moving to verse 56 we are told that Mary stayed with her cousin for three months. I am dealing with this birth story in this way to demonstrate something that is missing in Luke's story. Scripture suggests that Mary left the night before the birth of John. Do the math. Ask your wife "if she would leave her elderly cousin, especially under those travel conditions, the night before she gave birth to her first child?" Luke does however report that her neighbours and relatives rejoiced with her.

Now back to Zechariah. The eighth day had come and it was time for the child to be dedicated to God by the ancient ritual of circumcision. Always remember, this is the covenant that replaced the sacrifice of the first born child. Following the ritual, it was now time for the naming of the child. The men were going to speak for the mute father and name the child Zechariah. This is where clergy need to learn to read scripture through the eyes of theatrical production. Ladies, listen to how Luke, in the NRSV, records the voice of Elizabeth, "No! he is to be called John." The voice is firm, definite and commanding. In the King James Version we hear the softer voice of a meek woman, "not so, he is to be called John." Clergy need to read scripture as if directing a play in order to get away from writing boring monotone sermons. In answer to all the rebuttal from the relatives, Zechariah motions for a writing tablet and inscribes the name Jonathan (Yehovah is a gracious giver). Immediately, he regained the ability to speak and began to praise God.

Luke tells us the story of Mary's arrival at her cousin's home. Telling the story in real time enhances the beauty of her poetic praise. The voice of Mary touched the infant John who "leapt" in Elizabeth's womb. Please note, scripture does not say moved or kicked, but a much more active word, leapt, following which Elizabeth is filled with the Holy Spirit. It should be apparent by now that Luke did not hear this story from men. This is a woman's story. Could you imagine this being written in the Gospel of Matthew? The quality of Luke's writing is at least equal to that of the prophet Isaiah, "how beautiful upon the mountains are the feet of the messenger who announces peace, who brings good news, who announces salvation, who says to Zion, "Your God reigns" (Isaiah 52:7). Please listen anew to the female voices that were in total harmony with God.

Luke 1: 41-55

> "When Elizabeth heard Mary's greeting, the child leapt in her womb. And Elizabeth was filled with the Holy Spirit and exclaimed with a loud cry"

> Blessed are you among women, and blessed is the fruit of your womb. And why has this happened to me that the mother of my Lord comes to me? For as soon as I heard the sound of your greeting, the child in my womb leaped for joy. And blessed is she who believed that there would be a fulfillment of what was spoken to her by the Lord.

And Mary said,

> "My soul magnifies the Lord, and my spirit rejoices in God my Savior, for he has looked with favor on the lowliness of his servant. Surely, from now on all generations will call me blessed; for the Mighty One has done great things for me, and holy is his name. His mercy is for those who fear him from generation to generation. He has shown strength with his arm; he has scattered the proud in the thoughts of their hearts. He has brought down the powerful from their thrones, and lifted up the lowly; he has filled the hungry with good things, and sent the rich away empty. He has helped his servant Israel, in remembrance of his mercy, according to the promise he made to our ancestors, to Abraham and to his descendants forever."

If you were to hear the Magnificat in its proper Hebrew poetic form you would feel the power of the Holy Spirit even though you did not understand the language. In a like manner, Zechariah, after his mouth was opened, prophesied the future calling of his infant son. Luke records that "Zechariah was filled with the Holy Spirit and spoke this prophecy:

> Blessed be the Lord God of Israel, for he has looked favorably on his people and redeemed them. He has raised up a mighty saviour for us in the house of his servant David, as he spoke through the mouth of his holy prophets from of old, that we would be saved from our enemies and from the hand of all who hate

us. Thus he has shown the mercy promised to our ancestors, and has remembered his holy covenant, the oath that he swore to our ancestor Abraham, to grant us that we, being rescued from the hands of our enemies, might serve him without fear, in holiness and righteousness before him all our days. And you child, will be called the prophet of the Most High; for you will go before the Lord to prepare his ways, to give knowledge of salvation to his people by the forgiveness of their sins. By the tender mercy of our God, the dawn from on high will break upon us, to give light to those who sit in darkness and in the shadow of death, to guide our feet into the way of peace. The child grew and became strong in spirit, and he was in the wilderness until the day he appeared publicly to Israel" (Luke 1: 67-80).

Luke is the only writer who informs us of how Joseph and Mary came to be in Bethlehem. It was a census decreed by Augustus. But Luke also calls you to make a decision. Liberal Luke states that Mary was engaged (2:5) to Joseph. Not married! Luke does not fully realize the implications of a child born out of wedlock in Hebrew society. Matthew however, is quite specific in noting the couple did get married before they went to Bethlehem. Luke is also significantly different in that the Magi are missing, as is the story of the slaughter of the infants and the flight to Egypt. This is where most clergy merge the two birth stories. Those who attend but once a year see Magi, shepherds, animals, soldiers, the innkeeper's son, Curly, Larry and Moe, as well as a variety of cattle in the manger scene. All is as it should be for the hatch, match and dispatch Christians to go home reassured they do not have to come to church until Easter when Jesus will die for their sins and if he sees his shadow on the third day we will have six more weeks of winter. Clergy make note of the attendance, satisfied that the church was full, and the beat goes on.

Luke's beat however, is to record the beauty of the story for generations to come. The reader is told that the inn was full so Jesus was born in a nearby cattle stall. We have been left with an image of a clear star-light night and the newborn babe wrapped in a swaddling cloth. The heavenly host appears to shepherds in the field who make haste to visit Bethlehem. At this point, Luke's record is identical to that of Matthew's in that Jesus is dedicated on the eighth day in Jerusalem. He also mentions Simeon (heard) and the prophetess Anna (grace). After hearing the two prophesies Joseph and Mary return to Nazareth, not Egypt, and they are still not married.

Luke's gospel is the only one that records an incident in the early life of Jesus. It is worth noting as the story holds an interesting clue to the holy child's educational development. The story I am referring to is found in Luke 2:46, "after three days they found him in the temple, sitting among the teachers, listening to them and asking them questions." Anyone who has ever sat through a defense of their doctoral thesis knows exactly what is going on in the story. In those days, computers were not available, nor were the local print shops to produce copies for the defense team; the supplicant presented from memory, then defended the dissertation in the middle of a half dozen teachers. When Jesus next comes on the scene, John's voice is crying in the wilderness. We learn that John baptizes Jesus in the presence of people who hear the heavenly voice, "you are my Son, the Beloved; with you I am well pleased" (Luke 3:22).

This is the gospel that gives us detail to many other stories. We are told that Jesus spent forty days in the wilderness being tempted by *dee ab ol os* (the devil). On his return to Nazareth he went into the synagogue and, "as was his custom" read from the scroll. On this day he read from Isaiah "the Spirit of the Lord is upon me" Luke 4:18). When the people said, [hey, is this not Joseph's son,] Jesus said, [no prophet is accepted in his hometown]. When last we heard, Jesus was 12 years old, now he is 30 and appears at the Jordan to be baptized by John. Heaven only knows where he has been. Scholars believe Jesus studied and resided at Qumran among the Essenes with his cousin John. This is the most likely source of what is now the Sacrament of Baptism. It makes sense that this new sect would have a symbolic purification cleansing for new converts. Fundamentalists believe Jesus walked out of his father's carpenter shop to be baptized by John and God beamed down all the knowledge of the universe as he came up out of the water. I tend to side with the scholars. Following his baptism, and his wilderness temptation experience, Jesus proceeded to gather twelve disciples. Mark and Matthew disagree with Luke on the names of the disciples.

| Luke's disciples | Matthew's disciples | Mark's disciples |
| --- | --- | --- |
| Simon | Simon | Simon |
| Andrew | Andrew | Andrew |
| James | James | Philip |
| John | John | John |
| Philip | Philip | Philip |
| Bartholomew | Bartholomew | Bartholomew |
| Matthew | Matthew | Matthew |
| Thomas | Thomas | Thomas |
| James | James | James |
| Judas | Thaddaeus | Thaddaeus |
| Simon | Simon | Simon |
| Judas | Judas | Judas |

The story now moves to the Pharisee who invited Jesus to dine in his home. During this time a woman had courage enough to enter the Pharisee's home and silently present herself at the feet of the Messiah (Luke 7:36-50). She wept on his feet, dried them with her hair and anointed his feet with alabaster oil. The Pharisee moves the dialogue forward by speaking to others gathered in his home. I get the impression from the passage that the Pharisee was speaking in a soft, "I told you so" manner, saying in verse 39, "if this man were a prophet, he would have known who and what kind of woman this is who is touching him – that she is a sinner." Understand that Jesus would have replied with the same soft voice when he told the allegorical story of the two debtors. One debtor owed much and the other who owed very little. Jesus then asked the Pharisee which debtor would be more grateful having their debt cancelled. The Pharisee replied with the obvious answer, to which Jesus answered compassionately, "you are right." The story is simple to understand but what is often missed is the fact that this sinful woman had faith in Jesus. Her act was one of repentance which openly demonstrated her faith and gained this sinful woman her forgiveness.

In Chapter 9 we once again hear the sending story. It is an "on the job training" story. Notice the brevity of the account as Jesus is not part of the story. Luke, as in Mark, uses the beheading of John the Baptist as an interlude. Upon the disciples return there is a lack of detail which leaves the reader with the idea it was not an emotional experience for the disciples. This is sad as I have heard clergy explain that the disciples were faithless dimwits. Please read what scripture says and put the stories into perspective. Luke's feeding of the five thousand is not just another information story about the miraculous Jesus. Learn to read scripture for the light it sheds, not the bias it conveys. Christians need to see disciples, both then and now, as an integral part of Jesus' ministry. Bias denies disciple participation and can fool you into thinking Jesus can do everything by himself. If Jesus wants it, Jesus will do it is an attitude in the Christian church. At a meeting to develop an evangelistic outreach program in my first church a fundamentalist elder spoke up angrily saying, "if Jesus wants them to come to our church, he will send them." I said, "Hogwash!" Jesus called disciples for a reason. Disciples need to recognize Jesus for whom he is, "the Messiah of God" (Luke 9:20). We are the disciples, the ones who choose to serve and we are the ones who choose to obey the great commission.

The following is a passage that does not sit well with fundamentalist Christians. The disciple John said, "Master, we saw someone casting out demons in your name, and we tried to stop him, because he does not follow with us [belong to our club]. Jesus said to him, Do not stop him; for whomever is not against you is for you" (Luke 9: 49-50). In as much as the faith of the disciples continued to grow, their esoteric understanding of their calling still needed to grow dramatically. Had it not been for the Apostle Paul, the disciples may well have only evangelized the Jews in and around Jerusalem. I will speak more on this later as the original disciples never did fully trust Paul or believe he saw Jesus.

Listen to the exclusive, our club alone, dialogue that continues. Jesus had set his face toward Jerusalem. On the way, some disciples entered a Samaritan village to make ready for him, but the Samaritans were jealous because Jesus was going to Jerusalem and not Mount Gerizim. They did not receive him. Now listen to what happened when the disciples turned faith into religion. James and John reacted indignantly with, "Lord, do you want us to command fire to come down from heaven and consume them" (Luke 9:54). Jesus rebuked them and they went on to another village. Note how humans act when they are the ones in the inner circle. Also, notice how their faith had grown. James and John said, "do you want **us** to command fire to come down?"

Luke tells the story in Chapter 10 of a lawyer who tested Jesus with the question, "what must I do to inherit eternal life." The following is the answer from Jesus. He does not say that eternal life is inherited by faith in him as many fundamentalists believe. Jesus answered with God's requirements, "what is written in the law"? The law is Deuteronomy 6:4 - Yehovah is El, and Leviticus 19:18 - love thy neighbour. This passage is Hebrew Midrash. The lawyer is not trying to trick Jesus but is setting him up to explain by using an allegory within the people's comprehension. Chapter 10 also includes the story of Mary and Martha. You have heard it explained many times. All I would add is pay attention to how Luke allows the woman's voice to be heard.

Chapter 11 is the most widely used scripture in the Bible. Clergy say, "let us pray as Jesus taught his disciples to pray." Coming from liberal Luke it is understandable how he would interpret this as instruction. Unfortunately, he did not understand the part about vain repetition. Translating from the Greek:

Matthew reads,  "In this manner offer prayer."
Luke reads,  "Whenever you offer prayers say."

There is only a slight difference in the wording but it is distinct nonetheless. Always remember, Jesus' form of prayer was not some mindless repetition which eventually becomes meaningless. It was about communicating with God. It was about speaking and listening. The church has turned a model for prayer into vain repetition.

The use of Throckmorton's *Gospel Parallels* enables the Biblical students to capture a glimpse of the personal agenda of each gospel writer. It is also easy to establish the importance of a story which has been recorded by two or three writers, but what about the stories a writer chooses to exclude? The choice of inclusion or exclusion reveals much about that writer. Scholars have forever pondered why Luke omitted the walking on the water story recorded in both Mark and Matthew. It is referred to as "Luke's great omission." His "little omission" is the eternal punishment story in Mark and Matthew of "a great millstone around your neck." It must have been too distasteful for him. On the other hand, the "parable of the good Samaritan," and "the parable of the rich fool," were not included in Mark and Matthew.

Even though the millstone story may have been too harsh for Luke, the "repent or perish" stories in Chapter 13 were not, as they dealt with salvation. They are the harsh truth stories, the either/or stories. The chapter opens with Pilate's mutilation of some Galileans and the tower of Siloam falling on eighteen people. After being asked if these people were worse sinners than all others, Jesus said "no." Once again, the criterion for salvation is announced from the mouth of Jesus, "unless you repent you will all perish" Luke 13:5). This story is followed by a man who planted a fig in his vineyard which did not bear fruit. Jesus said, [give it one more chance and if it does not bear fruit, cut it down.] After healing a woman on the Sabbath Jesus called the leader of the synagogue a hypocrite because he was more concerned with rules than compassion for the sick. Being saved never was about professing the name of Jesus; it is about obedience to God's command to love. Over the course of time the church has taught us to hate the Pharisees, hate the Jews, as they were all bad and all disobedient, but in this chapter we find the opposite, "some Pharisees came and said to him, 'get away from here for Herod wants to kill you'" (Luke 13:31). It is easy to say, "the Jews killed Jesus," but I say unto you, "who killed JFK?"

The Lucan story of the Prodigal Son is a Sunday morning favourite in the Christian Church. Clergy focus on the rebellious son one year, the older son the next, and even the father from time to time. Inasmuch as there is valuable teaching from any perspective, you should know that stories about "a father" are usually about "the Father." What is not evident however, is an understanding of the story in the Hebrew context. First of all, it is not a real story. It is an allegory, a fable made up to convey a divine truth. Secondly, the reason for the story was to infuriate the scribes to the point of wanting to stone Jesus to death on the spot. If you know Hebrew culture, you would realize that the preamble to the story is not true. The younger son was not entitled to any inheritance other than the opportunity to live on the family farm and earn a reasonable living. Farms then, as today, are not divided on each succeeding generation. Younger sons during the Crusades went to the Holy Land to carve out their fortune and capture a piece of land because elder sons stayed home to inherit. The audacity of this boy to do such an indignant thing as to ask for a share would have sent the scribes into a rage.

This method of getting the scribal attention continues with the boy leaving the Hebrew family/community in favour of a promiscuous gentile society. Spending the money a foolish father gave him on wine, women, and song, (the fun things in life) infuriated the scribes even more. Taking a pig feeding job and eating their food was a slap in God's face. But now, the turning point in the story comes and the scribes get ready for the great punishment at the end of the story. You and I know however that repentance is the first step to salvation. The boy repents; he returns to the father; he rehearses his confession so that he does not miss a sin. One of the things Christians should not fail to see in the story is that the father not only sees his son returning, but saw him "a long way off." No matter how far you have gone astray, when you repent, the Father sees you. At this point the scribes are still waiting in anxious indignation for the condemnation. You need also to recall the 17th century painting by Rembrandt in which he portrayed the repentant son kneeling before his father with pious elders looking on. The painting conveys the bias of the scribes and the church leaders of the time.

The Biblical story is not as Rembrandt has portrayed. The father would not let the son kneel and grovel; the father would not let the son finish his confession; the father put his arms around the son and kissed him. Once again the scribes would have been furious so Jesus turned up the heat even more by having a family robe brought out, he put a ring put on his son's finger and sandals on his feet denoting that the child had been redeemed. The father ordered that the fatted calf be killed for the celebration, then, in the silence of a stunned crowd and infuriated scribes Jesus said in a soft voice, "this son of mine was dead and is alive again; he was lost and is found" (Luke 15:24)! The story does not adequately convey the silence. We do not see the heads of the scribes hung in shame for not seeing past their rules. Nor do we see the tears in the eyes of parents who continually pray for wayward children.

Imagine, if you will, a compassionate Jesus looking kindly at the crowd and after a painful moment of silence saying softly, "now his elder son was in the field." Read the passage if you are not familiar with it, then reflect upon the second purpose of the story. The first purpose was for the scribes and audience. Today, it is for pious rule oriented Christians. The second purpose is you! You are the reason for all the stories. Never mind the elder son as he is left in the same place as the crowd; on the outside. You are left on the outside to think about your response to the invitation to the banquet. It is a beautiful story which actually extends the invitation to the people of Israel and to you. I do not believe there is a better example of God's grace, of God's loving-kindness (hesed) anywhere. Please note, there are two actions in the story. One, the younger sinful child repents (turns) of his own volition. Two, the father received him with only a minimal confession. You are the elder son. You must make your own decision for Christ.

Luke conveys to us the tough stories very well. To all who believe that, in the end, everyone will be forgiven, no matter what they have done, please read the story of Lazarus and Abraham. It is what happens when you live a life of unrepentant sin. It also demonstrates that the nether world has been forbidden contact with the temporal world. This story is a perfect example of the results of a conscious disregard for Deuteronomy 6:4 and Leviticus 19:18. It also contains a sad truth foreshadowing the resurrection. The rich man wanted Lazarus to return and warn his brothers, but the answer was "no." Abraham said, "if they do not listen to Moses and the prophets neither will they be convinced even if someone rises from the dead" (Luke 16:31). Do you believe in the resurrection?

Chapter 17 reinforces the story of the prodigal son in that forgiveness has a prerequisite. It challenges much of what the church has professed over the ages. There is a dichotomy between sin and heinous crime. Heinous crimes are covered in the Old Testament under "sin unto death." The pardon for redeemable sinners was the mission of Jesus. This is made clear in the directive, "if there is repentance, you must forgive" (Luke 17:3). As Christians, we need to understand that the gospel needs to be preached so that people understand the need for repentance. Again, read the Matthew 25 story of the sheep and the goats and the story of Lazarus. The sin the rich man had committed was that he did not demonstrate his love for God by being obedient to the command to "love his neighbour."

## Entering Jerusalem

Luke continues with the healing stories and sayings as Jesus made his way to Jerusalem. On the first day of the week (Sunday) Jesus and his disciples entered Jerusalem and began teaching in the temple court by day and on the Mount of Olives by night. During the week Jesus drove the sellers from the temple court. He answered questions such as the legality of paying of taxes. As Passover approached, he sent his disciples to find an inn and prepare a room. During the Passover meal Christ followers are forever charged to remember the new symbolism of the bread, (representative of the body of the Messiah) and the wine, (representative of the sacrificial blood of the Lamb of God). Christians need to be reminded of the significance of this sacrificial remembrance and the depth of meaning it held for the early church. Melchizedek first desired to share the bread and wine with Abram as a sign of brotherhood in God. Bread and wine are the ancient symbols of those who believe in the one true living God. For Christians, they are the symbols now shared between those who believe God's Messiah has come to redeem the sins of the redeemable of the world. Please do not turn it into a private ceremony practiced only by your exclusive club. It is a remembrance shared between those who confess Jesus as Lord (Adonay) or Master (Kurios) and at least try to love their neighbour. While they were still sinners, Jesus shared the Passover with them.

Following the Passover the group moved to the Mount of Olives where Jesus, being heavy with grief, prayed to the Father. Verse 22: 43 is shown in brackets [an angel from heaven gave him strength.] The brackets indicate that early manuscripts bear no record of an angel. It is an addition first appearing in the middle ages. A poor translation does not make this distinction. Both Mark and Matthew have the praying in the garden story but neither one has the angels' story. Likewise verse 23:34 "Father, forgive them, for they do not know what they are doing" is also a scribal addition. Again, both Mark and Matthew include the casting of lots story but do not have the plea of forgiveness. Christianity is not a powder puff religion. Forgiveness comes with repentance.

Please read Luke's crucifixion account as if you are a forensic investigator. This is one of the ways Presbyterian clergy are taught to read; we call it a close reading. A close reading does not lead one into doubt or disbelief; it helps one to get a sense of the actions taking place in the whole story. One of the shortfalls of Christian preaching is that it takes a snippet (pericope) and preaches on it as if it was a stand alone teaching and can be taken from a specific teaching to the general principle. Short stories make it difficult to understand the nonchalant approach Pilate took to the accusations of insurrection in light of his duty to uphold the *Iuris Romani* (Roman Law). The whole idea of Pilate sending an accused individual to Herod is preposterous, and equally preposterous is the idea that Herod and Pilate became friends. People who caused insurrection were nailed to a cross as an example to others!

Luke records the crowd shouting to release Barabbas. Bar meaning son and Abba meaning father. It sounds strange that the Jewish crowd was shouting a proper noun Barabbas which means, "son of the father." Nonetheless, Pilate was the one who condemned Jesus, not the Jews. It is highly doubtful that Pilate was afraid of the crowd. Fear was not a quality of a Roman officer. They upheld the Roman law at all costs. Christians believe that Jesus was scourged mercilessly before being sent to the cross; a punishment that was abolished by the Emperor Constantine in the late fourth century. Although the witness accounts at the cross differ slightly, they all agree that Jesus died on the cross. This is an important theological imperative. Without death there is no resurrection and all is a scam. People in every age have argued that Jesus did not die on the cross but only swooned (fainted) and that is why he was not found in the tomb. Obviously, we do not have a corpse to examine but forensic pathology can determine if death did occur by examining the witness accounts of the crucifixion.

With thanks I will relate the findings of Lee Strobel (*The Case for Easter*) who sought to determine if it were possible for Christians to make the claim that Jesus did in fact die on the cross. In order to substantiate his claim, Strobel interviewed an individual who had the medical and scientific knowledge, one Alexander Metherell, M.D., Ph. D., to explain what happens to the human body on the cross. The following is a brief account of his findings.

The whole crucifixion process is designed to inflict as much excruciating pain as possible. The victim's arms are stretched out as far as possible, even to the point of dislocation. If they do not dislocate it will happen when the cross beam is lifted up and fastened to the vertical post. The nails are driven through the wrists to prevent the skin from ripping away and the victim falling head first. This causes tremendous pain as the nails rip the nerve connecting the "funny bone." When the cross beam is lifted, the body drops and the feet are then nailed causing more pain. This may not sound life threatening but the reality is that breathing is inhibited. As the body drops the individual inhales but does not have the use of the diaphragm to exhale. The only way to exhale is to push the body up by exerting force on the feet which inflicts more pain. Even the strongest individuals become too exhausted to push up and die from asphyxia. The process is not designed to last all day, just long enough to inflict unbearable pain and remind onlookers of their fate should they consider transgressing the Roman law. William Lane Craig, Ph.D., D.Th., will testify to the fact that if a Roman soldier did not carry out an order he too would suffer death.

The Christian record of witnesses states that Jesus breathed his last and committed his spirit unto God. This is what crucifixion is designed to do. When the soldiers assigned to duty were ready to leave they broke the legs of the other criminals so they did not have to wait much longer. With their legs broken, it was now impossible for them to push up to breath and so they died of asphyxia. The soldiers could literally witness the death within minutes. Scripture tells us that Jesus had already died so his legs were not broken. Now realize, that if a victim were to somehow survive, the soldiers on duty would be crucified for dereliction of duty. To ensure this did not happen, one soldier thrust his spear up through the side of Jesus, penetrating the lungs and heart. The mixture of water and blood was the result of that action. When Joseph of Arimathaea went to Pilate with a request to take the body down, there would not be any hesitation as Roman soldiers would never allow a body with any amount of life within to be taken down. The death of the Messiah is a reality as foretold in scripture. The Jews that became Christ followers would have never followed if it were a hoax.

Thursday

Again, the day was Thursday. Jesus died on Thursday. Luke records that Jesus was nailed to the cross before noon and about mid-day cried out, "Father, into your hands I commend my spirit... and he breathed his last" (Luke 23:46). Surprisingly, Luke does not name any of the women at the cross. He simply says, "the women who had come with him from Galilee" (Luke 23:56). Now remember, Thursday afternoon turns to Friday night at sundown. Joseph claimed the body and placed it in the tomb before the day of preparation (Friday) which began at sundown. At sundown, Thurs-day becomes Fri-day night. The next morning is Fri-day morning, the second half of the first day in the grave. Saturday night follows for the second night in the grave with Saturday morning dawning the second day. Saturday night and Saturday is the Hebrew Sabbath. At sundown Saturday the Sabbath is over, but it is night, Sunday night, the third night in the grave. At dawn, on the third day, Mary Magdalene went to the tomb where she was told that Jesus had risen, "remember how he told you… that the Son of Man must be crucified, and on the third day rise again" (Luke24:7)? Isaiah's 53:7 prophesy is fulfilled. Jesus' words are fulfilled, and we have a faith to be cherished in our hearts. The only debt we owe is to become a living demonstration of our faith by being obedient to the new commandment, "to love one another, as I have loved you" (John 13:34). Christians do not worship on the 7th day as do the Jews but on Sunday, the first day of the week, the day Christ was raised from the dead by God. Although Luke does not name the women at the cross, he names them at the tomb.

They are:

> Mary Magdalene
> Joanna
> Mary, the mother of James
> and the other women with them.

Luke makes it very clear that there were many others with the disciples who would have also been at the Passover. Luke also does something very bold in a chauvinistic world. He passes on to us the vulgar reaction of the disciples on hearing the news of the resurrection from women. Luke 24:11 has been traditionally softened to read "but these words seemed to them an idle tale." Luke's word choice was *leros* (ley ros). It is a strong word. It is a vulgar word. The Rev. Dr. Anna Carter Florence, preaching professor at Columbia Theological Seminary, Decatur, Ga., maintains that the word *leros* properly translated means "bull shit." The term "idle tale" makes the women's witness frivolous. It is male bias. Imagine, if you will, the fear and tension within the group of disciples when the women entered in unbounded joy making the announcement, "he is risen." This is what the angel at the tomb told the women, not the men who deserted. Peter however, had no sooner shouted "bullshit" in anger when he felt the truth in his heart and immediately bolted for the tomb.

The story of Jesus' revelation to disciples on the road to Emmaus is timeless. It also reveals to us the name of a previously unmentioned disciple named Cleopas who returned to Jerusalem to tell the others that Jesus has been raised. It is important to read the last few verses of Luke and realize that Jesus had returned as promised. After Jesus revealed his risen self, he does not say, "I will come again." Jesus gave his disciple the "great commission" and told them to stay in Jerusalem until they received the promised Holy Spirit. Imagine the joy in this group of people as they walk toward Bethany. Along the way, Jesus raised his hands, blessed them, and was carried up into heaven. The disciples returned to Jerusalem to await the Ruwach of God. Once again, it is from John 14 that Christians get the idea that Jesus will come again. John's hallucinatory gospel has caused more heartache and mis-understanding than can be comprehended. It should have never been included in the Christian canon.

Luke ends volume one of his gospel at this point. Next, is volume two, the Acts of the Apostles. The church fathers separated Luke and Acts so that the fourth gospel, John's gospel, might be kept with the real gospels.

# John

It should be of no surprise to hear that when it comes to John's gospel, I have some serious issues with the term, "witness gospel." There is a reason that Matthew, Mark and Luke are called "synoptic gospels." Synoptic means to be seen in the same way, with many of the same stories and much of the same wording. John's work is inspirational. By inspirational I mean like Mohamed, like Joseph Smith, the author of John's Gospel went up the mountain, smoked some really good stuff, and became inspired to write what was on **his** heart. Much of what John writes is correct but the fact remains, only ten percent of John's material appears in the other gospels. Ninety percent of the material in John is new. Another oddity is that John has Jesus make three separate trips to Jerusalem. They are recorded in John 2:23, 5:1 and 12:12. The synoptic gospels have Jesus move from Galilee to Jerusalem over the course of three years. Considering that John was written sixty to eighty years after the death of Jesus it is highly doubtful he was alive at the time of the crucifixion. Richard Bauckham argues that John is a credible eyewitness gospel but I could not agree with his theory that testimony made decades after the death of Christ was just as credible as the early testimony. As you read the gospel you should notice that John's audience is different than the synoptic audience. This is evident by the multitude of explanations inserted into the dialogue such as John 1:41, "we have found the Messiah (anointed one). A Hebrew audience would not need an explanation. A few other examples are 1:15 - 1:38 - 4:8 - 18:32 - 19:35 - 20:24. John is the gospel from which the church endeavoured to make Jesus God. John's purpose was to prove that Jesus was divine. However, the word divine means heavenly as were the sons of God. John opens his gospel by putting Jesus in the beginning as the Word, "and the Word was with God, and the Word was God." John establishes Jesus as the one through whom all things came into being. Unfortunately, Proverbs 8:22-36 establishes wisdom (the feminine aspect of God) as the one in the beginning through whom all things were made. John is not familiar with the Old Testament, Hebrew history, nor is he familiar with temple worship.

John's calling of the disciples is slightly different than the synoptic gospels. After Andrew is called he brought his brother Simon whom Jesus said was to be called Cephas (Cephas is Aramaic for rock). As I have stated, Jesus would not have changed the name of another Jew to a Greek or Aramaic name. Chapter 4 states that the Pharisees heard Jesus was making and baptizing more disciples than John the Baptist, but then inserts the qualifier, "although it was not Jesus himself but his disciples who baptized." This information is too important for the others to have forgotten. On three occasions (John 11:49, 11:51 and 18:13) John stated that Caiaphas was the "high priest that year." The office of Pope was copied from the office of the high priest. Both were offices held until death. John 3:16 is more than likely one of the most familiar Biblical passages quoted. John's theology claims that the world will be saved through him (3:17) and that salvation is obtained by a belief in Jesus. Now think of the Matthew 25:32-46. The goats believed in Jesus!

This claim is contradicted in John 6:44 making salvation a choice of God in concurrence with the son. This, as on many other occasions, John acknowledges a definite dichotomy between the Son and the

Father. Verse 6:65 is another example, "for this reason I have told you that no one can come to me unless granted by the Father." Nonsense! Statements such as these have been used by the church to promote predestination which means that you are chosen from birth to be saved and there is nothing you can do to change that. Presbyterians no longer believe this false teaching. Double predestination means that if someone is living on the street as a beggar or is living in a horrible situation, we are not to extend relief and consolation because it is God's will for that person to live in destitution. Therefore, if you help that person you are violating God's will. Thank heaven people are no longer stupid enough to believe that *leros* (lay-ros).

The Christian church at one time suffered from the accusation that Christ followers, in celebrating the Passover (observing communion) ate human flesh and drank blood. Thanks to John, the church had to battle for centuries to dispel the belief that Jesus said, "those who eat my flesh and drink my blood have eternal life" (John 6:32). Further doubt is cast when John 6:59 claims that Jesus said this while preaching in the synagogue at Capernaum. Leros! John's gospel has also suffered from Christian scribal influence. The familiar story of the woman caught in adultery (7:53 - 8:11) does not appear in the older manuscripts. Apparently, the church did not believe Revelations 22:18 and the threat that God would send plagues and remove from the Book of Life the name of anyone who adds to or deletes from scripture. It is only John who claims that if you have seen the Son you have seen the Father (10:35, 14:7 and 14:20). Christians blindly listen to a scripture reading one week that says, "no one has seen God at any time" (John 1:18 and 1 John 4:12), then listen the next week to a lesson that says, "and the Lord spoke to Moses face to face, as a man speaks to his friend" (Exodus 33:11). People listen but no one questions the contradiction between John and Moses. In John 1:29

we are told that John the Baptist said, "I myself did not know him." That is really surprising as the first chapter of Luke tells us that Jesus and John were cousins. John 20:21 declares that salvation is in the name of Jesus. However, Jesus tells the story of sheep and the goats and according to Jesus salvation comes from obedience to God's command to love our neighbour.

Other issues that make me suspicious of the credibility of John's gospel are to do with the crucifixion. First, is that the inscription on the cross was "written in Hebrew, in Latin, and in Greek" (John 19:20). Leros! The second thing is John's account of the women at the cross. The women at the cross include:

> Mary, the mother of Jesus;
> Mary's sister - Jesus' aunt;
> Mary the wife of Clopas; and
> Mary Magdalene.

The only woman to come to the tomb in John's account is Mary Magdalene.

When you read the other accounts, the eyewitness accounts they are not aware of Mary, the mother of Jesus, being anywhere near the cross. Personally, I cannot imagine God being so cruel as to send Mary to watch her son die by means of crucifixion. Heaven only knows what John was smoking but it must have been good stuff. In the morning of the first day of the week Mary Magdalene went to the tomb to prepare the body. Finding that the stone had been rolled away she returned and reported this to the disciples. The mother of Jesus, whose duty it would have been to clean and wrap the body has disappeared as suddenly as she entered. Please pay attention to the record of the people who were at the cross and the tomb in all four gospels. The list will follow. John also states that a mixture of spices, myrrh and aloes, weighing a hundred pounds was brought to prepare Jesus. Leros! Not only is that enough mixture to prepare the bodies of all the Roman soldiers stationed in Jerusalem, it would have been worth a small fortune. To put its value into perspective, a 15-ml bottle of myrrh sells in religious book stores for $82.50.

Now it may seem contradictory but I do believe much of what John wrote. There are many truths contained in the joy of his conversion but he must be understood as an over zealous convert trying to evangelize people to Christ. We experience the same thing today; people without a credible theological education, read the gospel and go out and proclaim Christ. It is not difficult. A good memory will enable anyone to cherry-pick desired verses and mesmerize gullible people. It is easy to preach love; it is easy to preach prosperity; it is easy to preach forgiveness and salvation; it is easy to convince people to send you a $1,000.00 seed of faith and claim God will reward you ten-fold. Leros! The message of God, the message of Christ Jesus, is "to love one another." We are taught to do unto others as you would have done unto yourself. People demonstrate their love for God by loving their neighbour. If you do not believe this statement then you better read the story Jesus told about the sheep and the goats. It is the key to salvation. In all fairness, the writer of John's gospel has given us the most profound commandment of Jesus. That is, "to love one another, as I have loved you" (John 15:12).

From the above it should be of no surprise to hear that I am suspect of the 90% of John's stories. Nonetheless, I believe his heart was in the right place. While examining your faith belief, ask yourself, "do the words in John's gospel parallel those of Jesus in the synoptic gospels?" Or, "do the words sound like an over enthusiastic Christian trying to bring others to Christ?" It is worth listing the accounts of those at the cross and at the tomb.

**Matthew's** list of women who witnessed the death of Jesus **at the cross**:

> Matthew 27:56
>> Mary Magdalene;
>> Mary, the mother of James and Joseph;
>> and the unnamed mother (Salome) of the sons of Zebedee.

Matthew's list of women who returned to **the tomb**:

> Matthew 28:1
>> Mary Magdalene;
>> the other Mary.

**Mark's** list of women who witnessed the death of Jesus **at the cross**:

> Mark 15: 40-41
> Mary Magdalene;
>> Mary, the mother of James the younger and Jose, and Salome;
>> and many other women who came with him from Jerusalem.

Mark's list of women who returned to **the tomb**:

> Mark 16:1
>> Mary Magdalene;
>> Mary, the mother of James, and Salome.

**Luke's** list of women who witnessed the death of Jesus **at the cross**:

> Luke 23:49, 55
>> Luke states "and the women who followed him from Galilee"

Luke's list of women who returned to **the tomb**:

Luke 24:10

Mary Magdalene

Joanna

Mary, the mother of James

and the other women

**John's** list of women who witnessed the death of Jesus **at the cross**:

John 19:25

Mary, the mother of Jesus;

Mary's sister - Jesus' aunt;

Mary, the wife of Clopas; and Mary Magdalene.

John's list of women who returned to **the tomb**:

John 20:1

Mary Magdalene

Most of Christianities theological beliefs are founded on the John's book which states all you have to do is confess Jesus (talk). It is contradicted by the words of Jesus which call us to action (works).

## The Acts of the Apostles

The book of Acts is part two. It is as it claims a record of eye witness accounts of the acts of the apostles. In actual fact, no one knows where, when or how Luke converted to being a Christ follower or exactly when the writing took place. During his travels Luke encountered both Peter and Paul. I suspect that it was not too long after Paul's death that Luke undertook to finish compiling his orderly account for the most excellent Theophilus. Luke would have taken

notes during his association and travels with Paul. Then he would
have gone back to search out his many eye witness sources. On
completing the Gospel according to Luke he would have referred
to notes taken while with Peter and Paul and other disciples. This
is where the Book of Acts begins. Luke affirms for Theophilus that
the great commission of Matthew 28:19 had been given to the eleven
disciples. This may be a clue as to the person of Theophilus as the
writing is in the form of a Greek apology. Apology means to write
"in defense of," not to apologize.

It appears as if the first fifteen chapters of Acts are records of eye
witness accounts, possibly Peter's as they include events witnessed
by a disciple. The first four chapters are far too eloquent to have
been written in Greek by the Hebrew fisherman Peter. At the end
of Chapter 4 there is a story about a native of Cyprus named Joses
(exalted) to whom they gave the name of Barnabas (4:36). Then in
brackets, some middle ages scribe wrote in, "son of encouragement."
Unfortunately, for clergy who do not know Hebrew, the name
Barnabas means "son of rest." Could it be possible that Luke was
telling us that Barnabas was lazy but the scribe cleaned it up?
Chapter 5 contains one of those stories never mentioned by clergy.
It is the story of Ananias (whom Jehovah has graciously given) and
his wife Sapphira (sapphire). Personally speaking, this is a story
designed to frighten converts into giving money for the support of the
emerging church. Now ask yourself, "does this sound like something
Jesus would do?" Or, "is it something men of power and authority
would do?" Apparently, the couple sold a piece of property and kept
part of the proceeds of the sale from the common church purse.
When they lied to conceal the deed they fell down and died in the
presence of the apostle's court. One can imagine the fear this story
would have put in the hearts of the illiterate in the middle ages. In the

words of Professor Peter Gomes, a good sermon title for this would be, *They Tried, They Lied, They Died*. Can you imagine clergy telling their congregations that unless they gave a full 10% tithe God would strike them dead? The story had its desired effect as Verse 11 states, "and great fear seized the whole church." Remember, at this point they believed Jesus' return was imminent so they could comfortably ask people to give away their possessions..

Luke's liberal witness lends support to the belief that the author of the Gospel of Matthew was a rabbi; "the word of God continued to spread; the number of disciples increased greatly in Jerusalem, and a great many of the priests became obedient to the faith" (Luke 6:7). Please get it out of your mind that all priests and Pharisees were bad. The Christian church started in Jerusalem by devoted Jews who accepted Jesus as the long awaited Messiah. Scripture tells us that many people were in Jerusalem for Pentecost. This was the day when Peter broke forth proclaiming the resurrection of the Lord. To me, this is the true "speaking in tongues" and not the incoherent babbling of holier than thou Christians pretending to be spirit led. Interesting speculation on my part would suggest that it is at this point, Pentecost, that Luke felt God touching his heart. Luke's inquisitive mind may have started searching at that point. Also, I would ask you to consider the reaction of the Jewish authorities who were only interested in their own well being and were willing to do anything to denigrate this emerging sect. As the sect grew, the need for someone like Saul became apparent. Emerging Christianity was not only a threat to the Jewish status quo but to the Romans who were determined to keep the *Pax Romanus*.

Luke does not tell us how he came to Christ, nor does he tell us how he came to be the traveling companion of Saul. Another traveling companion of Saul was Barnabas who also journeyed to Jerusalem with them. Understandably, the Jerusalem disciples were not only suspect of Saul (Acts 9:25-26), as he was the original inquisitor, but did not appreciate him baptizing gentiles who had not been circumcised. It is doubtful if the Apostles ever became comfortable with Saul or his ministry. During this time God was working to open the doors of salvation to all creation. Peter experienced the revelation that he should not call anything God had created unclean, as had become the Jewish practice (Acts 10:14). It is in Chapter 10 that Peter affirms that the gates of salvation are open to everyone. Notice that "doing" is part of the requirement! He proclaims, "I truly understand that God shows no partiality, but in every nation anyone who fears him and does what is right is acceptable to him" (Luke 10:34-35). Take note, our acceptability is via actions. Faith is active, not passive. Luke was a well-educated Greek who had embraced this theology because it was logical. Education and logic go hand in hand. Coupled with God's Holy Spirit working in him, Luke went to great lengths to pass on his witness to all generations.

Now listen to the order in which the following occur. First, Peter testifies that Jesus is the one ordained by God to judge the living and the dead. This is also the place where Christians find justification for doing nothing, "everyone who believes in him receives forgiveness of sins through his name" (Luke 10:43). Anyone who says they believe in Jesus and yet does not obey his commandment to love one another is a hypocrite looking for the easy road to salvation. Any charlatan can take these words and preach them to people who are looking for salvation without having to do anything except profess Christ. Proclaiming Christ must be seen in the context of obedience to the will of God which states that we are to love our neighbour. Maybe you have heard of the German Lutheran who coigned the phrase, "cheap grace?" By definition, "cheap grace is preaching forgiveness without requiring repentance, baptism without church discipline, communion without confession." Cheap grace is, "grace without discipleship, grace without the cross, grace without Jesus Christ, living and incarnate" (Dietrich Bonhoeffer, 1937). After spending more than a year and a half in a Nazi prison for his faith stand against Hitler, Bonhoeffer was executed on April 9, 1945. This happened one day after a short mock trial and one month before the German surrender on May 8, 1945.

Saul had experienced the revelation of Christ in Chapter 9. Chapter 10 speaks of baptizing converts into this new faith. Baptism is a New Testament word. It is not to be found in the Old Testament and was not a Hebrew practice. The Greek words for baptism used in the New Testament have the same meaning "to immerse," or "submerge." Bap-tid-zo (baptized) and Bap-tis-mah (baptism) mean total immersion. Sorry my fellow Presbyterians, we have fallen victim to the Popes' desire to rid Christianity of its Jewish roots by disregarding the God given command to dedicate a new born child on the eighty day. We follow the practice of baptizing someone who is not able to make their own decision for Christ. Baptism for the Roman church was a means of giving illiterate people and infant children something which promised salvation. It also gave the church the power to remove that gift by excommunication. It was a way to guarantee a continual stream of club members. Islam used a different way to build membership. Initially, Mohammed brought Islam to Arabia through war. After his death, Abu Bakr became the first Caliph. Tribesmen had a choice; convert to Islam or have their head cut off. After a few heads were lopped off, the tribes converted. Christianity originally offered a choice. One had to choose to become a Christian. Now, Christianity is a mess because we have baptized every baby, dog, cat and turtle to be found and we still preach salvation to the saved every Sunday. The church has given away Christianity and now wonders why no one wants that which has no value. Cheap grace!

Chapter 11 demonstrates that the disciples were still preaching in synagogues. This new sect had not yet begun to blossom by baptizing believing adults into a faith which was first named "Christian" in Antioch (Acts 11:26). In Chapter 13 we are told that Saul's name was changed to Paul (Acts 13:9). I rather doubt that Saul, or even Luke for that matter, knew his name had been changed. This was an attempt in the middle ages to deny our Jewish origins and heritage. Somehow, I get the impression that Luke was present to witness the dissension among the Jerusalem disciples with regards to Paul's conversion. The disciples, even though they had been commanded to go to every nation (Matthew 28:19) were keeping the newly forming church exclusive. It is after this that we learn that Luke became Saul's traveling companion and recording secretary. Thus far, Luke's writing had been third person omniscient but when the Spirit turned Paul back from going to Bithynia he went to Troas where Paul had a vision of a man from Macedonia pleading with him to come over to Macedonia. Suddenly, in Acts 16:10, there is a very distinguishable change in grammar. Luke writes, of Paul's vision, "**we** immediately tried to cross over to Macedonia, being convinced that God had called **us** to proclaim the good news to them" (Acts 16:10). Luke's sudden change to the terms "we and us" denote first person omniscient.

Somewhere, somehow, Luke became part of Paul's entourage. He does not appear to be called initially to evangelize, but to witness and record. His extensive record is an indication of his continued dedication to the evangelistic efforts of Paul. Luke's witness, in the form of a two volume apology to Theophilus, suggests an access to the upper echelon of Greek society. His work imparts a first hand eye witness account of the Apostles' actions. When you read Luke's witness remember that he not only has an eye for detail, but the ability to record the service of both men and women. Remember also, he is a Greek with many cultural differences. Imagine if you will the same story being told by Hugh Hefner and Jerry Falwell. There would be significant differences in the bias as well as perspective. One can see those differences in the Gospel according to Matthew and the Gospel according to Luke. Matthew writes with a chauvinistic male bias. Luke writes with a liberal bias.

It is interesting to note that Paul required Timothy to be circumcised at this point in his ministry, in order to bring him into the Hebrew covenant (16:3). By this time Paul's followers were many and willing to travel. In Chapter 20 we are introduced to a convert named Tychicus (*Too khee kos*) one of Paul's traveling companions who later wrote/recorded Ephesians. I will speak more of him in Paul's letter to the Ephesians. He was a fervent Christ follower to whom we owe much in terms of his letters written while Paul was under house arrest in Rome. Paul's eyesight was poor and he needed scribes to write his epistles (1 Corinthians 16:21). What is important to realize, is that Paul built the Gentile church under the premise that Christ's return was imminent. Then Paul had to backpedal and admit he did not know when Jesus would return (Hebrews 10:37). Converts today continue to equate their new found salvation with the return of Jesus. Our knowledge of Paul's teaching is limited but a distinct change is noticeable when converts began to die and Jesus has not returned. Paul's letters start to deal with this dilemma.

In Acts 21 Luke's eyewitness account records how the Jews in Jerusalem tried to kill Paul for bringing un-circumcised Greeks into the temple. In Acts 22 Paul tries to explain the wonder of his conversion on the road to Damascus, as well as the bright light that temporarily blinded him. We also learn that Paul had a sister and how her son warned him of the plot to kill him. Paul was taken, under heavy guard, to the governor Felix. After spending a few years in custody Paul, accompanied by Luke, was sent by ship to Rome. Paul's death remains a mystery as does the reason for Luke's failure to record the when and how. It is thought that Paul was put to death by Nero after the great fire in Rome, which was subsequently blamed on the Christians. It is truly a paradox that the followers of Christ thrived under persecution until the Constantinian Shift, when in 313; the Edict of Milan ended the persecution of Christians. In the year 380 the Edict of Thessalonica made Christianity the official religion of the Roman Empire.

The Emperor Constantine needed the support of Christians at the Battle of Milvian Bridge in 312. On looking up to the sun he saw a bright light and a cross bearing the words *In hoc signo vinces* meaning, "by this sign you will conquer." He ordered his army to paint the symbol *Chi-Rho* on their shields and from then on he was victorious. After the shift, Christianity became a prerequisite for a good government job.

Women, who had been a major part of Christian evangelism, were pushed out of the ranks as leaders in favour of men who saw the opportunity for power and advancement in the form of organized religion. Over the course of time, stone buildings came to define the word "church," and the *ekklesia*, the Greek word meaning church was lost. The New Testament meaning of *ekklesia* is, "a public assembly of people gathered for the purpose of worship." As in the Old Testament, God never wanted a building. God wanted to live in the hearts of believers.

Never forget that a significant turning point in the ministry of Jesus was when he walked out of the synagogue in Mark 6:6 (Jesus marveled at their unbelief) and never returned in favour of taking the word of God to the (*ekklesia*) people. One of the problems with Christianity is that we have made the worship of our buildings of uppermost importance, superseding even our faith. Many of our red brick churches are crumbling as die hard Christians hang onto old memories. Monuments constructed to the "Glory of God" have turned into stone synagogues void of the presence of a personal love for God, a reverence for the redeemer and a place to nurture our love for each other. People want to die before they see the death of their church rather than help with their resources.

## Romans

Through the evangelistic efforts of Saul/Paul the Church of Jesus the Christ spread throughout the world. As Paul moved from community to community churches were formed in two ways. First, Paul evangelized in synagogues amongst his own Jewish community. Then he turned his efforts to evangelizing pagans/Gentiles. We do not know what Paul said in order to convert Jew and Gentile into proclaiming Jesus as Lord and then to be baptized. What we do know is that Paul believed Christ was Lord (Adonay), Christ was the redeemer/Messiah; Christ was crucified, dead, buried and after spending three nights in the grave, rose on the third day and now sits at the right hand of God the Father Almighty. When you think about the simple logic of the resurrection statement, it is impossible to rise on the third day without spending three nights in the grave and a dead man cannot raise himself. It takes a second party.

Most Christians do not realize that the books of the New Testament do not appear in order of writing. Scholars are still debating the dates of writing for both the Gospels and Epistles. Marcus Borg lists the

Pauline books in this order and written between 48 and 58 AD: 1Thesselonians, Galatians, 1 Corinthians, Philemon, Philippians, 2 Corinthians and Romans. Although many Epistles claim Pauline authorship the above seven letters are universally agreed upon as being truly Pauline. When a letter speaks of an event or situation beyond Paul's death in Rome it could not have been written by him.

Remember that persecutions were on the increase and the Jewish people were trying to separate themselves from this new Christ movement growing within the synagogues. Also, the disciple Peter was executed in Rome in the year 64. As I have mentioned, people believed Jesus would return before the disciples died. As many of the faithful began to die, literate converts began to record witness stories and expand on Paul's letters. The Qur'an was constructed in a similar manner. Mohamed did not write anything. All of the Surah's come from friends, relatives, servants and enemies, all professing to remember the messages Mohamed said god passed on to him. Unlike the gospels, many Surahs's satisfied the needs of Mohamed at the time and the desires of all the future witnesses.

The dates of New Testament writings are still in hot scholarly dispute. Those who place Luke's authorship after the destruction of the temple in the year 70 AD are wrong. The writing of Mark's gospel was approximately 65 AD. Some believe that the Epistle of James precedes Paul's letters. I believe the Johannian writings to be 70 years after the crucifixion of Jesus (year 100) and that John could not possibly have lived that long. His writings are drug induced inspiration.

Not unlike Christians of today, evangelists focus on desire. This is not to cast dispersion upon scripture but to help us understand how the differences impact our understanding. Nothing can ever dispute the overriding message of love conveyed by Christ. Galatians 5:14, love thy neighbour, is a key passage illustrating how Paul understood the person of Christ, the son of God. The Old Testament is a multiple voice witness of God at work in the world with people chosen to be holy. God had been at work for some time before speaking to Abram. Possibly, the flood story represents the net end result of people living in un-redeemable sin; I do not know. What I do feel is that Christ came to clean the cob webs, so to speak, out of the Old Testament. Christ brought the message of love and redemption to all who would listen. The message seems so simple, "love one another." I am convinced that the only true message from the living God is the message of love.

Any religion that turns brother against brother is not of the Father. Imagine the lunacy of listening to a theology which teaches its adherents that the way to attain eternal life in paradise is to bomb and mass murder innocent human beings? Listen to Paul's words, "I am not ashamed of the gospel; it is the power of God for salvation to everyone who has faith, to the Jew first and also the Greek, for in it the righteousness of God is revealed through faith" (Romans 1:16-17). Which teaching is from God and which teaching is from a perverted man; the one that teaches love or the one that promotes death?

As you read Paul's letters you cannot help but get the impression that he knows it all. This is not to deny the truth of his witness, but to say he injects his own perspective. Early in my study of scripture I came to call him "know-it-all Paul." He was a Pharisee, the son of a Pharisee (Acts 23:6). Paul boasted that, "it is we who are the circumcision, who worship in the Spirit of God and boast in Christ Jesus and have no confidence in the flesh even though I, too, have reason for confidence in the flesh. If anyone else has reason to be confident in the flesh, I have more: circumcised on the eighth day, a member of the people of Israel, of the tribe of Benjamin, a Hebrew born of Hebrews; as to the law, a Pharisee; as to zeal, a persecutor of the church; as to righteousness under the law, blameless" (Philippians 3:3-6).

As Paul endeavoured to convince the Jerusalem disciples that he was an Apostle, he stated that he was born [prematurely] in time. A non-canonical book called *The Acts of Paul and Thecla* describes Paul as being of small size, bald, bow-legged, a large hooked nose with one Cro-Magnon eyebrow across his forehead. These personal features are reminiscent of Socrates. Neither man was attracted to the opposite sex. Paul was very vocal in his monogamous belief as well as his condemnation of homosexuality and prostitution (1 Corinthians 6:9). He was the perfect choice to pursue and persecute pesky Christians. Then, on the road to Damascus, Jesus himself had to stop the carnage Paul would have inflicted on the emerging church. Never forget, that like the inquisition, there have always been psychopathic little churchmen willing to torture innocent people in order to get an ecstatic orgasm. This is not an effort to discredit Paul's ministry. Rather, to give an understanding of his background prior to his conversion. What Paul became does not change. What he was going to do does change. Paul converted Greeks, Romans and Jews to Christianity. Like Christ, Paul does not endeavour to change the law but to move condemnation under the law to redemptive forgiveness in the law of love. Make no mistake, in Paul's eyes there is a definite difference between salvation and damnation. People are rewarded according to their deeds, not words (Romans 2:4-11).

Chapter 3 brings us to one of the most misunderstood passages by penny-pinching Christians who think that just coming to church and sitting in the pew is good enough. Paul speaks of "works prescribed by the law," and it is necessary to separate works of the law from good works. Works of the law deal with Hebrew dietary laws, travelling on the Sabbath as well as contact with Gentiles, etc. Good works involve deeds that demonstrate love for your neighbour. Whether or not Paul says "works of the law" or simply "works," they are one in the same. He is speaking in terms of his legalistic background in the law. The Book of James speaks directly to the misunderstanding of the relationship of salvation and works. Good works is a misunderstanding penny-pinching Christians love to cherish. Again, all of Paul's references to the word "works" are in the context of "works of the law." The Bible promotes good works.

One of the problems with taking a specific verse out of scripture and building a theology upon that verse is that the general context is lost. This has happened with Paul's beautiful verses of faith that teach us, "if thou shalt confess with thy mouth the Lord Jesus, and believe in thine heart that God hath raised him from the dead, thou shalt be saved. For with the heart man believeth unto righteousness; and with the mouth confession is made unto salvation. For there is no difference between the Jew and the Greek: for the same Lord over all is rich unto all that call upon him. For whosoever shall call upon the name of the Lord shall be saved" (Romans 10:9-13). However true, the fact remains that it is Paul's statement of faith. As such it cannot be taken as an all encompassing guarantee of salvation. The reality of James 2:17-20 must be evident as simple words of the mouth cost nothing. Also, the most hated story in the Gospels is the Matthew 25 eyewitness story of the sheep and the goats. These are the harsh words of Jesus. Passively professing Christ is not the way to salvation. Faith is not a passive verb, it is an active verb. Loving your neighbour is the way to salvation. Professing the name of Jesus is the first step. Living that profession requires Christians to do more than warm a pew for six or seven decades.

I have always enjoyed listening to Pastor John Hagee who speaks to Christians as if they were in the army of Christ. He feels that too many Christians spend their lives in boot camp wanting more and more training but never leave camp. He once said, speaking of Christians that only want to spend time in Bible studies and not do any thing else, "its time to get out of the diaper division and into army of Christ." This is what Paul was talking about; actively bring the witness of Christ to the Gentiles. People are to live according to all the teachings of Jesus, not sit in a comfortable pew forever singing happy clappy songs of empty faith. The church has never been built from inside a building but rather on the highways and byways of life. I would note also that in Romans 16:1 Paul commends "our sister Phoebe, a deacon" saying, "welcome her in the Lord as fitting for the saints." The word deacon (diakonos) is not gender specific; it is a title for the office of minister. As I have said, the church of Christ was built by the faithful service and martyrdom of men and women equally. After the Constantinian turn, men desiring power and authority said, [step aside ladies, there is power to be had and money to be made].

Paul's Epistle to the Romans could well have been his last letter even though it was written by his disciple Tertius (third) and the greetings in Chapter 16 may have been to the friends of Tertius. It is difficult to understand some names on the list as they seem strange to me. For example, in verse 11 Narcissus means "stupidity" as in narcotic. In verse 12 both names are feminine; Tryphena (luxurious) and Tryphosa (luxuriating) make me wonder just what is being said. Persis means a "Persian woman." And so, Paul's letter to the Romans ends. He is in prison awaiting execution. Tired and significantly blind, having to rely on disciples to write his letters, he leaves us a legacy of evangelism, suffering and courage. The sixty six books of the Bible are still a mystery wrapped in an enigma. The Old Testament has many authors writing from different perspectives and traditions. The New Testament is also a collection of eyewitness accounts and inspirational stories with an agenda. The synoptic gospels are eyewitness accounts of the life and purpose of the Messiah. Johannian theology struggles to prove the divinity of Christ. Pauline theology records the evangelistic efforts of a devout Jew who encountered the resurrected Messiah. The other letters deal with all the trials, tribulations and misunderstandings within a growing Christian community. The bottom line to all sixty-six books comes from Jesus himself when he said, to love one another. Jesus was reiterating God's command in Leviticus 19:18. Love for one another is always conjoined to our love for God. Read the following and you will get the picture.

Matthew 22:39 - Mark 12:31 - Romans 13:8 - 1Thessalonians 4:9 - 1 Peter 1:22

1 John 3:11, 3:23, 4:7, 4:11 and 2 John 1:5.

Predestination

Read Romans 8:29-30 and Ephesians 1:5 and 1:11. In a word, nonsense!

Predestination means that God has already determined that you will be saved or will go to hell. It also means that God has decided if you will be rich or poor, sick or healthy. Leros! If this were true, then evangelism under this Pauline/Calvinistic concept is a waste of time. After all, what is the point of professing salvation through Christ? What is the point in repenting if you are predestined to rot in hell? Calvin's double predestination would teach that any effort to save a sinner is contrary to God's plan for the individual's life and therefore would be opposing God. Know it all Paul got it wrong when he used the word predestined to describe his calling. It suggests that it was God's plan that Paul murder and torture people so that he could be converted on the road to Damascus. Predestination can only be understood in the general sense that God has predestined those who are redeemable to inherit eternal life. Paul knew he was saved and therefore destined for ethereal mansions.

# 1 Corinthians

Even though some scholars question Paul's authorship of 1 Corinthians the sentence structure demonstrates the same emphatic desire to be recognized as an Apostle as did the opening of Romans, i.e., one who has been commissioned by Jesus himself.

Romans 1:1
*Paulos doulos Iesous Christos kletos apostolos.*
Paul, a servant of Jesus Christ, called to be an Apostle.

1 Corinthians 1:1
*Paulos kletos apostolos Iesous Christos deeah thelema Thelos.*
Paul, called to be an Apostle of Christ Jesus by the will of God.

You will notice also that in 1 Corinthians and 2 Corinthians the introduction becomes even more compelling in that Paul adds *deeah thelema Thelos* "by the will of God". The introductions now read, "Paul, called to be an Apostle of Christ Jesus by the will of God." It is doubtful if the Jerusalem disciples were ever fully convinced of his calling. Peter and Philip definitely had problems trying to convince the Jerusalem disciples that Jesus died for all of creation, not just the chosen few. Consider, if you will, the number of denominations that believe their little club is the chosen club.

1 Corinthians is a beautiful witness, but be careful not to be drawn into a fundamentalist mind set. While I am not disputing Paul's Christology, be careful not to mistake Christ reverence for Christ worship. There is a difference. We revere Christ, we praise Christ for what he has done, but we worship God. We pray to God through Christ. Paul understands the dichotomy between Christ and God. To him, Jesus is the Son who sits on the right hand of God the Father. These words are definite; "if ye then be raised with Christ, seek those things which are above, where Christ sits on the right hand of God" (Colossians 3:1). Jesus is not God; he is our advocate before the eternal Judge. Having said this, the first chapters deal with Paul's rules and judgments. Don't forget, once a lawyer, always a lawyer.

You will notice Paul's fixation with sex and sexual immorality in Chapter 5. Paul must have been the prototype for the movies "The Forty Year Old Virgin." To be polite, Paul was trying to evangelize people who were the modern day equivalents of those who are "sexually liberated." Religious celebrations were all similar in that the lean meat, the beef or lamb, was not wasted. The entrails were burned and the meat was roasted. The people, all the people, had meat to eat, wine to drink, and what irked Paul, was people enjoying free sex. Even today, festive celebrations in New Orleans, Rio de Janeiro, Nassau and many other places are huge, colourful, noisy and raunchy celebrations culminating in sex with as many of the celebrants as possible. Understanding the culture of the time and the nature of worship will enable you to understand what monogamous Paul was up against.

In Chapter 7 Paul gives the attentive reader insight into the sexual practices of the Gentile communities. He condemns sexual immorality [by telling future Baptists that sex will lead to dancing] and that it is good to abstain from sex for a while in order to pray. Paul goes on to talk about separation and divorce. He tells widows to remain unmarried, as he is, but if they cannot control the urge, they should marry. Finally, at verse 7:25 Paul admits he is out of his league when he says, "now concerning virgins, I have no command of the Lord, but I give my opinion"… [don't enjoy sex]. Even though Paul remained a virgin he did have some insight into marriage when he said, "those who marry will experience distress in this life, and I would spare you that" (1 Corinthians 7:28). Is it any wonder I call him "know it all Paul?"

The beginning of Chapter 9 reveals more of Paul's desire to be accepted as an Apostle when he asks, "am I not an Apostle? Have I not seen Jesus our Lord? Are you not my work in the Lord? If I am not an Apostle to others, at least I am to you, for you are the seal of my Apostleship in the Lord." This is followed by what sounds like righteous belly-aching. I point this out not to discredit scripture but to show the humanity of his witnesses. For centuries God has had an ongoing relationship with humanity and the Bible is our witness. In all our sin and transgressions the Bible records the ongoing struggle God endures in order to save those who are redeemable. The Christian notion that there is nothing we can do to obtain salvation is nonsense. The individual makes the decision to repent. The individual makes the decision to love their neighbour. The individual makes the decision to help the less fortunate. People who rush to the bedside of the dying, or the heinous prisoner who is about to be executed, are wasting their time. The words of Ecclesiastes 12 make a definitive statement, "remember now thy creator in the days of thy youth" suggesting that grasping at straws is a waste of time. If you think that making a death bed confession, after living a life of sin, will gain you salvation then you are dumber than a box of rocks.

Soliciting these kinds of confessions only make the do-good-er feel like they have done something worthwhile. Ecclesiastes 12:1 does not instruct us to wait until the last minute and then only confess Jesus to appease those who peddle cheap grace. After all, confessing Jesus will shut them up.

In Chapter 12 Paul moves to speaking of spiritual gifts. God not only blessed humanity with mental, physical and creative gifts, God also blessed humans with spiritual gifts. Something as simple as a kind word, a heart felt hug at the right time, an unexpected act of kindness, are gifts we can all share. These gifts are given to everyone, not just Christians. A child of God who understands compassion will use their gifts accordingly. Paul was skeptical with regards to the gift of speaking in tongues. Possibly, he had a hard time believing that mindless incoherent babbling was a gift. Modern day Christians still try to impress others with this mindless form of prattle. Remember, Paul had met Jesus and if anyone should have been able to speak in tongues, or at least interpret the speaking, it would have been Paul.

1 Corinthians, Chapters 12 to 14 are the only places Paul deals with tongues. In short, Paul said [if no one is there to interpret, keep the mindless babbling to you]. What on earth is the sense of speaking incomprehensible rubbish if no one can understand it? People love to lift themselves higher than other Christian by pretending they are uttering messages from the angels. True speaking in tongues happened during the first Pentecost. When Peter spoke, everyone could understand his speech in their native language. Get it! Speaking in tongues is for understanding, not self-gratification. Read the beginning of Chapter 14. Paul forbids speaking in tongues. He is saying, [what is the point when no one can understand the babbling?]

The beautiful love poem of Chapter 13 is a continuation of spiritual gifts. Unfortunately, even the early Christians took the gifts too far and out of context. Imagine Paul speaking to Christians who were trying to out-do each other. The new Christians were bragging about who had the greatest gift. Paul dealt with these individual gifts by way of analogy to the human body and how all the parts work together in harmony. He opened the poem with a direct response to speaking in tongues. He says, "if I speak in the tongues of mortals and of angels, but do not have love, I am a noisy gong or clanging symbol." In a nutshell, the whole point of the "Word of God" is to teach us to "love." The greatest of all gifts is love. It doesn't matter how many times people hear the 1 Corinthians 13 there are still those who are hateful, talk spitefully behind the backs of friends, and refuse to stop acting like school children.

Paul did not write this passage for use at weddings. However, the passage is fitting for young adults about to commit to a life together. It is a lovely passage and yet, in my opinion, the most important verse is often mistranslated. I am referring to verse 13:13, which is the faith, hope and charity passage. This passage is typically translated two ways.

1. And now abide faith, hope, charity, these three; but the greatest of these is charity;
2. And now abide faith, hope, love, these three; but the greatest of these is love.

The Greek from which this is translated is *de nuni mino pistis elpis agape tauta treis de meizon touton agape*. Translators get hung up on the word *agape*, which can be translated as love or charity. Consider, if you will, the context of the whole passage and Paul's teaching on love. This is the "love is….." passage and Paul names many attributes of love, one of which is the condition that "love never ends" (13:8). The key to the passage is not *agape*. The key is the two forms of "these" *tauta* and *touton*. These three is translated from *tauta treis* (these three). The greatest of these is translated from *meizon touton* (of these). The demonstrative adjective "these" is the key. "These three" (*tauta treis*) denotes the nominative or accusative case. However, "the greatest of these" (*meizon touton*) denotes the genitive case plural masculine. This means there is a change in relationship. The words *tauta treis* denote three separate entities. The words (*meizon touton*) denote the three are grouped collectively as one unit. Paul is not saying "the greater **one** of these three." He is saying of the collective body there is a greater virtue, which is love.

To my way of understanding this passage, it should read, "and now abide faith, hope, charity, these three, but the greatest of these three (the collective) is love." This is the love poem. The greatest single virtue of all the gifts a Christian can possess is love. Love is the foundation upon which faith, hope and charity set us apart as children of God. Love is the foundation of all the gifts of the spirit in Chapter 12. Always remember, God has faith in humanity, hope for human salvation and a charity of understanding of human sinful ways. God's desire is that men and women learn to love each other (agape).

Ironically, a strong male bias shines through in verses 34-36. Briefly it says, "it is a shame for women to speak in church… and if a woman has a question she is to wait until she gets home to ask her husband" (1 Corinthians 14:34-36). If you have a Bible that has been properly translated it will show these verses in brackets. Brackets mean the verse is a scribal addition and not in the original manuscripts. Fundamentalists thrive on verses corrupted with male bias. It allows them to treat women like possessions.

Paul went on to ask the people the age-old question regarding life. He said, "if the dead are not raised, let us eat and drink, for tomorrow we die" (1 Corinthians 15:32). Now think about the immorality he was speaking against. Promiscuous couples would start to think about what they were doing. God ordained marriage between a man and a woman. Any other kind of union, bestiality, orgy, was not in God's plan for *iysh* and *ishshah* (man and woman). Humans live in the flesh but flesh does not inherit the kingdom of God. Before Paul closed his letter he made the statement the Hebrew people had been waiting for, "death has been swallowed up in victory" (1 Corinthians 15:54).

If we had the original manuscript written to the Corinthians we would see a definite change in hand writing as Paul wrote, "this salutation I now write with my own hand." It becomes obvious, through reading the Pauline letters, that the Apostle has surrounded himself with educated people. In that era the educated represented a minority of the population.

## 2 Corinthians

The opening of 2 Corinthians indicates a strong emphasis on the dichotomy of the trinity. Paul does not consider the trinity to be monogamous. God is God. The Spirit is the Spirit and the Son is the Son. In verse 4:14 Paul's understanding is clear; "the one who raised the Lord Jesus will raise us also with Jesus." Paul affirms in verse 5:16 the humanity of Christ but as Christ is now a new creation so we too will be a new creation. These analogies serve as evidence of God's desire to reconcile creation through Christ. In these passages we get a clear understanding of the man who lived as a human so that, in his divine person could present the redeemable before the Father.

Fundamentalists use verse 6:14 to justify segregation from a sinful society. They fail to realize that Paul felt Jesus' return was imminent so converts needed to separate themselves from those who preferred to live in sin. Paul was concerned for the welfare of new converts who might return to the old cultural practices. To think that Paul was teaching Christians to forever segregate themselves from society it totally incorrect. That kind of philosophy allows people like Charles Manson, David Koresh, and Jim Jones, to justify their actions by quoting a single passage of scripture. By isolating specific verses, taking them out of context, (cherry picking) a sociopath can justify murder, incest, rape, wife abuse, slavery and so on. This is not the intended use of "God's Word." Any teaching that directs an individual to harm or suppress others is not from God or his Son Jesus.

From time to time Christian clergy will become frustrated, as was Paul. Chapter 10 demonstrates some of Paul's belly-aching and boasting. It not only demonstrates Paul's humanity but also the reason the church made him a saint after he died. Historically, God has demonstrated the ability to turn human weakness into strength. Paul understands God's ability to use human weakness. It makes me wonder about those who say God has called them to be strong in terms of dominance, power and force. As Paul closes 2 Corinthians he is still teaching that Jesus will come in their lifetime and by the sounds of the letter he has invested much time and effort in their Christian community.

## Galatians

As was his custom, Paul's letter to the Galatians opens with the statement "I am an Apostle." Galatians gives the reader insight into the many unfaithful new converts. Frustrated with their backsliding, Paul makes a emphatic statement with regards to the message he has been commissioned to bring to the world. He states, "the gospel that was proclaimed by me is not of human origin; I did not receive it from human sources, nor was I taught it, but I received it through a revelation of Jesus Christ" (Galatians 1:11-12). This was a very harmful statement as many whackos now claim that their uneducated minds have been filled with God's word. Even though they only know a few verses of scripture they claim everything is a revaluation from God. Leros!

Paul also mentions seeing James (Jacob) the brother of Jesus. This has always seemed strange to me as, of the forty-two times the name James is used in the New Testament, this is the only reference to a James as the brother of Jesus. Leros! Greek translations for the noun James give several choices and only one choice suggests that this James is the half brother of Jesus and why half brother? Did Jesus not have whole brothers? Did Mary or Joseph die unbeknown to the disciples? Heaven only knows where that choice comes from as it would necessitate Mary's death and Joseph's remarriage, all of which are doubtful. This is also the only statement in scripture that indicates a relative of Jesus became involved in his ministry. Also, the way the statement is added into the text makes is suspect to the addition coming from a Middle Ages scribe who manipulated the statement from "James, a brother (adelphos) in the Lord."

Two observations with regards to Galatians 1:9 are, one, Paul calls this James an Apostle. Jesus' family did not believe or follow him and Jesus' brother was not one of the Apostles. Two, kuruis (Lord) and adelphos (brother) suggest this James was a fellow believer and more than likely the brother of John. These are the kinds of mis-translations the Roman church used to try to substantiate their truth of the gospels.

This passage also gives a time line to Paul's travels as he had been traveling in Arabia, possibly as far as Medina, which would take a substantial amount of time. Paul returned to Damascus after his sojourn in the south. He stayed there for three years then traveled to Jerusalem to visit Cephas (rock) who was building the Christ church in Judea. He then traveled to Syria evangelizing for fourteen years before returning to Jerusalem again.

In Chapter 3 Paul discusses the promise to Abraham in conjunction with the law that came hundreds of years later. As it was then, it is today, Christians and Jews live by faith. We are both heirs. Christians now have an inheritance in God's promise to Abraham as there is "no longer Jew or Greek... slaves or free... male or female; for all are one in Christ... heirs according to the promise" (Galatians 3:28-29). Christians have not replaced the chosen people. Paul's understanding of the person of Jesus comes in the form of an explanation that, "in the fullness of time God sent his Son, born of a woman, born under the law, so that we (Gentiles) might receive adoption as children" (Ibid., 4:4-5). Notice that Paul expresses the same theological perspective as the writer of Matthew, "that Jesus was born under the law." Luke is wrong in saying Jesus was illegitimate.

Of particular interest to Christians is the Christological imperative to love one another. As mentioned previously, it is not an accident that sentences have the same structure in the Greek language. Sentences with the same structure are usually copied. Paul writes in Galatians 5:14 "thou shalt love thy neighbour as yourself." Paul records the words of Jesus verbatim as they are recorded in Mark 12:31, Matthew 22:39 and almost verbatim in Luke 10:27 "and thy neighbour as thyself." Christians can believe what they want but "the whole law is summed up in a single commandment - "you shall love your neighbour as yourself." Like it or not, the people you criticize for not attending church may in fact be the sheep that inherit the kingdom of God. Please read again verses 5:19-21 to see who "will not" inherit the kingdom of God.

It is doubtful that Paul wrote the whole letter or just the closing. In verse 6:11 he writes, "see what large letters I make when I am writing in my own hand." This could also be a way of ensuring that others did not pass contradictory letters off in his name. In closing, Paul gave birth to an erroneous belief of punishing the body, self flagellation, were desired practices for Christ followers. The remark, "for I carry the marks of Jesus branded on my body," led to many disgusting practices in the church (Galatians 6:17). The only command ever issued by Jesus was, "to love one another."

## Ephesians

Once again, Paul differentiates between God and Jesus. In verse 1:17 he states "that the God of our Lord Jesus Christ... may give you the spirit." Also, the grammar in Paul's letter to the Ephesians is significantly different than his other letters which make me suspect that notes were taken by Tychicus and the letter written at a later time. It is a letter of encouragement as well as a plea for the people to denounce their pagan ways. The first part of the letter would have ended at verse 3:21, with the second part beginning at Chapter 4 as the theme shifts to unity and spirit. Recalling Psalm 133:1 Paul writes how David sang "how good it was for brethren to dwell together in unity." The word unity is only used three times in scripture, once in Psalms and twice in Ephesians, verses 4:3 and 4:13.

I think there were three primary reasons Jesus revealed himself to Paul. First, was to stop the authorized persecution of Jews who turned to Christianity. Remember, evangelism started in the synagogues, not with the gentiles. Second, Paul was free from marriage and able to travel in order to bring the gospel to the Gentiles. Third, his capability to evangelize stemmed from his complete understanding of the law and the prophets. Ephesians 4 demonstrates this understanding of God's will for all humanity. Listen to the beautiful way in which Tychicus expresses God's desire, "I... beg you to lead a life worthy of the calling to which you have been called, with all humility and gentleness, with patience, bearing with one another in love, making every effort to maintain the unity of the Spirit in the bond of peace."

For those of differing religious faiths, compare the above with the teaching of your faith. Inasmuch as Christians and Jews call the creator of the universe "Father," ask yourself, would a father ask his children to mindlessly murder each other? Part of the teaching in the Old Testament and the New Testament, reveals what happens when creation/men try to impose their interpretation of God's desire on others. These interpretations have always led to murder, mayhem, and war. These interpretations have always led to a struggle for power, despotic authority and riches. Ephesians, Chapter 4, is the perfect verse to hold in juxtaposition to Matthew 25; the sheep and the goats. This letter is not just about a Christian household, it is about the Kingdom of God.

Sadly, male bias demonstrates how the removal of one word in a translation can change the whole context of a passage. I have mentioned that Paul was abhorred with the sexual promiscuity of the Ephesians. He laboured long and hard to promote monogamous relationships in marriage. You will notice how the removal of the word *idios* (own) from the 5:22 passage changes the context from reciprocal relationship to the making of a woman into a slave who is nothing more than a chattel.

Ephesians 5:22 reads:

| Greek | *Gune* | *hupotasso* | *idios* | *aner* | *hos* | *Kurios.* |
|---|---|---|---|---|---|---|
| Transliteration | Wife | subordinate | own | husband | like | Lord. |
| Translation | Wives, submit yourselves unto your own husbands, as unto the Lord. | | | | | |

As in the Hebrew language, the Greek language has certain connotations to a variety of words. The Greek *"aner,"* meaning "husband" has a sexual connotation to it. Although the passage goes on to establish the husband as the head of the household in the decision making capacity, it does not support the idea that a wife is a slave, a chattel, or to be abused at the will of the husband. I point this out as men have used this passage incorrectly to subordinate the woman. The premise of this passage draws a parallel to Christ's relationship to creation as being similar to that of a man's relationship with his wife. The man is not called to lead by force, but lead with wisdom, as Christ leads with wisdom. If you belong to a denomination that uses a translation which leaves out the word *idios* (own) then you should find another denomination. Unconditional female submission is a load of male Leros. Christ is the "shepherd" who is responsible for the welfare of the flock just as the husband is responsible for the welfare of the family.

In the 1950s I was in my formative years. It was a time when the word divorce was almost never heard. If a woman walked into a police station with a black eye and swollen lip, she would have been told "to learn to keep her mouth shut." In a culture where human rights have been won at the cost of countless thousands of lives, do we in North America really want to let a false religion divide humanity in two, making a superior male class and an inferior female class distinction in God's creation? Remember, in Genesis 1:27 there is not such distinction in male or female or skin colour; "so God created man in his own image, in the image of God created he him; male and female created he them." Less than a generation ago an individual's rights and freedom were determined by skin colour. Humanity is getting better but it is a long slow process.

Paul is a product of his environment and upbringing. As such, he does not think to upset the status quo. He leaves that for future generations who are to grow in the unity of the Spirit and the love of God. Suffice to say, the Letter to the Ephesians tries to bring standards into a culture that has lost all morals and ethics. In doing so, Paul paints a portrait of a Christian family, a Christian community, and a Christian country who revere God as King. Who says that Christian ethics do not belong in government? Canada has lost the benefits of Christian ethics because politicians would sell their own mothers to buy a vote. You cannot unify a county by having two differing moral standards with equal rights and authority. I also believe you cannot unify a country by having two official languages. Politicians need to go back to school as you cannot divide one by two and get a whole. You get two halves.

## Philippians

This is one of Paul's prison letters which demonstrates Middle Ages shaping. The opening verse, 1:1 is directed to the church, to the overseers and the deacons. The Greek word for Bishop is *episcopos* (masculine) and the word for Deacon is *diakonos* (gender neutral). These words would have been unknown during Paul's life. They were substituted for "overseer" and "servant" as the Greek Church grew in form and structure. In this letter, Paul repeats several of his exhortations and boasts. He ends with commending the new church for their gifts of support.

## Colossians

As in previous letters, Paul opens with, "Paul, an Apostle of Christ Jesus by the will of God." It is noticeably different than Philippians where he says that he is a servant. Verse 3:17 again demonstrates Paul's understanding of the person of Christ, saying, "whatever you do, in word or deed, do everything in the name of the Lord Jesus, giving thanks to God the Father through him." This is how Christians pray. We pray to God in the name of Jesus our redeemer. This is in accordance with Jesus' words, "ask in my name" (John 14:13). Here again, Paul's instruction is echoed in verse 3:18, "wives, be subject to your **own** husbands."

Tychicus appears to be the messenger carrying this letter to the Colossians but that is in dispute even though much of the letter resembles the Letter to the Ephesians. Verse 4:18 says that Paul has written the salutation with his own hand but it is uncharacteristically short. Nonetheless, the letter is Pauline in nature.

## 1 Thessalonians

This is one of Paul's early letters, c. 45, preparing the people for the Kingdom of God. It should be noted that "the Kingdom of God" is a New Testament theme mentioned in sixty eight verses. Kingdom of God, Jubilee, love one another, are the overriding messages in scripture. The Kingdom of God is God's paradise and one does not get into paradise by murdering others. Like those of the Greek Orthodox faith, I do not try to explain the how and why of our sojourn on earth. I simply marvel at the fact that paradise awaits those who obey God's command to love one another.

Previously, I had explained the night/day order in the Hebrew context. Paul demonstrates this in his writing as all of his references to any given day are noted as "night and day." (Verses 2:9 and 3:10) On the other hand, Greeks, like Luke, (Acts 9:24 and 26:7) use the same terminology as we do and say, "day and night." I have also stated that Paul initially preached that Jesus would return while the converts were still alive. In 1 Thessalonians 4:13 Paul must back pedal to explain this inaccuracy. First of all, he refers to those who have died as being asleep (*koimao*). Then, in verses 4:13-18 he explains that when Jesus does come, and the archangel's call with the sound of God's trumpet, those asleep in Christ will rise to heaven first and then those who are still alive. The people are told that God will come like a thief in the night. In other words, no one knows. Those who make a living on end times prophesy are no more than thieves in the day. Again, Paul reiterates the teachings of Christ in 5:12-22. Read it as though Jesus were talking to you.

## 2 Thessalonians

This letter gives insight into the growing concern as to the time of Jesus' coming. In Chapter 2 Paul is trying to calm those who are shaken and alarmed by "other letters," not from Paul that say the day of the Lord is already here. The Church of Christ has always had to withstand the lies of Satan (the one who opposes). This short letter admonishes the people to keep the faith and live in imitation of his disciples.

# 1 Timothy

In this letter Paul explains that, "the law is laid down not for the innocent but for the lawless... for the unholy and profane, for those who kill their father and mother, for murderers, fornicators, sodomites, slave traders, liars, perjurers (1 Timothy 1:8-11). Paul acknowledges himself to have been a sinner with his blaspheming ways, with his persecutions which lead to death, but then affirms that, "Christ Jesus came into the world to save sinners" (Ibid, 1:15). Chapter 1 ends with the reason sinners are cast out of the community. Hymenaeus (belonging in marriage) and Alexander (man defender) are "turned over to Satan (adversary) so that they may learn not to blaspheme" (Ibid, 1:20).

One of the strongest statements of the person of Christ comes in 2:5, where Paul specifically declares, "there is one God; there is also one mediator between God and humankind, Christ Jesus, himself human, who gave himself a ransom for all." Ironically, the Roman church burnt people who were in agreement with this statement. The writer of the Gospel of John did nothing more than inflict pain and suffering into society for two thousand years by his delusion of grandeur in suggesting that Jesus was Yehovah.

Paul's moral perspective demonstrates his belief that officers, male and female, of the church should "be above reproach, married only once" (Ibid, 3:2 and 3:12). The Roman church invented the nonsense of celibacy for priests and nuns. It was nothing more than a money grab. Up until the middle ages priest married and so did Popes. The problem for the Roman church was that the children of those marriages inherited all the gifts and property given to the priests. Rome wanted everything so they instituted celibacy (Pope Gregory – 1079) which eventually made them one of the richest corporations in the world. Unfortunately, papal law could not suppress human sexual desires so priests took to violating boys. After all, girls would get pregnant and expose their priestly sin. (Some groups still adhered to the Old Testament practice of providing proof of virginity before marriage.) Priestly child abuse is one of those "sins unto death" which means those priest will all rot in hell. There will be no mercy for men who abuse children. For all those who have abused children, remember the millstone, it will be better than the punishment awaiting you.

I have affectionately made reference to "know it all Paul." In Chapter 6 his famous quote, "the love of money is the root of all evil" has proved to be true for two thousand years. In closing, Paul speaks to the "do nothing Christians" who feel just sitting in a pew singing happy clappy songs is the way to inherit eternal life. Verse 6:18 states that, "they are to do good, to be rich in good works, generous, and ready to share." Think about the people in your church. Think about yourself. Are you a sheep, or are you a goat? With what good works will you stand in judgment?

# 2 Timothy

In this second letter, Paul affirms that he is an Apostle and lifts up the name of Onesiphorus (profitable) for his acts of kindness and service in Ephesus. Although this letter is thought to have been written c. 100 it still addresses the issue of the coming of Jesus. In poetic form verse 2:11-13 reaffirms that,

> "if we have died with him, we will also live with him;
> if we endure, we will also reign with him;
> if we deny him, he will also deny us;
> if we are faithless, he remains faithful."

Christians are warned against "wrangling over words which do no good." Our several thousand Christian denominations are proof of the wisdom of this statement. Paul's male chauvinism is exposed again in verse 3:6 when speaking of people to avoid he says, "among them are those who make their way into households and captivate silly women."

Part of the reason for writing this book stems from Paul's prophesy that, "the time is coming when people will not put up with sound doctrine, but having itching ears, they will accumulate for themselves teaching to suit their own desires" (2 Timothy 4:3). The Christian church has had enough of the teachings to suit denominational desires. Chapter 4 finishes on a note of melancholy as Paul laments as one "who has longed for his [Jesus] appearing" (Ibid, 4:8). Ironically, Paul speaks contrary to the Christian concept of mindless forgiveness when he reminds people of the great harm Alexander the coppersmith inflicted upon him. We do not know exactly what Alexander did but he appears to have turned against Paul and his disciples and possibly testified against him in court. Nonetheless, Paul does not forgive him but tells his followers that "the Lord will pay him back for his deeds" (Ibid, 4:14). I think the whole community must have feared Alexander as verse 4:16 reveals that, "at my first defense no one came to my support, but all deserted me." Paul closes with an affirmation that Jesus will rescue him and save him for his heavenly kingdom.

## Titus

Once again Paul's opening affirmation is that he is an Apostle. He becomes vicious in his condemnation of Cretans saying that one of their own prophets said, "Cretans are always liars, vicious brutes, lazy gluttons" (Titus 1:21). Chapter 2 is still speaking to the customary sexual promiscuity which Paul abhors. He also directs the church to devote themselves to good works and to avoid stupid controversies. If people will not listen to reason, then, "after a first and second admonition have nothing more to do with anyone who causes divisions" (Ibid. 3:10). We see that Tychicus is working ceaselessly as Paul's messenger. In closing Paul continues to encourage the people "to devote themselves to good works" (Ibid. 3:14). Paul understands that a byproduct of the knowledge of salvation is the act of responding with acts of good works. Good works are a joyful act and reaction to the gift of salvation.

## Philemon

Paul is in prison, the end is near, and he writes with his own hand a note of encouragement to the house church of Philemon (one who kisses). He confesses keeping their slave Onesimus (useful) near him during his imprisonment. Confident that Jesus will not let him die in Rome without first seeing his return Paul asks that Philemon "prepare a guest room for me, for I am hoping through your prayers to be restored to you" (Philemon 1:22). It is interesting as well that Philemon mentions Luke or Lucas, both meaning "light-giving." It cannot be certain that the Luke/Lucas mentioned in 2 Corinthians 13:14, Philemon 1:24, Colossians 4:14 and 2 Timothy 4:11 are the same Luke who wrote the Gospel of Luke and the Acts of the Apostles but it is highly probable.

## Hebrews

The letter to the Hebrews is of unknown origin but the opening line, "long ago God spoke to our ancestors" demonstrates that the writer was a Rabbi or a Pharisee. The first two chapters are primarily prophesies from Psalms, Proverbs, Genesis, Exodus, Samuel as well as some New Testament witness statements. This writer is more than an educated individual; the writer is definitely a Hebrew giving witness to the long awaited Messiah. The writer understands that the resurrection of Jesus destroyed the power of death thereby freeing those held in slavery (Hebrews 2:14-16). The depth of the writer's knowledge of God is revealed in verse 4:12, "the word of God is living and active, sharper than a two-edged sword, piercing until it divides soul from spirit, joints from marrow; it is able to judge the thoughts and intentions of the heart."

Hebrews also recalls something we know very little about, that is, the priesthood of Melchizedek, informing us that Jesus is "a priest forever according to the order of Melchizedek" (Ibid. 5:6). Melchizedek means my king is Sedek or king of righteousness. He was the King of Salem who met and blessed Abraham. Chapter 7 states that Melchizedek also means, "King of righteousness," as well as "king of Salem" and "king of peace." I rather suspect that these are copyist inclusions and not in the original text. I say that because an educated individual writing to a Hebrew audience would not say the obvious.

In Chapter 8 the writer repeats Jeremiah's prophesy in 31:31-34 of God's promise to establish a new covenant with the house of Israel. In Chapters 9 and 10 we are told that Christ's sacrifice was a "once for all" and intended to include people of every nation as Jesus is the mediator between creation and the one true living God. Our God does not desire any burnt sacrifices as recorded in Hosea 6:6. We are told that a priest cannot take-away sin. Only God forgives sin. Hebrews 10:16 reminds us of the Jeremiah 31:33 promise of a new covenant written on our hearts by God. The writer also believes that Christ's return was imminent (Hebrews 10:36-38).

The evidence of that covenant is expressed in a believer's faith as declared in Hebrews 11:1, "faith is the substance of things hope for, the evidence of things not seen. The chapter goes on to list the things done in faith in the Old Testament. Chapter 13 enforces our call to live in love by not neglecting "to show hospitality to strangers, for by doing so some have entertained angels without knowing it" (Hebrews 13:2). There is no clue as to the writer's identity but it appears that the individual is part of the inner circle of evangelists. Considering the fact that Paul initially evangelized in synagogues it is reasonable to think that the writer is a Rabbi. Like Paul, the writer calls people to "obey your leaders" (Hebrews 13:17).

## James

For some reason, a pastor will have a preference for certain books in the Bible. The Gospel of Mark and the Letter of James touch me more than the others. I understand their point of view and manner in which these books communicate God's word. The Letter of James was one of the books that just barely made it into the Christian canon. The writer of James (Jacob) was not the brother of Jesus. As you read this book, you come to understand that the writer has caught a glimpse of the heart of Christ and that there is a possibility that he was a lawyer as the use of new analogies reveals an educated and abstract mind. I admire the conciseness of the analogies and the way he explains the relationship of works with regards to salvation. James is the one who coined the phrase "The Royal Law" (James 2:8). Teachers who truly interpret scripture correctly make the Royal Law of love the foundation upon which your faith in God's word and the gift of Christ Jesus are understood.

One of the most misunderstood concepts in scripture is the relationship between good works and salvation. We have all heard the phrase "you cannot get to heaven by doing good works." That is true. This idiomatic expression has been used to justify thousands of pew warming Christians from extending relief and consolation to others. It justifies keeping all their money within their dying church so they can survive a few months more. The writer of James is brutal in exposing the truth of good works. Faith and good works go hand in hand. In verses 2:14 he writes, "what good is it... if you say you have faith but do not have works." Remember, "faith, hope, and charity, these three, but the greatest of these is love" for others (1Corithians 13:13).

It is refreshing to see how James continues as if this had been part of a discussion among converts who wanted the benefits of salvation but did not want to do anything or part with their money. He may have even been criticized for his good works, so he responded to the group's crucial claim that "faith alone will guarantee salvation" with; "you have faith and I have works, and I by my works will show you my faith" (James 2:18). Earlier in the discussion James asked, "can faith save you, [can you show me your faith without good works]? If a brother or sister in naked and lacks daily food and one of you say to them, go in peace; keep warm and eat your fill, and you do not supply their bodily needs what is the good of that?" Calling them empty Christians, he makes the conclusive statement, "faith without works is dead" (James 2:20). James understands the relationship of faith and works.

As the early church began to grow and develop their unique set of theological beliefs, it was important to establish that faith is the first step. However, faith without works is a dead faith. Good works overflow from a heart that truly believes. In this way it is a continuation of the Hebrews 11:1 passage, "faith is the substance of things hoped for, the evidence of things not seen." We all hope for peace in the world, love to abound, pain and suffering to be no more. The question is, "how do we contribute to world peace and the relief of suffering?" The Word of God came in a new way to bring the message of love to a starving people. James is an educated individual who understands the full implications of the ministry of Jesus. Once again, the message of the Bible is not to kill those who differ from us, but to learn to love all people. This does not mean that we let an enemy murder those who disagree with us then mindlessly forgive them? Sometimes, the only way to stop violence is with violence. President Theodore Roosevelt used an old African proverb several times during his presidency. It is actually, "speak softly and carry a big stick."

One of the anomalies of the industrial age is that it has lead to a very large group of people commonly referred to as "the middle class." Prior to the nineteenth century the world was comprised of the rich and the poor. Distinctions between the poor, the enslaved, and the rich, were very little. In Rome as in Asia, when difficult or dangerous work needed to be done, the rich would hire the poor. In that way, if they got hurt, the poor worker would simply be thrown off the property and replaced with another. In a master/slave relationship a household slave or farm slave actually had more status than a poor man who was free. Slaves had value; they were property. It was into this culture that Jesus brought a message of a better place; of a Father who had prepared a mansion for those who did not resort to evil or idol worship. This is the context into which the message of Chapter 5 is speaking. As it is today, the poor cannot do a thing when treated unjustly by the rich. There are of course instances of justice, but for the most part the poor suffer from the rules of law. To those people, in every age, James has a message for the poor who must endure, and for the rich who persist on profiting from the helpless. The message to the middle class has always been, "pure religion and undefiled before God and the Father is to visit the fatherless and widows in their affliction, and to keep yourself unspotted from the world" (James 1:27).

Of particular interest to me is a teaching of Jesus in Matthew 5:34-37 that James has come across and is passing it on. Considering that it only appears in Matthew's gospel it makes me wonder if he knew the writer of Matthew. James understood that many cultures swear by "a dead mother," or swear by "the name of their god," or anything else that might add credibility to their statement. Both Jesus and James tell us not to "swear by heaven" or "by earth" or by "any other oath," but let your "yes" be yes and your "no" be no, so that you many not fall on condemnation" (James 5:12). Is it not ironic that for 2,000 years the church and our courts of law have required us to put our hand on the Bible in order to swear an oath?

# 1 Peter

Civil unrest had escalated for the forty years following Christ's death. Finally, a fatal war had broken out against the Romans. In 70 A.D., the Roman army commanded by Titus with his second in command, the future Caesar, Tiberius Julius Alexander, destroyed Jerusalem. By this time Peter was an old man and had lived to see the fall of Jerusalem. When you read his letters, be aware of the heart warming and heart breaking memories he carries within. Listen to how Peter understood the person of Christ; "through him you have come to trust in God, who raised him from the dead and gave him glory, so that your faith and hope are set on God" (1 Peter 1:21).

Listen to how the theology of "you can do nothing to obtain salvation" is challenged as he tells us to, "rid yourselves, of all malice, and all guile, insincerity, envy, and all slander. Like newborn infants, long for the pure spiritual milk, so that by it you may grow into salvation, if indeed you have tasted [communion] that the Lord is good" (1 Peter 2:1-3). Listen how Peter understands the salvation of humanity as he parallels the calling of all people to the calling of the people of Israel. To those who come to have faith in God Peter said, "you are a chosen race, a royal priesthood, a holy nation, God's own people, in order that you may proclaim the mighty acts of him who called you out of darkness into his marvelous light. Once you were not a people, but now you are God's people; once you had not received mercy, but now you have received mercy" (1 Peter 2:9-10).

The temple had been destroyed, the Jewish people had been scattered into every nation. Peter was evangelizing all who would listen, Jew and Gentile alike. Once again wives are told to accept the authority of the husband in some translations. However, Peter is saying the same thing as Paul in verse 3:1, that wives submit to *idios aner*, their "own husbands" which is spoken with a sexual connotation. One cannot deny that male bias has prevailed over the centuries and in verse 3:7 even Peter refers to women as, "the weaker sex." But please understand, the Bible does not make women slaves, servants or chattels. Any group or religion that does is not from God. Please consider the culture when you read Peters words in Chapter 3 when he says, "do not adorn yourselves outwardly by braiding your hair, and by wearing gold ornaments or fine clothing." Consider how many people in society today can afford to wear gold and fine clothes. Even secular groups who stick to the "simple old ways" allow their women to braid their hair. Religion was not meant to keep people in the past. We are to use the gifts God has given us for good and not for evil. Those who work hard and earn a good living are entitled to that life; they are called however, to be good stewards; to share a portion of their earnings with those who are less fortunate.

In closing, Peter tries to somehow rationalize the age old question of why do good people suffer and bad people flourish. I do not have an answer. Maybe Forrest Gump came the closest when he said, "it happens." As I said, Peter was very old as his closing acknowledgment reveals that his letter was written through Silvanus.

# 2 Peter

2 Peter opens with Simeon Peter, as servant and Apostle of Jesus Christ. The older manuscripts do not have the word Peter, affirming that the church changed all the Hebrew names to western names thereby differentiating the good guys from the bad guys. We do know that during the reign of Pope Damascus in 382, St. Jerome changed the name of Yeshua of Nazareth to Jesus of Nazareth. At this point in time the Roman Catholic Church did not exist.

In a way, it does not matter how the church decided to name the letters and gospels, the fact remains, they are still witnesses to God at work in the world through Jesus the Christ, the beloved. We will never know which statements are factual and which are inspirational (pipe dreams). There is one overriding message from start to finish; the one true living God is a God of love who desires peace in all creation.

Peter speaks of false prophets and false teachers. The early church fathers who tried to determine which letters and gospels were credible enough to include in the canon had to deal with hundreds of documents, many of which were rejected. When I come to a passage such as 2 Peter 2:4 where it says "if God did not spare the angels when they sinned, but cast them into hell and committed them to pits of deepest darkness," I become suspect of the passage when I cannot find anything else in scripture to support that statement. Statements like these reveal a different nature to God. Never forget, the Roman church used every horrible myth they could think of to drive fear into a people God called them to love.

In closing, 2 Peter warns people to be careful of those who would deceive, as by this time the stories and myths were abundant. By this point in time all Peter can do it ask the people to remain faithful and wait, strive for peace and refrain from sin.

# 1 John

The letters of John were not written by John the disciple. Nonetheless, the writer understands that all have sinned. 1 John warns of the "antichrist" three times giving the church an unseen enemy to fear. In his letter it is apparent the world is turning against Christianity and the struggles are just beginning. This is a sign of a later date of writing. One of his strenuous warnings is about hatred when the writer affirms that there is a difference between redeemable sin and sin unto death. Verse 3:15 states "all who hate a brother or sister are murderers, and you know that murderers do not have eternal life in them." When Jesus was preaching forgiveness there was no need to differentiate between sin unto death and redeemable sin. Jesus came to redeem sinners and they knew what he meant.

The beginning of Chapter 4 directs the people not to believe every spirit. They were to test the spirit to see whether it is from God or not. I have always been suspect of clergy who begin their talk with,

"I have a word from God for you." At the very least they are elitists. It is odd that John contradicts Paul who wrote in Romans 3:23 and 5:12, that "all have sinned and fallen short." John tells the people that, "whosoever is born of God does not commit sin… because he is born of God" (1John 3:9). Later, at the beginning of Chapter 5 John states, "everyone who believes that Jesus is the Christ has been born of God." Please realize a theology that takes the responsibility off you for making a personal decision for Christ is a human construct. Admittedly, many of the scriptures will say that you have been chosen or destined, but the fact remains, if that were true, there would have been no need for God's Messiah. You cannot put the blame for your failure to attain salvation on anyone but yourself. Salvation is as Jesus said, "when I was thirsty, you gave me water; when I was naked, you clothed me, when I hungered, you gave me food to eat." If you do not believe me go back and read the Matthew 25 story that Jesus told. Ask yourself, "what did Jesus say?" Then ask yourself, "did Jesus forget to say these other things?" 1 John 5:18 says again, "we know that those who are born of God do not sin." If so, can you name one person, other than Jesus, in the history of the world that was born of God? You are responsible for your own damnation or salvation.

# 2 John

This is the second shortest book in the Bible which is followed by the shortest book in the Bible, 3 John. The letters of John sound like he was an itinerant preacher; "I was overjoyed to find some of your children walking in the truth" (2 John 1:4). I say this because John writes that he will not waste paper and ink because "I hope to come to you and talk with you face to face" (2 John 1:12). Again he warns of deceivers and instructs the "dear lady" that anyone who does not bring the command to love should not be welcomed into her home.

# 3 John

His third and shortest letter is still dealing with deceivers and infighting. Upset with the preeminent disposition of Diotrephes (nourished by Jove) John writes that the man is to be reported to the church. Again, his letter is short expecting that he will come soon and speak with them face to face.

# Jude

Jude opens with a typical greeting differentiating between God and the person of Christ. After reading this statement throughout the New Testament you cannot help but get the idea that the Trinity, as we know it, was a creation of the Bishops in 387 AD. First formulated by a decree of Emperor Constantine, the First Council of Nicaea in 325 AD formulated the *hypostasis* (the unity of the Father, Son and Holy Spirit). However, it was not ratified until 387 AD after Bishop Arius died. Arius had cited John 14:28, "I go unto the Father, for my Father is greater than I." This passage prevented the passing of the Doctrine of the Trinity in 325 AD. After his death, all positive writings of Arius were destroyed and the church kept only the negative allegations and made Jesus God.

There is a difference from what the church wants the Bible to say and what the Bible actually says when read in the original Biblical languages, i.e., Hebrew and Greek. Even the Gospel of John which set the Trinity idea in motion contradicts itself many times. Also, Paul writes in 1 Timothy 2:5 that, "for there is one God, and one mediator between God and men, the man Christ Jesus." As Dorcas taught us, "read the words," and "listen to what the words say." Through this work you will have heard some of the objections Luther voiced against the Roman church in his attempt to get the church to start preaching the truth of scripture. As the late Rev. Dr. Les Renault would often say, "the church of Christ has survived in spite of the Christians." Surely this is God's doing.

## Revelations

The Revelation of John is either from God or a man high on hallucinatory drugs. Steven Spielberg would be hard pressed to dream up this stuff although if he could buy the stuff the writer was smoking I'm sure he could. Although I cannot make a definitive declaration as to the authenticity of the book I do side with the church fathers who wanted to keep this book out of the canon. This is end times apocalyptic literature of which I have never been interested or felt was credible. You would have to make that decision for yourself. There are many clergy who have made a lot of money with their interpretation of the writer's hallucinatory trip into the world of fantasy.

# Conclusion

In the Presbytery of New Brunswick, Canada, the Biblical issues I have raised would be grounds for the charge of "resurrecting the old heresies." What this charge means is, "the church has decided how passages are to be understood and there is no room for reasoned argument." Even when blatant contradictions exist, blind faith must prevail. I have demonstrated that the Bible is not God's word but that God's word is contained within the Bible. You have seen that the Bible does not say Jesus is God but the son of God. You have seen where humans have seen God face to face and lived. This book has demonstrated how Maundy Thursday is celebrated on the wrong night and how Jesus did in fact die on the cross and spend three nights in the grave before God raised him to become our heavenly advocate. Christ is indeed the way but not the way the church would have you believe.

Rev. Dr. James K. Stewart

# Recommendations

It seems that the recent Past and the current Present, in literary circles, are constantly being assailed with the questioning of every aspect of our spiritual selves. We members of Society had always been told "the absolute Truth." We wouldn't be lied to by those we've been taught to admire, would we? Yet our senses have been tickled and shocked into new thinking recently, as our beloved icons of Art, our holiest and most iconic Architecture have been presented in new ways through many literary breakthroughs, in the last 50 years.

Hold onto your hats and get a firm grip on your chairs as James K. Stewart takes us on the most amazing roller coaster ride of thought stimulation. Watch as he unfolds a new picture of what lies within the pages of the Holy Bible, hidden in plain view for centuries.

Remember that those who have educated us in the Past are the same folks who gave us •the burning of the Library of Alexandria • the bloody centuries of numerous Crusades • the repeated Slaughters of The Innocents • the gory and despicable Inquisition • being the silent partners of the WWII Holocaust.

Exercise your Free Will; pull back the "Oz Curtain" and be prepared to be enlightened. Thank you, Jim, for the opportunity to finally see the Light. **The Bible According to Jim** is destined to be a new "must-have" in millions of libraries, I'm sure.

B. Andrew Downes, CLU, CH.F.C. CFP,
Mississauga, Ontario (Retired)

*The Bible According to Jim is* an easy to read, plain talk, thought provoking analysis of the Bible. It explains the meaning of Bible passages based on translations from the original Hebrew and Greek. It deals with what the words say and not the words as interpreted over the years. It provides perspective and a foundation for understanding, or questioning, all faiths. Logical arguments are provided for his reasoning. The narrative is a mixture of fact, opinion and many humorous and amusing asides. The male bias and the blame of women for all of man's sinfulness are exposed sometimes with shocking examples.

Whether, or not, you agree with the content, it provokes the motivation for further examination and study of the Bible and one's own beliefs.

Patricia Mandy, RN BA MPA CHE, Dundas, Ontario

Thank you Jim on behalf of all the women in the world for your interpretation of creation! George & I have been fighting over your book but he has finished so I have it all to myself. It is very interesting reading. (I always knew I was an equal).

Sandie Arlein, Listowel, Ontario

Printed in the United States
By Bookmasters